Seeing Through
the Mother Goose Tales

Seeing Through the Mother Goose Tales

❦ ❦ ❦ ❦ ❦ ❦ ❦ ❦ ❦ ❦ ❦ ❦ ❦ ❦

Visual Turns in the Writings of Charles Perrault

❦ ❦ ❦ ❦ ❦ ❦ ❦ ✳ ❦ ❦ ❦ ❦ ❦ ❦ ❦

Philip Lewis

Stanford University Press, Stanford, California 1996

Stanford University Press
Stanford, California
© 1996 by the Board of Trustees of the
Leland Stanford Junior University
Printed in the United States of America

CIP data are at the end of the book

Stanford University Press publications are
distributed exclusively by Stanford University Press
within the United States, Canada, Mexico, and Central America;
they are distributed exclusively by Cambridge University Press
throughout the rest of the world.

Published with the assistance of the Hull Memorial
Publication Fund of Cornell University.

For Catherine Porter

Acknowledgments

In 1991–92 the goodwill of three colleagues in the College of Arts and Sciences at Cornell University, Dean Don M. Randel and Associate Deans Elizabeth Adkins-Regan and N. Gregson Davis, made it possible for me to take the kind of fully protected leave that academic administrators normally have to forgo. This book is the product of that year of freedom.

An abbreviated early version of Chapter Two, entitled "L'Antisublime ou la rhétorique du progrès," appeared in French in *Rhétoriques fin de siècle*, ed. François Cornilliat and Mary Shaw (Paris: Christian Bourgois, 1992), 117–45. A segment of Chapter Three was published in altered form as "Writing to the King: Charles Perrault's Dedicatory Epistle for the Dictionnaire de l'Académie" in *MLN*, 107 (1992): 673–97. A shorter and preliminary version of Chapter Four appeared under the title "Food for Sight: Perrault's 'Peau d'âne'" in *MLN*, 106 (1991): 793–817. I am grateful to the editors of these publications for allowing me to rework and use this material here.

P.L.

Contents

Seeing Through
the Mother Goose Tales

Introduction

This book attempts to ferret out some connections between the two roles for which Charles Perrault (1628–1703) has come to be known in the cultural and literary history of France: that of an influential player in the development of the arts under Louis XIV, and that of a celebrated author of short stories. The three essays of Part I deal with work in which Perrault offers interesting and capacious perceptions of the "splendid century"— work on the basis of which one can make a case for regarding him as the veritable founder of modern French literary history. In studying the stance he adopts and the discourse he forges in commenting on the arts and letters, I have made use of significant writings that deserve more attention than scholars have given them heretofore: his unfinished memoirs, the four-volume *Parallèle des anciens et des modernes en ce qui regarde les arts et les sciences* (1688–96), the two-volume *Les Hommes illustres qui ont paru en France pendant ce siècle* (1697, 1700), and the slim but intriguing *Pensées chrétiennes* (written during the last decade of the author's life). The distinctive feature or leitmotif I have drawn from these works is an intellectual bent, a turn of mind, a conceptual pattern that manifests itself in a practice of compromise formation. Through this practice, Perrault domesticates—mutes, recuperates, reappropriates—the original, radical, rigorous concepts he encounters in other writers of his century. My fundamental hypothesis is that a rearticulation of this characteristic mind-set recurs with striking insistency in his *Histoires ou contes du temps passé* (1691–96). In each chapter of Part I, I attempt to flesh out the formulation of this hypothesis enough to convey a precise sense of the rationale behind it and to point toward the potential for its expression or emplotment in the tales.

Part II offers readings of a representative group of fairy tales—"Peau d'âne" (The Ass's Skin), "Cendrillon" (Cinderella), "Le Petit Chaperon rouge" (Little Red Riding Hood), "La Barbe bleue" (Bluebeard)—along with comparisons that suggest approaches to three others: "Le Petit Poucet" (Thumbkin), "Riquet à la houppe" (Riquet with the Tuft), and "Le Chat botté" (Puss in Boots). In these three chapters, I have resisted the temptation simply to deploy this hypothesis as a grid that can be applied to each tale so as to produce a ready-made allegory. My practice of resistance consists in analyzing each story with the same, quite conventional narratological apparatus, and thereafter in comparing the tales with one another on the basis of these structural accounts. The readings in which the narratives' messages, positions, and allegorical dimensions eventually emerge are further elaborations of—commentarial expansions upon—these structural/comparative analyses. Since the narrative schemes and structural comparisons that preside over my readings are generated independently, without regard for my central hypothesis about the recurrence of the Perraldian mind-set, the readings they spawn should, in principle, serve as discovery or testing techniques, that is, they should reveal whether the *Contes* do or do not reconstruct conceptual compromises akin to those I have unearthed in the nonfictional corpus.

In reality, of course, the integrity of the interpretive process cannot derive solely from a methodological contrivance. If only because the basic plot sequence in which the narratological framework is grounded incorporates, in itself, a bias toward social equilibrium that can be understood as a kind of built-in compromise, the relation between my hypothesis and my procedure is not unproblematic. I would therefore be the first to counsel against placing too much stock in the critical approach, even while advocating the commitment to analytic rigor and consistency that underlies its use. Ultimately, the reader's judgment on the utility and plausibility of my general hypothesis will have to be fairly complex. Bearing upon the pertinence, coherence, and elucidatory power of my readings, first of Perrault's expository writings, then of his narratives, that judgment will finally have to reckon with the supposition of historical continuity between the two textual veins of his work.

Readers familiar with the history of the *Contes* realize that this supposition is especially delicate in Perrault's case, owing mainly to the insurmountable confusion enshrouding the authorship of the prose tales. Modern-day editors of the *Contes*—Gilbert Rouger, Jean-Pierre Collinet, François Flahaut, and Marc Soriano—have tended to converge toward a consensus view, according to which a certain collaboration between Charles Perrault and his youngest son, Pierre, was ultimately dominated by the father. Charles both originated the process by choosing and telling the tales to his children (perhaps encouraging his teenage son to undertake the project of writing them down) and exercised control over the publication of the definitive edition, in 1697. His contemporaries were already assuming that the father put his hand to the texts by the time the collaborators began revising them and composing the versified *moralités*. In any case, for my purposes Charles Perrault's active, vitally influential role in the composition of the *Contes* suffices to attach any continuity we may uncover between them and his nonfictional writings to a biographic base, and thereby warrants my assumption that Perrault's writerly career constitutes one of the viable contexts of interpretation to which readers of the tales can and should appeal.

Underlying the attention I have given to Perrault's career and to the ties between the *Contes* and his other, quite substantial writings is an interest in the role he deserves in modern accounts of seventeenth-century French literary and cultural history. It therefore seems appropriate to situate my study vis-à-vis the two major contemporary interpretations of Perrault's fiction—by Marc Soriano and by Louis Marin—that have contributed decisively to revealing his work's richness and to bolstering his status among seventeenth-century authors. Notwithstanding my many debts to the monumental scholarly investigations of Marc Soriano and my sympathy with his emphasis on the folkloric background of the *Contes*, I have approached Perrault from a vantage point that is relatively far removed from his remarkable psychobiographical thesis (initially developed in the pioneering study *Les Contes de Perrault: culture savante et traditions populaires*; 1968). My opening take on what is at stake in Perrault's writings derives primarily from the *Parallèle*, a polemical work that—by its organization and themes—tends to impose the standpoint of the intellectual historian, interested in the handling of ideas and concepts. The informing principle that I posit as a key to

Perrault's thinking appears on the level of argument and discursive strategy. As such, it has no immediate relation to the unconscious structural principle, visible in effects of coupling and doubling, that Soriano perceives in an analysis of relations within the Perrault clan.

Louis Marin's reading of Perrault (in *La Parole mangée* and a number of interpretive essays) also centers on the *Contes*. Like Soriano, who anchors his readings in the folkloric sources of the tales, Marin draws extensively on historical background that is largely external to Perrault's writing. In *La Parole mangée* (1986) he pushes the focus away from Soriano's interest in the gestation of the tales and toward the forms of understanding at work in the reader's interpretation of the finished text; he thus tends to privilege, not specific sources for particular texts, but semiotic, political, and theological horizons of Perrault's time. A brilliant exploitation of the *Logique de Port-Royal* underlies his claim that the tales expose and explore the complicities between the rationalist theory of representation and the exercise of power in the orders of ideology and politics. On the level of reading procedure, there is an evident kinship between Marin's work and mine, since I take his approach to exegesis—attending to the structural processes of narrative fiction, but plying this semiological analysis to an exceedingly thorough, patient, multifaceted rereading of the text, its details and its signifying effects—to be exemplary. If, on the other hand, the inflection of my readings differs globally from his, it is largely because my starting point and ongoing frame of reference are distilled from within Perrault's work. As I have noted, owing to this initial interest in a characteristic mind-set, the design of my study is quite close to the project of traditional monographic inquiries that begin by searching for a certain continuity and homogeneity within an author's corpus. Thus, in very reductive terms, it might be said that Marin has elaborated something of a Pascalian reading of Perrault, whereas my own attempt is to set forth the lineaments of a Perraldian reading of Perrault. Neither of the two projects is more justifiable than the other, and while they are by no means mutually exclusive, they are caught up in a productive tension with each other that will require further attention in the opening chapter of Part II.

While the full-blown interpretations of Perrault's tales elaborated by Soriano and Marin served as my principal foil in the elaboration of Part II, my appreciation of Perrault's fairy tales has also benefited greatly from a broader horizon of reading that has taken hold in recent years. Lying rather more in the domain of cultural history or "cultural studies" than that of intellectual history, this work has been pioneered by the eminent American scholar Jack Zipes. In remarkable historical studies of fairy tales and children's literature, Zipes situates them in the light of Norbert Elias's theses on how the processes of acculturation and education serve familial and societal stability in the modern European nation-state. In the framework deployed by Zipes in *Fairy Tales and the Art of Subversion* (1983), Perrault's work holds an inaugural position to the extent that it draws the material of popular folktales, transmitted in a diffuse oral tradition, decisively into the mode of highly refined writing. By appropriating and inflecting the narrative contexts and messages of popular tales, Perrault makes his published versions potentially very significant vehicles of mediation between the political and cultural elite and the lower classes.

Scholars engaged in cultural studies insist on situating collections of tales like those of Perrault and his storywriting contemporaries (notably women such as Catherine Bernard, Marie-Catherine d'Aulnoy, and his niece Marie-Jeanne Lhéritier) as a period-specific phenomenon; the goal of commentary about them is to bring out their full sociopolitical or ideological resonance. To do so, it is necessary to grasp their entrenchment in social history and in the processes of representing that history. Above all, this entails tracing their connections to the many enduring forms of popular culture—folklore, to be sure, but also songs, plays, lives of saints, accounts of public events, the hastily composed and disseminated stories of chapbooks, images, illustrations, rituals, and so forth—and then analyzing the diverse meanings and perspectives that storytellers carry over from the past and weave together in constructs for their own audiences. Such a scholarly undertaking proves to be exceptionally fecund in the work of Catherine Velay-Vallantin, whose extraordinary study *L'Histoire des contes* (1992) pursues in a specifically French context the line of inquiry developed by Zipes on a broad, cross-cultural horizon. In her first chapter, Velay-Vallantin insists on reading Perrault's "La Barbe bleue" through the permutations of a storyline that she finds not only in folktales, but in popular songs of various regions of France. Explicitly rejecting a dominant focus on authorial creation, textual structure, or reader's reception, she attempts to show how the formidably rich network of motifs and associations that come to be crystallized in Perrault's character, Bluebeard, grows out of a long historical process of reciprocal exchanges among authors, texts, and readers. Literary critics and historians have much to learn from the dauntless breadth and cumulative insight of her work.

In the readings of Perrault's tales I have proposed in Part II, I have not attempted to carry the historical investigations of scholars like Zipes and Velay-Vallantin further. Nor have I been tempted to privilege them over the Perraldian perspective that I attempt to develop in Part I of this book. Having assumed, however, that Perrault's experience and representation of his time would correlate with and corroborate the sociohistorical theses of their inquiries, I have unhesitatingly appealed to their insights in the conduct of textual exegesis. Ideally, then, the coherence of the commentaries on the tales offered here will not derive solely from my approach to textual analysis; I hope it also reflects its dependency on the patient historical scholarship that unveils, in its slowly evolving depth and complexity, the innumerable effects of cultural sedimentation that Perrault's texts artfully represent.

PART I

Turns of Mind: Perraldian Compromises

1

The Cartesian Turn:
Perrault Against Descartes

I n 1661, more than thirty years before the *Mother Goose Tales* began to appear, Charles Perrault published a short story entitled "Le Miroir, ou la métamorphose d'Orante."[1] Appearing at a moment when the writing of portraits and self-portraits was a fashionable pastime, this tale recounts the life of Orante, a brilliantly skillful and unstintingly accurate, if overly frank, practitioner of the verbal portrait. Orante makes a strong, provocative impression on the people he describes—an impression that depends on how they look. He inspires the love of a dazzling young woman named Caliste, who revels in his elaborate, impeccably exact descriptions of her superb beauty; she practices a kind of narcissism without a mirror, hearing her beauty spoken by Orante rather than seeing it. Watching over the couple as a kind of fairy godfather is none other than the god of love, who admires Caliste's beauty and Orante's talent for provoking women to embellish themselves. But alas, the fate of the beautiful Caliste is to prefigure the horrific defacement of Madame de Merteuil in the *Liaisons dangereuses*: like Merteuil, the gorgeous girl is deformed by the ravages of smallpox. This exposes her to neglect by Cupid and to verbal assault by the depictive poet Orante: he is so caught up in his uncompromising mimetic destiny that he scrupulously describes her dreadful ugliness to her. Her angry response is to stab him repeatedly with a hefty hairpin; enduring her ire, the mortally wounded poet, still chattering away, slowly expires while pursuing his aggressive description of her deformities.

Afterward the god of love, who still cares for Orante, arrives on the scene of the debacle. He is too late, we are told, to bring the poet back to life; the dead man's soul has already taken flight from his body. But the god is resourceful and manages to preserve Orante's marvelous art of graphic exactitude by having his body converted into a mirror. This mirror is, moreover, a distinct improvement over the live portraitist. A stable, impassive instrument, it simply reflects, reproducing images perfectly without the evaluative, accusatory edge of the portrait in words. Moreover, the mirror provides the god a double satisfaction: it not only takes over Orante's function of prompting seductive women to perfect their beauty, but affords the god himself an experience of narcissistic captivation; the mirror reflects both self and other with felicitous effects of pleasure and provocation. The shift, then, from descriptive speech to mirror image takes on a strongly positive connotation; the mirror, by virtue of the enchanting relations of self-reflection it makes possible for its viewer, occupies a privileged place in the order of visual representation.

The Prestige of the Visual

Charles Perrault produced this early story more than twenty-five years before launching his major polemical and critical work, *Le Parallèle des anciens et des modernes*.[2] Published over a decade during which the Quarrel of the Ancients and the Moderns reached its most strident level and then, after 1694, subsided, the *Parallèle* consists of five somewhat stilted dialogues. Conceived as a systematic reply to Nicolas Boileau and the partisans of the Ancients, they are given over to orderly debates in which the deck is transparently stacked in favor of Perrault's contention that the artists and thinkers of his times were equal or superior to those of antiquity. If the writerly activity exemplified by Orante in Perrault's youthful tale seems to resonate harmoniously with the mature work of the apologist for contemporary art, it is not simply because Perrault adorned his story with a lesson or commentary praising the art of portraiture in the novels of a modern writer, Madeleine de Scudéry. Much more vitally, it is because the *Parallèle* ascribes to poetry a fundamentally representational function. In volume 3 of the *Parallèle*, Perrault's spokesman, the Abbé, treats the work of verbal art quite unreservedly as a painting or a picture. "La Poësie," he writes, "n'est autre chose qu'une peinture agréable" (Poetry is nothing other than a pleasing painting; 3: 7–8; 199).[3] Poetry has a pleasure function that is primarily visual: "Celuy qui lit ou qui écoute reciter un poëme bien fait," the Abbé notes in his next response, "n'a qu'à livrer son imagination aux images qu'y forme la Poësie, sans faire autre chose de sa part, que de les regarder" (One who reads or hears a well-wrought poem recited merely needs to give one's imagination over to the images that poetry forms within it, without doing anything other than looking at them). Clearly Perrault, who argues forcefully for according to painting an esteemed status equal to that of the belles lettres and who makes the heightened appreciation of painters and their works a key component of his apology for the Moderns, is closely aligned with one of the most striking trends in seventeenth-century thinking about art: its tendency to anchor itself in the authority of the visible, to treat visual experience in its diverse aspects—the pleasures of looking or being looked at, the form and formation of images, the bonding and communication at work in eye contact—as a pivotal human activity and source of value. Among the celebrated literary examples of this trend in France, we might cite what critics term Racine's poetics of the gaze, an expressive instrument that takes the eyes and discourse about them as the communicative channels of passion and its representation, or La Bruyère's probing analyses of facial images and of the exchange of looks in his Caractères, or again, Pascal's thoughts about perspective, the laws of which guide us to analytically satisfying points of view in geometry or architecture or pictorial art but elude us in ethical inquiry. With their line on the diverse components of the field of vision, these classical writers anticipate a point Freud will pursue in describing the dynamics of the gaze and the order of scopophilia, the zone of voyeurism and exhibitionism where sight is the transmitter of sexual drives to pleasure and pain. Much like Racine, Freud treats the look or gaze as a pathway or channel that makes for a kind of convertibility or network of equivalence linking the act of seeing, the seen object, the image of seeing, and the image of the object: all four of these distinguishable phenomena within visual experience are subsumed and thereby bound in an associative chain by the single word vision. Well before the seventeenth century, this key term had acquired its vast range of designation and connotation.[4]

The promotion of the visual was not, to be sure, simply a development in the world of art; the trend was ubiquitous and was connected, in the seventeenth and eighteenth centuries, with the gradual emergence of aesthetics (from the Greek *aisthetikos*, pertaining to sense perception) as an autonomous sphere of reflection. An early signpost was offered by the field of optics, where pioneering work by Kepler, Galileo, and Descartes presided over a general tendency to accredit representation by mirrors and lenses. Descartes, for example, stresses the scientific work made possible by telescopes in *La Dioptrique*. The general trend in this emergent science ran counter to the Platonic depreciation of the senses—sight chief among them—that was inherited from medieval philosophy and remained a skeptical commonplace in the moralist tradition.

Echoes favorable to this new scientific confidence are quite evident in Perrault's discussion of optical devices in the *Parallèle*. The book as a whole not only accredits the visual and an axiology that it informs; it reflects the wide range of that value system's operation through a somewhat eccentric feature of its global structure. The first four dialogues make up a homogeneous ensemble on the horizon of aesthetics: in the first two (1688), discussion moves from general considerations about the authority of the Ancients to the domain of the plastic arts; then in 3 (1690) and 4 (1692), Perrault deals with the verbal arts. In these two dialogues, he opposes eloquence to poetry in terms that, while they leave intact the conventional categorizations of classical rhetoric, anticipate preoccupations with the differences between speech and writing that will intensify in the work of Rousseau.

But then, at the end of a period corresponding to the time of composition of the celebrated fairy tales (1691–96), Perrault produces a fifth and late dialogue (1697)—the oddball, as it were—in which the arts play a relatively minor role. Here the advance of knowledge and science becomes the central concern, and unsurprisingly, praise for optics and the optical instruments of modern science is effusive. The conversation of the disputants touches upon many different areas of inquiry and technology: astronomy, astrology, geography, navigation, mathematics, warfare, fireworks, physics, medicine, and philosophy (including logic, ethics, and metaphysics). Far and away the dominant subject is philosophy itself, and the key evaluation of Ancients and Moderns involves measuring Descartes against Aristotle. Descartes is not just the main representative of seventeenth-century thought; he is the only one; and for the Modernist, Cartesian rationalism appears to be the only late-century position to be reckoned with. This situation allows us to draw one significant conclusion forthwith, before coming to grips with the somewhat complicated, quite ambivalent critical assessment that Book 5 eventually elaborates. The *Parallèle* testifies very clearly to Descartes's preponderant influence; and Perrault's comprehensive sweep across the philosophic and scientific terrain gives us a sense of what a popularized, recuperated Descartes could look like to a cultivated public in the 1690s.

Visualization in Descartes

From the stance that Perrault adopts in his defense of the Moderns, Descartes's work appears to have provided a crucial conceptual underpinning for the seventeenth century's privileging of the visual. In his work on optics, the elevation of sight and light is thematized—made spectacular, we might say—from the start. It is relevant to recall, for example, the opening proposition of *La Dioptrique*, introducing the discussion of light and visual mechanics: "Toute la conduite de notre vie dépend de nos sens, entre lesquels celui de la vue étant le plus universel et le plus noble, il n'y a point de doute que les inventions qui servent à augmenter sa puissance ne soient des plus utiles qui puissent être" (Our approach to life depends entirely on our senses, and since sight is the most universal and noble among them, there is no doubt that the most useful inventions possible are those that serve to increase its power).[5] We might also underscore Descartes's elaborate mechanistic account of human vision in his early treatises on the world—*Le Monde ou traité de la lumière*—and on man—*Le Traité de l'homme*. The effort he puts into explaining the role of the animal spirits in eyesight is so phenomenal that readers of the popular *Discours de la méthode* may very well wonder why that example, rather than the more controversial account of the circulation of blood, is not used when Descartes, in Book 5, makes his move from metaphysics to physics and presents his summary account of the laws of nature. The conjoined analyses of sight and light in these works of the young physicist signal an association that is crucial in Descartes's metaphysics, and that persists as an unwavering constant in the visual metaphorics and thematics of French classicism.

But the explicit accent on the visual in Descartes is doubtless less revealing than the more subtle moves he inscribes in his text when his thought strives to be, in a strict philosophical sense, *foundational*. An important case worthy of numerous afterthoughts is that of the famous method itself. Its first and grounding rule is the rule of *évidence*—of that which stands out to or for sight, that which is directly, immediately perceptible. A skeptical Descartes asks what we learn about knowledge from looking inside the mind detached from past assumptions and from sensory experience, and given over to self-inspective intellection. We discover, Descartes asserts, that the indubitable idea that commands our allegiance has to be clear and distinct. Since at that preliminary stage his exclusive models for such a transparent, self-evident truth are those of algebra and geometry, the distinctive mark of a clear idea tends from the start to assume a certain kind of visual contour, to figure the clear idea as unmistakably delineable form or shape. From the standpoint of geometric abstraction, the idea of such a clear idea incorporates its visualization: ideality is visual; the idea is to be seized and evaluated in its appearance as an *image*. The act of perception involves a subject's contact with an object that may indeed be carried out by the senses of touch or hearing, but the disclosure of truth in the form of ideas—no matter how narrowly it may be restricted to the self-contained sphere of the mind—emerges in the appearance of that object to sight. The conception or positioning of truth as immediacy that is not oneness requires the delicately differential touching achieved by vision.

A second, complementary case occurs in the *Méditations métaphysiques* soon after Descartes has reached the point of asserting the *cogito* as a proposition he cannot deny. Since not even the evil genius can delude him into thinking he does not exist as long as he is thinking, Descartes is able to assert his existence in thought: the proposition *ego sum, ego existo* is necessarily true, he asserts, whenever he pronounces it or conceives it in his mind ("quoties a me profertur, vel mente concipitur, necessario esse verum").[6] One might already glimpse here, in the reference to conception in the mind, a certain slippage toward visualization, toward the ideality of mathematics, toward what the third Meditation identifies as the proper notion of the idea: an image of things, as opposed to volitions and judgments, which involve the action of the mind adding something to a simple idea. But in the *cogito*, conception is not yet image formation; it is only the barest, hardly shaped or figured positioning of a simple thought in the mind; seeing is not yet operative in the proposition itself: "I am" at this point is not yet "I see." The truth of the proposition is a function of its uninterpreted articulation in ordinary language. (The text of the second Meditation allows us to use this term advisedly, as the celebrated passage about a ball of wax contains two references to the use of ordinary parlance, or *loquendi*, forms of everyday speech not normally subject to question.)[7]

Descartes's problem as a thinking being is the extreme difficulty of getting any further than knowing that he is when he says he is; it is the difficulty of knowing that he exists continuously, of knowing what he is, of drawing attributes for the thinking subject out of propositions like "I think" or "I am." He manages to advance just a bit in the famous passage about the ball of wax that dominates the second half of the second Meditation. There he discovers the primacy of introspection and homes in upon the crucial gesture of inspecting his own mind. The wax brings perception—primarily sight—into play as if it were coincident with thought itself. The conclusion elaborated in the penultimate paragraph goes much further than the predictable assertion, elaborating on the *cogito*, that seeing the wax object confirms the truth of the existence of the subject. The slightest apprehension by the subject of its seeing suffices to provide this verification: "For if I judge that the wax exists from the fact that I see it, it certainly follows still more evidently that I exist myself, from the mere fact that I see it. For it might be that what I see is not really wax; it might be as well that I do not even have eyes for seeing something; but it cannot happen that when I see, or when I think I see (*which I no longer distinguish from seeing*), I who am thinking am not something."[8]

Descartes's parenthetic remark—"quod jam no distinguo" (what or which I no longer distinguish)—notes the equivalence for the introspective subject of the clauses "when I see" and "when I think I see." What we glimpse here is no longer just a possible slippage: *differentiation* is set aside; the displacement onto seeing of that undeniable thinking that evinces the subject's existence presses thinking and seeing into coalescence and near-equivalence. After this opening or folding or displacement of thought onto sight, of cogitation—*cogito*—into visualization—*videam*—Descartes proceeds, in the third

Meditation, to situate the rule of evidence as the first derivation from his meditation on the *cogito*: "In this first knowledge, there is nothing except a clear and distinct perception of what I assert."[9] And when he reaches the point of asserting the objective reality of ideas, the visibility of the idea is again a crucial conclusion: "So that natural light shows me perspicuously that the ideas are in me as images."[10]

What commentators call the *cogito* derives from Descartes's contextualization or sublimation of the *cogito* itself: it is the representation of knowing thought carried out by this fundamental step within the itinerary of the *Méditations*, the move from the *cogito* to the rule of evidence, from the proposition asserting existence to the conception or vision of the mind's existence, from knowledge inherent in the speech of the subject to knowledge in the form of an image. Recourse to this metaphorical shift or shuttle or *tropos*, whereby the sayable is shunted into the visible, speech into image, assertion into figuration, knowledge into representation, the mind into the sphere of natural light, exerts a far-reaching yet subtle hold over the discourse of Cartesian idealism; far-reaching, in structural terms, since, as we shall see, the Cartesian subject, as soul or spirit, constructs its relation to the material world through the same metaphoricity or process of envisualization, controlled by the same rules and procedures. While this metaphoric relation is expressed in foundational terms in the rule of *évidence* and in the doctrine of the objective reality of ideas, in general Descartes's ontology strives to make the linkage or articulation between thought or idea and image or picture a natural, inevitable, thus almost invisible pattern or structure, no more subject to doubt than ordinary language. It is this thought-configuring movement of sublimation, which makes for the rule of metaphor and for the primacy of the metaphor positioning thought as vision, that I call the Cartesian turn.

The pertinence of the term *turn*, as opposed to trope or metaphor, lies in its capacity to evoke not only the formal cast of Descartes's reflection, but also its historical significance, as a turning point in the history of philosophy. A particularly salient contextualization of the *cogito*, which moreover repeats the Perraldian tack of situating Descartes's metaphysics in relation to modern science, is offered by Martin Heidegger's essay "The Age of the World Picture."[11] For Heidegger, Descartes initiated the turn of modern science and research away from its ancient and medieval precedents by interweaving in his work two decisive events: "the world is transformed into picture and man into *subiectum*."[12] In the conjunction of these two developments, Heidegger perceives the simultaneous and interdependent emergence of objective science, which construes the world as an object for man's examination, and of anthropology or anthropomorphism as the framework for the philosophical interpretation of life-experience. Heidegger's rendering of the *cogito* picks up on the coalescence of thought with vision that we have been stressing here. The thrust of his reading is, however, pointedly historical, inasmuch as it accentuates Descartes's abandonment of the theologically centered metaphysics sustained by (Christian) scholastic philosophy in favor of a truth grounded in the position of the knowing subject. The *cogito* is thus articulated in response to an imperative to endow the *subiectum*, assuming the role of truth's unshakable ground with self-certainty:

What is this something certain that fashions and gives the foundation? The *ego cogito (ergo) sum*. The something certain is a principle that declares that, simultaneously (conjointly and lasting an equal length of time) with man's thinking, man himself is indubitably co-present, which means now is given to himself. Thinking is representing, setting-before, is a representing relation to what is represented (*idea* as *perceptio*). . . .

Every relation to something—willing, taking a point of view, being sensible of [something]—is already representing; it is *cogitans*, which we translate as "thinking." Therefore Descartes can cover all the modes of *voluntas* and of *affectus*, all *actiones* and *passiones*, with a designation that is at first surprising: *cogitatio*. In the *ego cogito sum*, the *cogitare* is understood in this essential and new sense. The *subiectum*, the fundamental certainty, is the being-represented-together-with—made secure at any time—of representing man together with the entity represented, whether something human or non-human, i.e., together with the objective.[13]

In this commentary designed to explain the mutual interdependence of Descartes's epistemological subjectivism and his scientific objectivism, Heidegger pinpoints with consummate acuity the linkage within the sub-ject of the ground (*sub-*) to its projection or thrownness (*ject*). The linkage makes it not a simple presence, but always already a representation, not an idea without form or relation to an object, but "*idea* as *perceptio*" or image; it is a subject seizing its self-certainty in its imaging of itself for itself, and it is this historically durable and momentous articulation of a certain minimal, indispensable (self)-representation—of a fold within the fabric of subjectivity marking its permeability to the work of difference—that repeats itself as and in the wake of the Cartesian turn.

Thinking as Feeling

No doubt one should not lose sight of a shadow that the Cartesian turn leaves in its wake. The turn toward the external order of representation in the ball-of-wax passage leaves in the background another Descartes, whose *cogito* is distinguishable from the sublimated *cogito* of the historically influential—since recuperable—Descartes principally in question here. Over against the dominant (thematized, doctrinalized) thinking of a philosophic subject who undertakes, in the latter part of the second Meditation and throughout the third Meditation, to construct an articulation of his certainly apprehended existence with the objective world, the *ego sum, ego existo* and the practice of radical doubt briefly set forth an original, primitive experience of thinking as it appears to itself that is not yet, as we noted above, assimilable to seeing. In the opening chapters of *Généalogie de la psychanalyse*, Michel Henry situates the key to what he interprets as Descartes's essential, grounding intuition or apprehension of being or life in an assertion Descartes makes in the second Meditation, just before the shift in purview that the ball of wax brings into play. Descartes has been pursuing his attempt to clarify the nature of the "existing thing" revealed in the *cogito*, emptying his thought of anything subject to doubt, granting that he may be duped by his imagination or by his own creator, and finally going so far as to suppose he is sleeping. Even at that point when all mental representations have to be ascribed to illusion, he writes, "It *seems* to me that I see [*at certe videre videor*], that I hear, that I am warm, this cannot be false; properly speaking, that is what in me is called *feeling* [*quod in me sentire appelatur*]; and that, considered in these precise limits, is nothing other than *thinking*."[14]

According to Henry, the critical distinction here is between *videre*—which depends on a relation of *ek-stasis*, that is, on the constitutive structure of representation, the differential movement that places what is seen before a gaze—and *videor*—a passive see(m)ing internal to thought and fundamentally different from the seeing of *videre*: "*Videor* désigne la semblance primitive, la capacité originelle d'apparaître et de se donner en vertu de laquelle la vision se manifeste et se donne originellement à nous" (*Videor* designates the primitive seeming, the primary capacity of appearing and self-sensing through which vision initially emerges and becomes perceptible to us).[15] And as the two propositions that succeed the *videre videor* indicate, its order is that of feeling and thinking:

C'est donc dans le sentir que Descartes déchiffre l'essence originelle de l'apparaître exprimée dans le *videor* et interprétée comme l'ultime fondement, c'est comme sentir que la pensée va se déployer invinciblement avec la fulgurance d'une manifestation qui s'exhibe d'elle-même en ce qu'elle est et dans laquelle l'*épochè* reconnaît le commencement radical qu'elle cherchait. . . . *Videor*, dans *videre videor*, désigne ce sentir immanent au voir et qui fait de lui un voir effectif, un voir qui se sent voir.[16]

It is thus in feeling that Descartes detects the original essence of appearing expressed by *videor* and interpreted as the ultimate ground; it is as feeling that thought will invincibly unfold with the compelling force of a manifestation that reveals itself as what it is and in which the *épochè* recognizes the radical beginning that it was seeking. . . . *Videor*, in *videre videor*, designates this feeling that is immanent to seeing and that makes it a real seeing, a seeing that senses itself seeing.

The concept of perception by the five senses, which embraces the activity of sight designated by *videre*, is then separate from this primitive, radically interior sensing or self-sensation,

le se sentir soi-même qui donne originellement la pensée à elle-même et fait d'elle ce qu'elle est, l'originel apparaître à soi de l'apparaître. Le se sentir soi-même en lequel réside l'essence de la pensée n'est pas seulement différent du sentir qui s'appuie sur l'*ek-stase*, il l'exclut de soi et c'est cette exclusion que formule le concept d'immédiateté. Mais l'*ek-stasis* fonde l'extériorité, elle est son développement en soi.[17]

The self-sensing that gives thought to itself at its origin and makes it what it is, the original appearing to self of appearing. The self-sensing in which the essence of thought resides is not only different from the feeling that is based on *ek-stase*, it excludes it from itself, and this exclusion is formulated in the concept of immediacy. But *ek-stasis* grounds exteriority; it is its development in itself.

In its grounding core, the thinking that comes to itself in the cogito is thus an affectivity, a surge of self-apprehension within the tightly bound immediacy of "auto-affection," of the self-feeling that Descartes probes further, in elaborating on the psychic processes he terms the passions of the soul, when he takes the acts of will proper to the soul to be identical with its perceptions of the desire that the will effectuates.[18]

For Henry, the Cartesian itinerary we have followed in ferreting out the turning of thought into vision is to be understood not merely as a turning point—Heidegger's perception of Descartes positioning modern man as a subject and the world as a picture—but more critically as a turning away from the authentic revelation achieved in the *cogito*: the turn away consists in substituting the relation of the *cogito* to its *cogitatum* for the *cogito* itself; it is a fall of the subject's radical interiority into representation, an absorption of the *videor* by the *videre*. Henry thus criticizes Heidegger for reducing the *cogito* to the subject's act of self-representation and for reducing the *ego* of Descartes's *ego cogito* to man. But from the standpoint of seventeenth-century Cartesianism, his account of Descartes's infidelity to his own meditation is interesting because, for Descartes's followers and adversaries alike, it exposes a problem of understanding, a source of indetermination or confusion concerning fundamental concepts: terms such as *aperception*, *clarté*, and *distinction*, applicable to the initiatory coming into presence of feeling in a context devoid of light or sight (as in a "pure" experience of pain) also function readily with their "standard" meanings in the sphere of *ekstasis*, and by extension, terms such as *passion*, *pensée*, and *âme*, used to designate the order of the originary experience of thought as feeling, likewise tend to bring that experience onto the register of representation. One of Henry's telling illustrations is precisely the term *passion*. In its original acceptation, *passion* designates a rudimentary passivity inherent to feeling as self-sensation (self-sensing comes to itself in and of itself; it is passive insofar as its attending to itself simply happens in itself, insofar as it appears to itself without the intervention of any separate agency, external or internal). Thus the word *passion* covers and unites conceptually both the "actions" and the "passions" of the soul sensing itself in its primordial appearing to itself as the affectivity—an activity that is passivity—of thought. By contrast, however, in the very same articles of part 1 of the *Traité des passions*, Descartes repeatedly recognizes a general sense of the word *passion*, used to designate perceptions the soul "reçoit des choses qui sont représentées par elles" (receives from the things that are represented by them).[19] Thus his psycho-physiological discourse on the passions is already fully caught up in a framework of representation that treats the body and the soul as agents acting upon each other.

Another salient example analyzed by Henry is the term *clarté*, which connotes illumination and which is opposed to confusion and obscurity in the order of *ekstasis*, of cognition and intelligibility.[20] But in the invisible order of feeling, of primitive affectivity and immediacy, where the sharply delineated contours of representation before a seeing subject are not yet in question, *clarté* is in a sense identical to confusion and obscurity; it marks the effect of self-sensing experienced as the integral coalescence of thinking-feeling-being, as a taking-hold—rather than a bringing-into-focus—that in its oneness is necessarily and irreducibly confused and obscure. As Henry points out in his brief commentary on Malebranche,[21] in the development of Descartes's thought and of Cartesianism, the fundamentally introverted *cogito* that unfolds prior to the intervention of the Cartesian turn—of the ek-static slide into representation—leaves a semantic residue that cannot be fully eradicated. To the extent that radical doubt and the seeming but unseeing *cogito*, even if betrayed, persist or return as the informing commencements to which Descartes's successors refer, it is necessary to assume that traces or after-effects of the obscured or forgotten understanding of terms such as *passion* and *clarté* can emerge in the (self-)representational rearticulations of the Cartesian turn itself.

Perrault's Descartes

To perceive Descartes's informing presence in French writing during the reign of Louis XIV, one might wish to study, in the first place, how these rearticulations get refined or skewed in a theoretical register—as, for example, in the theory of representation elaborated in the *Logique de Port-Royal* or in Pascal's critique of Cartesian epistemology. In the register of literary practice, however, reappropriations of or resistances to the Cartesian turn are less transparent and more elusive. If we set aside ritual acknowledgments saluting Descartes's rationalist method and his provisional ethics, his inflective presence in the literature of French classicism is a relatively muted, modulated one. Its principal manifestation—unavoidably rather superficial—derives from the gradual diffusion of the reigning metaphor representing thought as vision or image into the general thematic accreditation of sight, light, and well-delineated visual form. The narrative substance of "Le Miroir, ou la métamorphose d'Orante" forms a spectacular instance of this thematization. By treating the inanimate mirror as a distinct improvement over the living portraitist, the tale forcefully underscores the prestige of the visual.

If Charles Perrault's writerly activity affords us an exceptionally revealing vehicle for studying late-century Cartesianism, it is primarily because it presents an explicitly marked relation to the Cartesian underpinnings, enabling us to look for a directly telling linkage. It is helpful, moreover, that the marking, a late-career testament from a privileged witness of the culture of the splendid century, occurs in writings in both of the registers mentioned above—theory in the *Parallèle* and his *Pensées chrétiennes*, literary practice in his occasional poetry as well as the *Contes*. It is also noteworthy that in deploying the pliable structure I am calling the Cartesian turn, Perrault persistently and artfully reinvested the trajectory leading from understanding (*intellegentia*) to imagination (*imaginatio*) with an axiological, if not polemical edge. In "Le Miroir," the itinerary leading from precisely stated knowledge to clear pictorial representation appears to subtend a simple allegorical statement about the ends of portraiture. The narrator unhesitatingly associates himself with Cupid's standpoint, depicting as an artistic advance the move from the verbal portrait produced by the witty Orante to the more perfect and alluring, yet also less aggressive and invasive visual representations reflected by the mirror. A massive repetition of an equivalent judgment, enunciated from the standpoint of poetics and cultural history, has been documented by Elizabeth Berg in her study of the relation between eloquence and poetry in the *Parallèle*. In dialogues that helped inaugurate a movement toward the autonomy of aesthetics in the late seventeenth century, the Abbé accounts for the higher esteem in which poetry is held by contrasting the orator's rhetoric to the poet's imagery: to move from the former to the latter is to advance toward greater pleasure, dignity, and security.

But what about Perrault's explicit attention to Descartes the philosopher in the final dialogue of the *Parallèle*? As we saw earlier,

Perrault leaves us no doubt that he leans heavily on the Cartesian tradition of his time, and if the epistemological Descartes who assumes and reasserts the primacy of the visual in the conception of thought is treated superficially, he is nonetheless an important legitimizing and structuring ground for Perrault's value system. Yet the *Parallèle* is complicated, to some degree at least, by the recourse to dialogue; and the interest of the debate in Book 5 stems largely from the critical slant taken not only by the Abbé, Perrault's spokesman, but also by the Abbé's usually naive crony, the Chevalier, and even to a certain extent by their adversary, the Président, a defender of the Ancients. Once the Abbé has finished explaining why Descartes's physics is superior to Aristotle's, the Chevalier begins assailing the Abbé with his insistent objections to the Cartesians. The Descartes who looms in the background appears to be less the idealist discovering the shape and significance of his own thinking than the dualist struggling to deal with the mind/matter dichotomy. The resistance to Descartes generally revolves around an objection repeated ad nauseam by the knight: the Cartesians flounder when they try to explain how a corporal being can think or know, or how it is that men have spiritual souls while beasts have only material ones, or how beasts can feel or know while lacking judgment or reason. The problem zone is indeed that of dualism as it emerges not so much in Descartes's foundationalist discourse about questions of epistemology and ontology as in the last two books of the *Discours de la méthode* or the later Meditations (5 and 6), in less rarefied discourse on questions of metaphysics and anthropology. In this orbit, elaborating the relations of mind to matter and of soul to body occasions obstacles, gaps, and complexities incomparably more forbidding than those of the inspection of the mind.

This challenge to Descartes prompts the Abbé to change his strategic course. Instead of defending Descartes against the ancient philosophers vaunted by the Président (Aristotle, Democritus), he locates him in the past vis-à-vis the Moderns of his own time. The latter have continued to advance philosophic understanding, thanks in part, he notes (5: 173; 327), to the analytic and scientific methods developed by Descartes. It is thus possible for the Abbé to adhere to some Cartesian principles and procedures, including the critique of received ideas, while nonetheless laying out in considerable detail reservations about certain Cartesian ideas that Perrault expresses more economically in the *Pensées chrétiennes* (paras. 11–12, 57–59). His critique, if incidental remarks are set aside, incorporates three main objections, all of which have at least a nominal connection to the status of sight and vision:

1. One of these criticisms mounts an attack, which is elaborated more seriously in the *Pensées chrétiennes* (paras. 11–12), on Descartes's ontological proof (based on the innate idea of a perfect being) of the existence of God in the third Meditation. Its interest lies not so much in Perrault's strong preference for the cosmological proof of God's existence (reasoning back from the existence of the universe to the necessity of a creator) as in the caricatural construal of the ontological proof. The Chevalier situates it as a derivative of fallacious claims about clear and distinct ideas: "Je pense qu'il y a un Dieu, & par ce que cette pensée ou idée me paroist tres claire & tres distincte, donc il y a un Dieu" (I think there is a God, and since this thought or idea seems clear and distinct to me, there is then a God; 5: 194; 322). The fustian reasoning here simply reverses the movement of the fourth Meditation, where Descartes hinges the general validity of the criteria of truth—clarity and distinctness—he had identified by scrutinizing his experience of the *cogito* on his equally indubitable idea of God. Yet the exchange among the three interlocutors yields a remarkable consensus on a central issue: adopting a simple-minded understanding of the first rule of the method presented in Chapter 2 of the *Discours de la méthode*, all confidently dismiss the principled link between truths that are certain and ideas that are clear and distinct.

2. A related objection apparently targets the third rule of the method, which requires the ordering of thoughts "en commençant par les objets les plus simples et les plus aisés à connaître" (beginning with the simplest, most readily known objects). The Abbé blames Descartes "d'avoir voulu nous expliquer dans le détail l'essence & la constitution des corps simples" (for having wanted to explain to us in detail the essence and constitution of simple bodies; 5: 165, 325). He goes on to explain that the human mind, aside from forming simple ideas (presumably fundamental terms that remain undefined, such as space, time, number, and element), is capable of two operations, dividing and assembling (it would not be difficult to show, using rules 2 and 3 of the method and parallels between the appeals

to architectural metaphors in the *Discours* and the *Parallèle*, that Perrault's viewpoint here is loosely Cartesian). It is possible to achieve knowledge of an object only by dividing it "en son genre & en sa différence" (into its genus and its species; 5: 166, 325). Thus, for example, in pursuing the knowledge of man and animals, one proceeds with division after division "jusqu'au souverain genre, qui est L'Estre, lequel ne pouvant plus se diviser en genre & en différence, ne peut plus aussi estre défini, ni bien connu, par consequent" (until reaching the sovereign genus [or type], which is being; the latter, since it is no longer divisible into genus and species [type and characteristic], is therefore neither definable nor knowable; 5: 167, 326).

Implicit in the curiously scholastic operation that leads Perrault to construct his own version of the tree of Porphyrus (reproduced in the *Pensées chrétiennes*, para. 81) is a resistance, also perceptible in the Abbé's denunciation of the practice of radical doubt (5: 195–96, 333), to the very premises of the foundationalist analysis that leads back to and then through the *cogito*.[22] For the commonsensical characters of his dialogue, if the reductive process of disassembly that leads to the simple origin—the inaugural ground or building block—of a cognitive construct such as physics or metaphysics can present the basic object or experience it discloses as a certainty, it is nevertheless unthinkable to endow it with clarity in their sense of the term, precisely because a truly simple entity, in its oneness, is indivisible. Had Perrault studied Descartes's discussion in the *Principes de la philosophie* of what happens when someone feels intense pain, he would no doubt have been unreceptive to the qualifying proposition in which Michel Henry anchors his definition of the particular clarity proper to the *cogito*: "encore qu'il n'aperçoive rien clairement que le sentiment ou la pensée confuse qui est en lui" (whereas he perceives nothing clearly except the feeling or indistinct thought within him).[23] The bias built into Perrault's tree of Porphyrus, isolating l'Estre as an unknowable genus-without-species, disallows this clear apperception of a feeling or inchoate thought; its frame of reference, detached from the elemental sentiment appearing on the hither side of representability, requires the ground of visibility introduced by the Cartesian turn.

3. Perrault's most forceful, elaborate, and historically significant objections to the thought of Descartes center on the theoretical

difference between man and animals.[24] Like La Fontaine and many others, Perrault protests against the account of animals as machines or automatons set forth in Chapter 5 of the *Discours de la méthode*. Citing cases of animal behavior, he insists that denying feeling, reason, and knowledge to animals is counterfactual, that differentiating man from animals has to be based on human "intelligence"—that is, on the mental faculties that enable man to work with abstractions and universals. "La différence essentielle de l'homme consiste à pouvoir se faire des notions abstraites & spirituelles de toutes choses, & sur tout de Dieu" (The essential characteristic of man consists in being able to form abstract and spiritual notions of all things, and especially of God; 5: 209–10; 336). What makes this issue pivotal, however, is the turn the debate takes when its focus narrows to the question of spirituality: do animals have a soul, and if so, of what sort? Hesitant to assert that animals have a spiritual soul, Perrault falls back on the guarded claim that it is reasonable to accord them hypothetically a corporal soul. Given this tentative stance, his problem is not to prove the hypothesis, but merely to show that it is plausible.

An Ambivalent Mirror: Imagining the Animal *Cogito*

Since the Abbé's case for the animal soul has to be made in response to the commonsensical objection that experience makes it hard for us to conceive of corporal thinking, it is not surprising that he sets out to question the conditions under which an idea or phenomenon may be relegated to the status of the inconceivable or the impossible. His point in this passage (5: 217, 338), as he resists hasty or ill-informed dismissals of the unthinkable, resonates intriguingly with Boileau's notion of the sublime, a strange quasi-concept— neither a style nor a rhetorical practice, but simply a turn of expression—that I shall examine in considerable detail in Chapter Two. Boileau initially associates the sublime or marvelous dimension of the great work with two familiar motifs—first, the immediate connotation of elevation, of a powerful uplifting effect, and second, the arresting experience of the ineffable or inconceivable, the inexpressible effect designated by the famous cliché, "je ne sais quoi," that is, literally an "I don't know what it is," or more colloquially "that special something but I can't say what." The elusive "je ne sais quoi" escapes or blocks or overwhelms the mind's representational grasp and records allusively the impact of experience that lies beyond the awesome analytic frontier where a positive definition or delineation of an idea or image or event or figure of language becomes impossible. In this uplifting poetic movement of inspiration and psychic integration that Neil Hertz calls, in *The End of the Line*, the sublime turn, the swell of an overpowering, figure-effacing brilliance inundates the space of the Cartesian turn and suspends its delineatory movement. To the extent that the sublime turn toward inspiration, spontaneity, immediacy, and fulgurant illumination overrides the ek-static, scopic, spectral, figural formation of truth with an upsurge of arresting revelation, its movement is the symmetrical converse of the Cartesian turn from revelation into representation: its beckons backward toward the commanding, initiatory appearance of truth, undifferentiated and undeniable, that is encountered in the *cogito* itself. In Perrault's resistance to Descartes, can one detect any intimation of an interest in that rarefied experience, any inclination to accompany Boileau in allowing, within the sphere of artistic representation, a certain reversal or suspension of the Cartesian turn?

For the most part, the Perraldian position in the *Parallèle* is the one we expect: his defense of sublime style and his resistance to the sublime go hand in hand with the Modern's loose Cartesianism, marked by his emphasis on rational, analytic understanding and plausible, technical explanations. Thus the Abbé's appeal to the inconceivable or inexplicable in order to ascribe verisimilitude to any view—his or Descartes's—of the mind/body and man/beast distinctions seems unexpected and paradoxical. The quite Cartesian example that he adduces to explain his point makes it at once all the more intricately intriguing and, in approach, typical of Perrault's strategy in the *Parallèle*. For his reflection centers on the way the mirror—figured in "Le Miroir, ou la métamorphose d'Orante" as the very emblem of visibility—functions as an optical instrument. Suppose, he says, you had never before seen a mirror or any image-reflecting surface, and somebody told you that in another country there are very thin objects that represent perfectly—even better than a painter can—anything one sets in front of them. You would find the idea astonishing and essentially inconceivable, but would you be right to claim that it is impossible?

The Abbé's suggestive simile measuring the refractory idea of a

corporal soul against this amazing mirror typifies Perrault's intellec-
tual posture because it is anchored not so much in analysis or argu-
ment as in his incessant appeal to comparison and analogy. If the
display of this analogical bent is unsurprising insofar as the ongoing
differentiation of Ancients and Moderns is concerned, and if it is
also, as I shall show in Chapter Two, quite consistent with Perrault's
views on rhetoric and eloquence, it is still remarkably extensive and
insistent. In its insinuatory form, the rhetorical question about the
reflective power of the mirror vis-à-vis the person who has never
encountered one resembles Molyneux's famous question for the
eighteenth-century *philosophes* about what a man blind since birth
would see if he suddenly acquired the faculty of sight. The rhetori-
cal gambit enables the Abbé to play upon his interlocutor's wish to
avoid the stigma of relative ignorance or imaginative naiveté. His
implied message is amply clear: you may find thinking bodies or
corporal souls inconceivable or awe-inspiring because neither your
experience nor your faculties have prepared you to understand
them; yet your inability to conceive of them does not make them
impossible; it only makes you ignorant or inexperienced or weak-
minded. In short, one person's blindness does not mean that others
cannot see.

The full interest of this one invocation of the mirror in the
Parallèle becomes apparent, however, only when the Chevalier reacts
by questioning, precisely, the Abbé's recourse to rhetoric: "mais
enfin ce n'est qu'une comparaison" (but, ultimately, that is only a
comparison; 5: 218; 338). Forced to recast his analogy in argumen-
tative terms, the intrepid Abbé treats his interlocutors to this rather
complex reasoning:

Si la seule disposition des parties de certain corps, leur donne la faculté de
representer toute sorte d'objets, pendant que tous les autres corps sont
privez d'une faculté si admirable, il ne doit pas y avoir de l'inconvenient
que la seule disposition des parties de certains corps leur donne la faculté de
sentir & de connoistre, pendant que tous les autres corps sont privez d'un si
grand avantage. Vous me direz qu'il y a bien de la difference entre la faculté
de representer des objets, & celle de les connoistre, & moy je répondray
qu'il y a aussi bien de la difference entre ce qui rend un corps capable de
representer des objets, & ce qui le rend capable de connoistre les mesmes
objets; & que si le simple poliment qu'on donne à une glace brutte de
miroir, en la frottant, luy communique le pouvoir de former les images de

toutes choses, on ne doit pas s'estonner que l'ame d'un animal, quoyque corporelle, soit capable de sentiment & de connoissance, si l'on considere l'admirable construction de toutes les parties du corps de ce mesme animal, la maniere ineffable dont ses sens sont organisez, la vitesse des esprits vitaux et animaux qui le remüent (5: 219–20; 339).

If the mere organization of certain bodies gives them the capacity to represent any kind of object, while all other bodies are deprived of such an admirable capacity, there should be no problem if the mere organization of the parts of certain bodies gives them the capacity to think and to know, while all other bodies are deprived of such a great advantage. You will tell me there is quite a difference between the capacity to represent objects and the capacity to know them, and I shall answer that there is also quite a difference between a body's capacity to represent objects and its capacity to know them; and that if the simple polishing of the surface of a natural mirror endows it with the capacity to form images of all things, we should not be surprised that the soul of an animal, although corporal, is capable of feeling and knowledge, [especially] if we consider the admirable construction of all the parts of the body of this animal, the ineffable way its senses are organized, the quickness of the animal spirits that invigorate it.

This passage is remarkable because it rises to a theoretical level passably rare for Perrault and his time. Under the general term of difference, it names a discontinuity that can be figured as a divide or a gap, and then proceeds to delineate a context for the work of difference. The Cartesian objection anticipated by the Abbé—who is fully aware of the contrast between the insensitive, inanimate mirror and the active, sensing animal—posits the difference between representing and knowing. Now it is just such a distinction within intellection—the difference between knowing existence and visualizing it—that separates the *cogito*, as the primitive ground of knowledge, from the mind's idea or conception of the *cogito*, which brings that immediate knowledge into the realm of a certain interior representation or visibility. But where the foundationalist Descartes, struggling against the radical doubt he has unleashed, is at pains to validate the continuity of thought and perception, to reduce the original gap between self-sensation and self-representation, to posit a rigorously controlled overlapping of the "I think, I am" with an uplifting "I see," Perrault's spokesman, with his contrast between the mirror and the animal body, seems to underscore, not the coalescence of representation with feeling and knowing, but an essential and irresolvable difference between them. Indeed the Abbé marks the difference doubly, since he grafts onto the discontinuity between representation and knowledge what he takes to be its cause, the less complex, more mechanical nature of the reflecting body versus the nobler, more dynamic, and more intricate resources of the knowing body.

A difference of this kind is, to be sure, what returns to the fore in the realm of human thought when we trace the move from idealist ontology to dualist anthropology in the work of Descartes. Lying beyond the Cartesian turn and thus within the order of representation that it continues to shape, such a difference comes into play early in the sixth Meditation, for example, when Descartes distinguishes the formation of images and ideas from reasoning or pure intellection ("primo examino differentiam quae est inter imaginationem & puram intellectionem").[25] Here Descartes anchors the crucial opposition of spirit to body in the difference between the enabling ground of representation, visibility, and that of knowledge, mind. The latter engages reason, intelligence, and communicative powers that Cartesian rationalism reserves for man, whereas animals, while lower than man, can perfectly well be endowed with a primitive faculty of representation. In this differential mode that is crucial to the discourse of rationalism on the unique nature of man as a thinking, speaking being whose essence is spiritual, the image has to be, as it were, reseparated from cognition and discourse, and then reintegrated into their elaboration through what amounts to a remobilization of the Cartesian turn. The position of the imagination—defined by Descartes as an "application of the cognitive faculty to an intimately present body" (applicatio facultatis cognoscitivae ad corpus ipse intime praesens)[26]—is thus secondary and derivative in relation to the primacy of thought, speech, and knowledge. As a process of envisualization or image-formation, the Cartesian turn now consists in this embracing application of mind to body, which is carried out by what is twice represented, in the succeeding discussion of geometrical figures, as the "attentive" or "focusing" mind (aciem mentis). The turn within the mind-body relation that makes for the fusion of cognition with imagination once again relies, as it did in the *cogito*, on the subtle slippage of thought into vision.

By contrast, when the Abbé expounds on the form and function of an animal soul, he implicitly relocates the groundwork in which knowledge is anchored. The shift, corresponding precisely to Heidegger's gloss that locates the Cartesian turn inside the cogitation of the founding *cogito*, is already evident in his extended comparison of animals and men (5: 197–211; 333–37): "Quand je regarde mon chien, & que mon chien me regarde, les images que nous concevons l'un de l'autre, sont également corporelles & materielles" (When I look at my dog and my dog looks at me, the images we conceive of each other are equally corporal and material; 207). Here, as in the passage cited above in which the mirror situates the mechanics of representation as a natural phenomenon involving nothing more than the play of light on a reflective surface, the Abbé's example places the starting point of the beastly and human animals' perceptive experience, not in thinking or feeling, but in the forming of images occasioned by sight of an object. The representation of objects that can be achieved mechanically, as a result of well-arranged physical parts, is the ground on or out of which "la faculté de sentir et de connoistre" emerges. Is it then reasonable to read the conjunction of *sentir* and *connoistre*, repeated near the end of the quoted passage by the reference to an animal soul "capable de sentiment & de connoissance," as a marking of equivalence comparable to the linkage of thinking to feeling in the *cogito*, and thereafter, still more venturesomely, to grasp in the movement from representation to knowledge within the animal's material soul a reversion toward a grounding apprehension of being as self-sensation, thus a reversal of the Cartesian turn?

At least two claims built into Perrault's text open the way for such a reading. The first is implicit in the primary argument through which he allows his spokesman to adumbrate, after Descartes, the lineaments of a modern, proto-materialist psychology that the eighteenth-century *philosophes* will detach from the metaphysical framework to which Perrault remains devoutly committed. The Abbé seeks essentially to point out that the possibility conditions for the operation of a corporal soul are observable in animal bodies. He punctuates the argument in the middle by introducing the Cartesian's objection that representation without thinking does not produce knowledge in a strong sense—that is, insofar as it differs from representation. In answering, he invokes the admirable complexity of the psychic organism, a neurological system in which the movements of sensory impulses and relations to objects or stimuli are vital. To the extent that feeling and knowledge are assimilated to those thoroughly integrated corporal movements, they are, as in the *cogito*, at one with each other. These psychic impulses can be understood as fundamental signs of existence, and thus as the irreducible components of what I shall call hereafter "the animal *cogito*."

The second claim, more elaborate and delicate, is articulated immediately after the passage comparing the material soul to the mirror. The Abbé is pursuing the vein of reflection that grasps the animal *cogito* unfolding from a representational base that is already in place. The principle to which he appeals harks back to the Cartesian account of the mind-body relation ("an application of the cognitive faculty to an intimately present body") and resonates with the Heideggerian embedding of the *subiectum* in an object-relation, in a "being-represented-together-with" the entity represented. The Abbé asserts in regard to man, then repeats in regard to beasts, that there is a necessary commensurability or congruence between a conceptual faculty and its object ("il faut qu'une puissance, comme je viens de le dire soit proportionnée à son objet"; 5: 221; 339). In the case of animals, which can achieve via imagination a restricted knowledge of "choses materielles & individuelles" but not the higher knowledge of "choses spirituelles et universelles" (5: 206; 335) accessible via intelligence, this means that the shape and medium of their knowledge correspond in nature to those of the object: if the animal soul can reasonably be defined as material, it is because the animal has the capacity to produce material representations of single material objects. Presumably, then, it is only as such, as an isolated object, that it can perceive itself.

The obvious weakness of this rationale is that it so readily allows the difference between knowledge and representation to dissipate. Its still considerable interest lies in the direction the Abbé's account of corporal reflection takes as it quickly glides back into the modeling of knowledge on visual perception. The predictable folding of animal cognition into the already present substructure of representation effectively reverses the outward thrust of the Cartesian *cogito* from the interior appearance of thought into visualization. Yet with that inward movement toward a grounding core of reflection that makes it the always already operative structure of cognition, the Abbé also appears to draw back from the materialist challenge with which the animal's psychophysical *cogito* confronts the primacy of spirit in Descartes's foundationalism and to restore, indeed strengthen, the predominance of the Cartesian turn. In effect, only for a moment, and in vague terms, does his effort to conceive of the animal *cogito* escape from the relation of a viewing subject to its object; and when the visual relation in which it is decisively reinscribed returns, its effect is to confer upon the animal *cogito* a structure not parallel to the immediate self-sensing of Descartes's founding spiritual *cogito*, but rather already aligned with the envisioning warp of the Cartesian turn.

Owing to the irrepressibility of the Cartesian turn within Perrault's attempt to articulate his resistance to Descartes, the Abbé's stance in the *Parallèle* ultimately entails the unwitting compromise that offsets his overt contestation with a deep-seated compliance. Although Perrault's apparent confidence in his critique of Descartes is not devoid of a certain fatuousness, the revelatory potential of his effort to force a further reckoning with the animal/human distinction should not be underestimated. The passage we have just examined in which the Abbé's resistance begins to flounder remains noteworthy for two reasons. First of all, it exposes the fundamental thrust of Perrault's critical intuition about Descartes in its simplicity and force: his speculation on animal knowledge opens onto an impulse—a need that Descartes meets with the Cartesian turn—to impose on the *cogito* itself, reduced to its foundational core, a reflexive or representational vector. Alternatively, this can be understood as an inclination to give up the search for a deeply fundamental ground of knowledge and to situate the *cogito* at a higher level, already fathomed by the order of representation. At that level, where the issue is no longer the relation of subject to object, but that of mind to body, Perrault does manage to oppose Descartes unequivocally: allowing only for the "proportionality" of mind to mind and of body to body, he effectively rigidifies the dualism that Descartes sought to overcome by structuring the imaginative faculty as an "application" of mind to body.

Beyond this, the Abbé's arbitrary assumption of likeness between subject and object puts an ultimately atomistic twist on Perrault's materialist fantasy. In reducing and binding the primitive moment of animal cognition to a single, simple material cognatum, the Abbé blocks whatever interior reflexive or self-sensing apprehension the animal might experience at the point of its inception as reflection, thereby depriving the bestial subject of the possibility of making the kind of connective, self-and-world-building turn into representation that the Cartesian *cogito* makes possible for man. While the animal *cogito*, bound by the isolated material object and thus actualizable only in punctual recurrences of the same perceptive experience, apparently does dissolve into feeling, it is not so much the feeling of thought freely seizing itself in its vital self-sentiency as simply the mechanically ordered sensation of instinctual process. As such, as affectivity caught up in the mindless, repetitive chain of stimulus and response, how can this feeling be conjoined with cognition and made constitutive of consciousness? The question here is not precisely an echo of the one raised by the Cartesian *cogito*: how does feeling come to fold back on itself in a movement of self-sensation? The mystery is not so much how a certain primitive representation for a seeing subject can inhabit this affective milieu as what such a representation might be: can it be anything other than the discontinuous play of discrete material images affecting the seeing body according to the laws of the nervous system?

The problem here is that the Abbé's speculations, while they sidestep the difficulty of describing animal consciousness directly, are inextricably immersed in his extended comparison and contrast of the animal soul to the mirror. Although the beast's capacity for representation can be likened to the optical mechanics at work in mirroring, the capacity for knowledge that makes animals more sophisticated and nobler than the impassive physical object involves a representational mechanics—evoked by the mythic first encounter with a mirror—that remains ineffable ("la maniere ineffable dont ses sens sont organisez"). The grounding perception at work in the animal *cogito* is precisely the restrictive, unthinking image-formation figured by the object-depicting mirror, endowed with its extraordinary power of exact representation. Clearly, that marvelous mirror can no longer quite stand here for the superiority of stable visible representation, as it does in the story of Orante's metamorphosis. Instead, because the Abbé conveys his ambivalent posture through the discourse he constructs around the mirror, it assumes a pivotal articulatory function. When contrasted with the animal body, the mirror figures simultaneously the inferior status of mimetic representation in relation to the higher plane of knowledge and understanding and the anchoring of that knowledge in a ground of visual representation. When considered in itself as the Abbé's singular example situating knowledge as a function of experience and perspective, the mirror illustrates both the splendor of the perfectly faithful imaging and the need to leave a space for the unfamiliar, the incalculable, or the inconceivable in the account of the truth. In its ambivalence, then, the mirror takes on the paradoxical potential to symbolize no less what sustains than what collapses the critical gap between representation and knowledge. Insofar as this crucial difference continues to inhabit intellection, it challenges the adequacy of mimetic representation for the expression of truth and disputes the value of clear and distinct ideas, perhaps even to the point of beckoning toward an unthinkable ground that escapes from clear apperception in the *cogito* itself. Yet insofar as the difference gives way to the integration of knowledge and representation, it signals a reinforcement of the Cartesian turn and of the values associated with visualization. It is, then, as if the *Parallèle's* mirror occasions a staying of the continuist movement that undergirds the value of visualization, even as it continues to emblematize that value; it is as if, for Perrault, the price of resisting the Cartesianism that undergirds the privilege of the visual in his axiology is his own retrenchment in the Cartesian turn.

Sublimations of the *Cogito*: The Inconceivable in Literature

If Perrault's resistance to Descartes ultimately lapses into compliance, the balancing act that at once denies and reasserts the convergence of visual perception with understanding, that overlays the original metaphoric construal of the *cogito* (knowing as vision) with its inverted equivalent (vision as knowing), does put a characteristically Perraldian twist on the Cartesian turn. For the purpose of situating this claim about Perrault's manner of appropriating the most exacting thought of his time, it seems relevant to point out, in advance of the analysis I shall offer in Chapter Two, that in dealing with Boileau and the sublime turn, he takes a closely analogous tack in much the same fashion, that is, with the same, acute attention to the explicitly disputed points and with little, if any, discernible awareness of the points of convergence.

In the fourth dialogue of the *Parallèle*, the two partisans of the

Moderns, the Abbé and the Chevalier, are criticizing examples of
the sublime or marvelous that Boileau, following Longinus, found
in Homer's epics. As a counterexample worthy of the term sublime,
the somewhat cavalier Chevalier suggests nothing other than the
marvelous one finds in "contes de Peau d'asne" (4: 120; 227), that is,
more or less popular or vulgar folktales, and as his particular exam-
ple, he mentions not the gold-defecating ass we find in Perrault's
versified tale "Peau d'asne," but rather the seven-league boots of
the prose tale "Le Petit Poucet." In the reasoning that eventually
emerges in this quite curious passage, Perrault's power play consists
in advocating his own diluted sublime, which is essentially the gran-
diloquent rhetoric that Boileau disdainfully regarded as *sublime
style,* while simultaneously appropriating Boileau's strong sublime,
grounded in inspired authorship.

As the Abbé's commentary recognizes, the marvelous elements
of the fairy tales, such as the magic boots, do retain something of the
inconceivable or unfathomable experience and striking, poetically
gripping quality that the sublime turn brings into play. Yet that may
be only a secondary point. For since the tales persistently fold the
inexplicable or imponderable back into the dominant order of rea-
son and verisimilitude, they bend toward a compromise formation
that leaves in place, though comfortably under artistic control, an
unresolved tension between the sublime and sublime style, between
the marvelous of a compellingly illuminating figure or inconceiv-
able experience and a naturalized marvelous, as it were, that is sub-
ject to rational, technological understanding. In its structure and
import, this double-edged operation recalls the Abbé's attempt to
defend the idea of a corporal soul by constructing an account of
animal cognition. His initial move is to validate the notion of the
inconceivable as it is illustrated by the marvel of mirroring; yet this
inconceivable factor is dissolved into a rational, functional account
as the mechanics of reflection are described. These two opposed but
articulated views of the mirror underlie the more complex compro-
mise formation that relates—in a crisscrossing or chiasmatic config-
uration—the Cartesian *cogito* to the animal *cogito.* The latter, an-
chored in the physical and subject to technical understanding,
nonetheless retains its marvelous, ineffable aspect, while the former,
although anchored in the indivisible ground of being that Perrault's
ontological schematic situates as inaccessible, can nonetheless—via
the Cartesian turn—order the cognitive field of representation.

Thus whether the dialogues of Perrault's *Parallèle* confront the Cartesian turn into representation or the sublime turn away from it, they work their way toward compromise formations or configurations that turn upon the same fundamental opposition, that of the conceivable to the inconceivable. The Chevalier's allusion to the fairy tales suggests that Perrault's fictional constructs in the *Contes* may also turn upon this opposition, situated as that of the marvelous to the rational. It happens, moreover, that the tale to which the Chevalier refers, "Le Petit Poucet," can be read not only as a typical case of this compromise, but as an allegorical narrative of its formation. The daring move that ultimately enables the hero to triumph consists in stealing the magic boots worn by the ogre who is trying to kill him and his brothers. That theft of the magic boots would be Thumbkin's seizure of the marvelous or sublime that displaces it into the realm of the clever hero's *esprit*. As for the term *esprit*—variously translatable as mind, spirit, soul, wit, intelligence—it is already the locus of a formidable compromise formation. On the one hand, the term points to the consummate strategic intelligence of Perrault's savvy heroes, who acquire the eloquence and mastery of the *honnête homme*, the perfect gentleman whose art of living is subject to codification and whose reasoned outlook privileges scientific understanding; this dominant rational *spirit* clearly falls within the perspective of sublime style, rhetoric, poetics, eloquence. Yet this very same spirit or "spirituel" also reserves within itself a subordinate but ineradicable space for a still unassimilable force, for spontaneity, inspiration, mystery, folly, and chance; it remains open to the work of a strong, irrecuperable sublime. The key term spirit—*esprit*—thus becomes a kind of signifying crossroads or condensation point, comparable in articulatory power to the mirror in the Abbé's speculations on corporal knowledge. Its semantic capaciousness enables Perrault to deploy and sustain the difference between the sublime and sublime style even while his dominant line is, so to speak, a sublimation of the sublime, a construction that drains the surpassing energy of the sublime turn into a vision of art as a craft, a pleasureful exercise. But can the spirit of the fairy tales also subject the Cartesian turn to a compromise formation comparable to this one and to those we have ferreted out of the *Parallèle*?

A number of Perrault's tales weave allegories of the spirit, as it were, in which the twists or reversals in the narrative effectively rearticulate his sublimation or recuperation of the Cartesian *cogito*.

The emblematic case of this allegorical operation is a formidably suggestive story entitled "Riquet à la houppe," a comical hero-naming title that means roughly "Richard (or perhaps Ricky) with the tuft of hair on his head" and identifies the determined protagonist as a wealthy runt.[27] The story tells how a marriage gets made—a marriage between Riquet, a cleverly eloquent and *spirituel* but hideously ugly prince, and a stupendously beautiful princess who is woefully stupid (or *mindless*, we might well say). The fairy godmother has empowered the young man endowed with *esprit* to make a gift of mind or spirit to the woman he loves; and symmetrically, the young woman who has beauty is empowered to bestow beauty or handsomeness upon the man she loves. The text seems to allegorize transparently the terms of Perrault's discourse on art and beauty in the *Parallèle*. The narrator's explanations link *esprit* unmistakably to speech as a discursive practice, and beauty to the prestige of the image, of pictural representation; and there is also a hardly subtle connection of the verbal to the male characters and the visual to the females, as the two queens and the two princesses are initially preoccupied with the visible qualities of beauty and ugliness. Riquet's triumph in the tale consists in exercising his verbal and spiritual talents well enough to bring his eventual wife through her resistance to his ugliness and, by inducing her to commit herself through performative speech, to obtain from her the reciprocal gift that makes him handsome. It looks like a victory of *esprit*, of mind, asserting its priority and control over the perceptual; the exercise of *esprit* eventually determines through what light or perspective objects will be seen and appreciated. So the scenario of exchange and the narrative structure seem to confirm the empire of a male-dominated order in which the hero's speech reduces the heroine to a certain practice of vision or re-vision that runs essentially counter to the tale's first *moralité*, which reasserts the priority of the visual, of perspective, of sight driven by desire: "ce que l'on voit dans cet écrit," notes the *moralité* at the end, "est moins un conte en l'air que la vérité même" (what we see in this text is less an ephemeral tale than truth itself; 285).

But of course, upon closer examination, the story turns out to be much trickier than this, and does contain evidence to support the lesson of that first *moralité*. Although Riquet, the hero, is the efficacious practitioner of spiritual speech, he takes his most forceful stand on the preeminent value of beauty. "La beauté," he tells the Princess, "est un si grand avantage qu'il doit tenir lieu de tout le reste" (Beauty is such a great advantage that it must hold sway over all the rest; 282) The power his successful speech acts confer on her is the power to make him objectively lovable, to create him as an object of her desire in the realm of the visible. "Vous pouvez me rendre le plus aimable de tous les hommes" (you can make me the most lovable of all men; 283), he tells her, enabling her to move into a position of self-mastery and appropriative desire as she carries out her commitment to him. Or again, on the level of the Cartesian opposition between the human and the animal, at first glance the Princess appears to pass through a metamorphosis from the animal—the term for her insistent self-qualification is *bête*—to the human as she receives the gift of gab; but we also find Riquet going through a similar metamorphosis, since he was born so ugly, according to the tale's opening sentence, that he seemed to lack human form. His humanity is not, moreover, simply the effect of her spoken wish; it is still more immediately the effect of her gaze constituting his humanized appearance: "La Princesse n'eut pas plus tôt prononcé ces paroles, que Riquet à la houppe *parut à ses yeux* l'homme du monde le plus beau, le mieux fait et le plus aimable qu'elle eût jamais *vu*" (No sooner had the Princess pronounced these words than Riquet *appeared to her eyes* as the handsomest, shapeliest, and most lovable man she had ever *seen*; 284–85; my italics). At the end of the tale a further account of this metamorphosis shifts the intervention of love that occurs in "Le Miroir, ou la métamorphose d'Orante," where the mirror image is valorized, into the realm, still visual, of illusion: according to some, the narrator tells us, "l'amour seul fit cette Métamorphose" (love alone produced this metamorphosis; 285). After this, a long sentence reports what the Princess saw in Riquet, how his disturbing bodily features appeared charming to her. Among those features were his eyes: "Ses yeux, qui étaient louches, ne lui en parurent que plus brillants. . . . Leur dérèglement passa dans son esprit pour la marque d'un violent excès d'amour" (To her, the fact that his eyes were crossed just made them seem more brilliant. . . . To her mind, their abnormality was the mark of a violent excess of love). Now this astonishing transposition reconstitutes the visual as the channel for the undeniably determining force of love, whether or not one reads there a veritable visualization, or we might say envisualization or insighting, of *esprit*, a reconstitution of the mind as a seeing mind that looks out and, through vision, imposes its imaginative frames on the bodily world, so as to make the world a kind of eroticized eye.

"Riquet à la houppe" thus displays a vacillation between two currents, one associating the power and mastery of a masculine order with intelligence and reasonable speech, the other promoting the value of a feminine order, presented in the conventional association with visibility and wish-fulfilling beauty. A great many other components of the story could be grafted onto this central opposition. But the basic structure of an exchange between speech and sight—between the verbal and the visual—that turns out to be motivated by desire suffices to introduce precisely the kind of complication that the Abbé generated with his ambivalent mirror in the *Parallèle*: the supreme value of the image, of beauty, is indeed asserted, but only to be modalized and left under a cloud as the tale gradually discloses its dependency on the verbal and its susceptibility to illusion.

Yet it remains arguable that this tale, like "Le Petit Poucet" and the ambivalent passages in the *Parallèle*, simply introduces a discontinuous factor—the sublime, the work of difference, illusion—that resists and perturbs a dominant value or perspective—rhetorical eloquence, mimeticism, well-wrought form—without seriously threatening to undermine it. Indeed, one could presume that the order of representation resulting from the Cartesian turn would thrive on meeting the challenge and compromising with it. Such literary compromises—built around a fluid, commodifiable concept of *esprit*—promote the elaboration of a unified neoclassicism that reintegrates the deep and radical reflection on inspired art we encounter in Boileau into the edifice of a complacent cultural rationalism. Similarly, Perrault's easygoing and ambivalent Cartesianism paves the way for the construction of the rationalist aesthetics he espouses in the *Parallèle* precisely by loosening the tightly articulated Cartesian turn and appropriating its yield in the form of themes or local insights. By forgetting the vigilant rigor with which Descartes structures and verifies the passage from saying to seeing, by dispensing with the methodic analysis of experience in the service of truth in favor of constructing elaborate comparisons and analogies that promote an accommodation of reason with verisimilitude, Perrault

manages to restructure the relation of the verbal to the visual, en-
abling them to function as the polar terms of a reciprocal exchange.
That drastic relaxation of the foundationalist, scientific impulse is
perhaps typical of what happens to philosophical reflection in the
hands of a so-called man of letters; it is certainly anticipatory of the
pattern that thinkers from the eighteenth century onward would
appropriate in representing the passage of ideas into art as a process
of sublimation.

2

The Sublime Turn:
Perrault Against Boileau

The crucial factor in Charles Perrault's long career as an influential man of letters was his close relationship in the 1660s and 1670s with Jean-Baptiste Colbert, Mazarin's successor as the chief minister of finances and state affairs under Louis XIV. Thanks largely to the Colbert connection, Perrault became a key adviser to Jean Chapelain, the aging poet responsible for recommending artists who were to receive subsidies from the king; he was also a central figure in two of the academies that helped apply cultural life to the service of the monarchy, the Académie des inscriptions et belles-lettres (the "petite académie") and the Académie française. Although Perrault had lost some favor at court even before Colbert's death in 1683, he was decisively marginalized thereafter, losing his position in the "petite académie" and his royal pension. Nevertheless, he continued to play an important role in the Académie française and thereby to stay abreast of most aspects of French cultural life. It seems probable that Perrault's assiduous work in the academy and his unrelenting vigor as an apologist for modernity were motivated in part by a wish to reestablish some of his lost credit with the monarchy. In any case, the interest he shared with nearly all the artists and intellectuals of his time, the glorification of Louis XIV, remained both at the core of the activity on which this chapter will focus—his dispute with Boileau (1688–94) during the most heated phase of the Quarrel of the Ancients and Moderns—and at the nub of his differences with Racine over the dedicatory letter for the *Dictionnaire de l'Académie française*, which will be taken up in Chapter Three.

The Rhetoric for Louis XIV's Century

The basic general problem to which Perrault, Boileau, and Racine had to be attentive can be stated quite simply: how should the king and his reign be described and praised? It is rather more on this horizon of an authentic debate—where the issue centers on discourse, on style and context, on rhetoric—than in the domain of controversy about achievements of the already triumphant Moderns (whose obvious advantage, dictated by the royal propaganda machine, was clear to all) that a significant opposition between Perrault and Boileau emerged. In "Le Siècle de Louis le Grand," the 532-line panegyric poem read before the academy in 1688 that sparked Perrault's bitter feud with Boileau, Perrault adopts the historical stance that he maintains in his two major end-of-career works, *Le Parallèle des anciens et des modernes* and *Les Hommes illustres qui ont paru pendant ce siècle*. As the titles of the poem and second book indicate, the framing concept is that of the *siècle* or century, and as the two book titles suggest, Perrault's rhetorical strategy as an apologist for the century of Louis XIV is oriented by his focus on great men, whether of antiquity or of modernity, whom he treats as actors determining the course of history. Perrault benefited from a privileged vantage point among late-seventeenth-century writers. His lengthy experience in public life, his concern with representing the modernity of his age in specific and positive terms, his largely successful attempt to review the artistic and scientific achievements of the age in the *Parallèle*, and his wide-ranging retrospective portrayal of the great men of the century in the *Hommes illustres* converge to make the perceptions and judgments he elaborates—with the approaching end of the chronological century clearly in mind (volume 2 of *Les Hommes illustres* appeared in 1700)—as unique and constitutive a gauge of the sense of the ending seventeenth century as an accomplished witness could fashion in the 1690s. Taken together, moreover, the *Parallèle* and the *Hommes illustres* make a noteworthy contribution to the development of literary and cultural history as a distinct genre or discursive formation.

The literary history of seventeenth-century France has recently benefited from some probing scholarly attention to the fin-de-siècle or turn-of-the-century motif as it has been defined by inquiry into the self-conscious literary decadence that sprang up when the nine-teenth century was coming to a close. Among the several essays devoted to the seventeenth century in Pierre Citti's collection, *Fins de siècle*, two contributions—by Jean Lafond and Alain Viala—carry out a valuable reconsideration of the problem of periodization and trace in broad strokes the background against which the Perraldian line on the seventeenth century should be set. From their findings one may distill the following points:

1. At the end of the century, when the dictionaries of Antoine Furetière and the Académie française provide clear frames of refer-ence, the term *siècle* is still shuttling between two senses: (a) an arbitrary chronological slice of 100 years; and (b) a period of unspec-ified length determined by a particular historical continuity. Viala describes the evolution of literary activity over the first two-thirds of Louis XIV's reign as one that gradually produces the mythical no-tion of "le siècle de Louis XIV" or "le grand siècle." This develop-ment brings the two meanings closer together. Its eventual effect is to prompt writers late in the century and in future eras to envision the entire seventeenth century as a periodic unit deriving its secular identity from the aura of the French monarchy and its institutions. Pursuant to this inaugural definition of the seventeenth century as the century of Louis XIV, the institutions that sustained national history would henceforth tend to conceive of centuries through a search for identifying traits or threads that could clothe the 100-year chronological sections in structural coherence.

2. The mythic seventeenth century created by artists who co-operated in the glorification of Louis XIV corresponds roughly to a period of consolidation during which the rise of the centralized state and the flowering of French neoclassicism went hand in hand. As Lafond shows, neither the start nor the finish of this period is readily datable, and neither phase displays significant collective con-cern with the "turn-of-the-century" phenomenon. Both, in fact, have the look of periodic subsections: perhaps 1620–50 for the beginning, 1680–1715 for the end. In the 1680's and 1690's, when the idea of "le grand siècle" became a commonplace, it is clear that a sense of fatigue and atrophy, of waiting for the end of Louis' ex-hausting reign, was an underlying, if weakly articulated factor in the intellectual climate. It is just as clear, however, that the period was

not devoid of significant artistic and cultural achievements. In particular, it gave birth to the intellectual currents that, according to Paul Hazard's *The European Mind, the Critical Years, 1680–1715*, were to fecundate the enlightenment and thus emerge as the defining traits of the eighteenth century. Hence Lafond's conclusion that the somewhat confused passage through a temporal transition or turning point is an irreducibly double-edged conjuncture of ending with beginning, of decline with renewal, of closure with opening.

3. Literary history is obliged, then, to account for the coexistence, indeed the coalescence, of contradictory impulses that Lafond perceives, for example, in La Bruyère, a stern partisan of the neoclassical doctrine calling for imitation of the Ancients. If the later editions (1689–96) of the *Caractères* are still anchored in the critical pessimism of "Des ouvrages de l'esprit" and the dejected belatedness expressed in its opening "tout est dit," they can nonetheless harbor (in "Des jugements," 12: 107) a formidably optimistic vision of the future, predicated on a notion of progress characteristic of the Moderns.[1] Similarly, as Viala suggests, if *Les Hommes illustres* (1697, 1700) displays a concern with chronology, generations, and periods that begins to bring the turn of the century into focus, the time consciousness that informs Perrault's biographic sketches hardly resembles that of late-nineteenth-century writers adrift in melancholy and anticipation of an epochal rupture. Rather, it puts into play a curious practice of recuperation (Viala aptly evokes an "oxymore historique") since Perrault, in order to construct his vision of a triumphant modernity, has to subject both his past antipathies and his observations of present realities to the compromises dictated by eulogistic discourse: his project requires him, on the one hand, to include applause for the achievements of his adversaries in the Quarrel of the Ancients and the Moderns, and on the other hand, to paper over the pronounced social, economic, and moral deterioration of the French state in the 1690s.[2]

Classicism and Rhetoric

To appreciate the rhetorical posture Perrault adopts in writing about his century, it does not suffice to observe that his perceptions of an elusive and elongated *fin de siècle* are ambivalent and in some respects contradictory. Since the whole of volume 2 of the *Parallèle* addresses the question of eloquence—that is, the theory, practice, and evolving status of rhetoric—in an intellectual and institutional context that is proper to the second half of the seventeenth century, the position Perrault elaborates has to be understood as a response to that context, at once synthesizing and modernizing the views of his contemporaries.

Owing to its central place in the education dispensed in the *collèges*, classical rhetoric prospered well into the eighteenth century. Its precedence over poetics, inscribed in Richelieu's charge to the newly created Académie française to produce a dictionary, a grammar, a rhetoric, and a poetics, is still fully intact in Fénelon's *Lettre à l'Académie* (1714).[3] Yet insofar as the cultural era of Louis XIV drew its identity from the doctrines and literary masterpieces of neoclassicism (thus from a movement that had triumphed in the 1660s and 1670s and began to wane by 1685), its reconstruction of the general rhetorical apparatus within which literary discourse was fabricated (a major part of the process consisted in filtering a Latin-based enterprise into French) put a distinctive stamp on the sphere of rhetoric devoted to style or eloquence (*elocutio*). The dominant posture, doubtless rooted as much in the valorization of logic, order, and simple clarity found in the work of Descartes and the thinkers of Port-Royal as in the rhetorical heritage of the classical tradition (Aristotle, Cicero, Quintilian, et al.), censures stylistic effects—ornament, embellishment, oratorical flair—that smack of exhibition or inflation. As Boileau admonishes in *L'Art poétique*: "Soyez simple avec art,/Sublime sans orgueil, agreable sans fard" (Be simple with art, sublime without pride, pleasing without makeup).[4] When *L'Art poétique* invokes rhetoric explicitly (with respect to tragedy in the first part of chant 3), the poetician sympathizes fully with its fundamental concern with reception, yet is quick to warn against the effect of pompous verbiage upon

> Un Spectateur toujours paresseux d'applaudir,
> Et qui des vains efforts de vostre Rhetorique,
> Justement fatigué, s'endort, ou vous critique.
> Le secret est d'abord de plaire et de toucher.
>
> A Spectator always weary of applauding
> and who, justifiably tired of the vain efforts of your rhetoric,
> dozes off, or criticizes you.
> The secret is first of all to please and to move.

In Fénelon's *Dialogues sur l'éloquence* (ca. 1680),[5] the dual requirement of imitation—of nature, as well as of Greek and Roman models—espoused by Boileau is applied specifically and at length to eloquence in its primary guise, the art of oratory. Elaborating a relatively complex, content-oriented account of eloquence, Fénelon defends the injunction to please in the delicate case of preaching by arguing that pleasure serves to prepare the listeners to respond to the sermon's ultimate mission, which is to touch their hearts; and even more insistently than Boileau and such contemporary poeticians as Dominique Bouhours and René Rapin,[6] he underscores the infelicity of visible artfulness. Along with his openly reserved attitude toward rhetoric—"vous n'attendez pas que je vous explique par ordre le détail presque infini des préceptes de la rhétorique; il y en a beaucoup d'inutiles: vous les avez lus dans les livres, où ils sont amplement" (you do not expect me to provide an orderly account of the almost infinite detail of the precepts of rhetoric; there are many useless ones: you have read them in books, where they are supplied in abundance)[7]—Fénelon manifests a revisionist tendency to emphasize *inventio* at the expense of *elocutio*, and to address the latter, not in terms of stylistic technique, but merely through an enumeration of desirable qualities and effects.

Thus, while the axiology of French neoclassicism put a rationalist critical inflection on the understanding and appropriation of rhetoric, it seems evident, as Aron Khibédi-Varga contends,[8] that it presupposed and worked within an integral relationship between the broadly conceived spheres of rhetoric and poetics. A telling piece of evidence here is the kinship of the two major works Boileau published in 1674, *L'Art poétique* and his translation of the *Traité du sublime*, which in the seventeenth century was attributed to Cassius Longinus.[9] Although it is precisely the sublime that was to be pivotal in the late-century period, running from 1688 to 1710, during which Boileau pursued his unflagging defense of the Ancients, it is important to note that the body of Longinus's treatise, in its broad conception as well as through its definitions, examples, and commentaries, is given over to rhetoric and style. Longinus's pointed discourse on the sublime emerges in a few key passages of the work; and for him, as well as for modern readers, the central challenge—and the spur that makes his thought original—is to articulate rhetoric with the sublime, to negotiate between the lowly nuts and bolts of artistic technique and the high altitudes reached by the work of genius. Moreover, it is clear that Boileau relished the broadly inclusive range of the *Traité du sublime*. He deemed its positioning of rhetoric to be fully consonant with his own work as a rule-writing poetician of classical reason and restraint, resistant to the uncontrolled flights of fantasy he saw in much writing of the preclassical period in France, and openly at war with preciosity in the literature of his own time.

The Longinian Sublime

If Longinus's treatise offers original and exemplary insights into the essence of great writing, one such contribution, Boileau suggests in his preface, lies in its deep appreciation of a fundamental value, that of majestic simplicity. The accent on simplicity emerges in a passage devoted to the meaning of the substantive, *le sublime*, which Boileau opposes to the affectations of sublime style: "Par sublime, Longin n'entend pas ce que les orateurs appellent le style sublime, mais cet extraordinaire et ce merveilleux qui frappe dans le discours, et qui fait qu'un ouvrage enlève, ravit, transporte. Le style sublime veut toujours de grands mots; mais le sublime se peut trouver dans une seule pensée, dans une seule figure, dans un seul tour de paroles" (By sublime, Longinus does not mean what the orators call sublime style, but this quality of the extraordinary and the marvelous that strikes us in discourse, and that enables a work to carry us away, to entrance us, to transport us. Sublime style always wants more big words, whereas the sublime can be found in a single thought, a single figure, a single turn of phrase).[10] With an example from Corneille's *Horace*, Boileau amplifies his accent on simplicity while stressing its bond with sincerity, authenticity. When old Horace is asked what his son should have done instead of fleeing the three Curiaces, the father answers, "Qu'il mourût" (would that he had died). Boileau comments that this response "est d'autant plus sublime, qu'il est simple et naturel, et que par là on voit que c'est du fond du coeur que parle ce vieux héros. . . . Ainsi c'est la simplicité même de ce mot qui en fait la grandeur" (is all the more sublime because it is simple and natural, and because we thus see that this elderly hero is speaking from the heart. . . . Therefore it is the very simplicity of this word that makes for its grandeur).[11]

The sublime appears, then, not as a style, not as a rhetorical practice, but simply as a turn of discourse; it can only be defined indirectly, elusively, evocatively, by its immediately compelling effects of force and authenticity. Yet Boileau, following the lead of Longinus, mobilizes numerous examples in order to generate a sense of the sublime, as well as to describe textual practices—rhetorical and stylistic—that enable the artist to build toward the production of sublime effects. Production and authorship are the primary conceptual levers here. Indeed, the preface's first and foremost example of the sublime is none other than the presumed author, Cassius Longinus. Of that great man "digne d'être mis en parallèle avec les Socrates et les Catons" (worthy of comparison to the likes of Socrates and Cato), Boileau writes: "ses sentiments ont je ne sais quoi qui marque non seulement un esprit sublime, mais une âme fort élevée au-dessus du commun" (his feelings have an inexpressible quality that marks not only a sublime spirit, but a soul far elevated above the ordinary).[12]

So forthwith, two motifs: elevation, the immediate connotation of sublimity, and the "je ne sais quoi," the celebrated phrase by which not only Boileau but Pascal, Bouhours, and many other writers allude to the impression made by the inconceivable, the ineffable that escapes or blocks the mind's representational grasp. The "je ne sais quoi" situates the sublime as a "limit notion," a term marking the analytic frontier at which positive definition or delineation of an idea or image or event or figure of thought becomes impossible. Approaching this limit brings into play a paradox that Longinus knowingly assumes and addresses in his treatise: the very instruments of rhetoric, representation, or expression that make possible the production of the sublime and inform the attempt to make it accessible through learning are not fully adequate to the task of circumscribing it theoretically and making it the object of artistic practice; its mode of inscription can only be that of presentation or, more aptly, exemplification; and discourse about the sublime can never address it directly, will always be discourse about the approach to it, about the conditions under which it appears, rather than discourse that captures the sublime itself. Already in Chapter 2 Longinus is venturing formulations that sustain the opposition between artistic competence and natural genius, while nonetheless resolving the tensions between them,[13] and in Chapter 8, the much glossed division of the five sources of the sublime between natural gifts (strong thinking and passionate feeling) and technical competence (mastery of figures, of style and usage, of harmonious composition of the whole) rearticulates the paradox marked by the "je ne sais quoi"—one must somehow allude to that unfathomable offering of natural genius that cannot be named or explained—as the structure presiding over the entire treatise.

Now, these salient initial motifs—elevation and indefinability—are by no means the only significant points to be drawn from Boileau's portrayal of Longinus. Stressing the author's dual role as the critic who discloses the sublime and as the writer who is sublime, who exemplifies or "instantiates" the sublime in his work on the sublime, Boileau accords at least two-thirds of his preface to what some might rush to dismiss as biographical criticism. But two factors give the focus on authorship, on the presence of the author in the text, a compelling and passably original twist. The first and structurally primary one is that Boileau forcefully and strategically immerses himself in the work and thought of the translator. In his capacious, audacious account of that task, he admits to carrying the translator's sympathetic identification with the author beyond self-effacing fidelity and scrupulous understanding, and into a still more concerted act of appropriation:

Quelque petit donc que soit le volume de Longin, je ne croirois pas avoir fait un médiocre présent au public, si je lui en avois donné une bonne traduction en notre langue. Je n'y ai point épargné mes soins ni mes peines. Qu'on ne s'attende pas pourtant de trouver ici une version timide et scrupuleuse des paroles de Longin. Bien que je me sois efforcé de ne me point écarter en pas un endroit des règles de la véritable traduction, je me suis pourtant donné une *honnête liberté*, surtout dans les passages qu'il rapporte. J'ai songé qu'il ne s'agissoit pas simplement ici de traduire Longin, mais de donner au public un *Traité du sublime* qui pût être *utile*.[14]

So however small Longinus's volume may be, I believe I will have made a noteworthy gift to the public if I have provided a good translation of it in our language. I have put every care and effort into the task. But let no one expect to find here a timid and scrupulous rendering of the words of Longinus. Although I have tried never to deviate from the rules of accurate translation, I have allowed myself an *honest freedom*, especially in the passages he cites. I thought it was not a matter of merely translating Longinus here, but of giving the public a translation of Longinus that could be useful.

Boileau is skeptical of unduly literal translation. From the impossibility of conveying the force and subtlety of the original by rendering its messages as exactly as possible, by reproducing strictly the meanings the author conferred on his text for his public, he infers a need for creative translation: in order to make the French version meaningful for the modern, seventeenth-century audience, he has discreetly supplemented the authorship of Longinus with his own authorial purview, warranting the adjustment he brings to the message of Longinus with his own intention toward his readers ("donner au public un *Traité du sublime* qui pût être utile"). By that assertion of his own involvement, Boileau effectively puts himself behind and into the text of Longinus that he is offering in French. Accordingly, his preface serves as a text of authorization, the confession of a translator drawn toward a kind of after-the-fact coauthorship; it allows us to take ideas and analyses in the *Traité du sublime* as insights to which Boileau is subscribing on his own account, via his freely appropriative practice of translation, as well as by his unreserved praise for Longinus; it thus sanctions our pairing of *Le Traité du sublime* with *L'Art poétique*.[15]

The second reason why Boileau's emphasis on the value of authorship is exceptionally compelling flows naturally, so to speak, from the first. For the perspective Boileau takes on with Longinus when he implicates himself in his noble author's text is none other than the treatise's own preoccupation with authorship, its remarkable attention to artists' immediate, experiential relation to their work. Sensitivity to the creator's presence in representation or in discursive action is the pervasive ground of Longinus's commentary on examples of the sublime; and the predominant concern with the author in Boileau's preface is evidently a particular case of his appropriation of Longinian insight as his own. This appropriative relation implies, of course, that in order to appreciate fully the solidarity between Boileau and Longinus as spokesmen for the authorial order, we have to examine the text of Longinus through which we can now perceive Boileau to be speaking in his turn.

The Example of Sappho

Two analyses of authorial experience in the treatise stand out as particularly revealing evocations of the sublime: first, the treatment of Sappho in Chapter 10, and then the treatment of Demosthenes in Chapter 16. Neil Hertz analyzes both cases in his shrewd reading of the treatise in *The End of the Line*. In the case of Sappho's ode, Hertz shows how Longinus takes motifs he repeatedly associates with the sublime—violent power and the risk of death—and links them with the poetic doctrine of organic unity. We encounter what Hertz calls "the sublime turn" in the "shift from Sappho-as-victimized-body to Sappho-as-poetic-force,"[16] that is, the disintegrative force of violent action and looming catastrophe is somehow reversed as that fearful moment of passion—desire carrying its victim to the point of death—is captured by the sublime surge of the author's voice, is remodulated as the harmonious, unifying power of great poetry. Boileau's translation records quite beautifully both Longinus's keen, identificatory admiration for Sappho and the bond he senses between the sublime she embodies and a profound experience of passion or pathos: "Voyez de combien de mouvements contraires elle est agitée. *Elle gèle, elle brûle, elle est folle, elle est sage*; ou elle est entièrement hors d'elle-même, ou elle va mourir. En un mot, on diroit qu'elle n'est pas éprise d'une simple passion, mais que son âme est un *rendez-vous de toutes les passions*; et c'est en effet ce qui arrive à ceux qui aiment" (Note how many competing impulses agitate her. *She freezes, she burns, she is mad, she is wise*; either she is entirely beside herself, or she is going to die. In a word, we might say that she is not taken with a simple passion, but that her soul is a *meeting-place of all the passions*; and that is indeed what happens to those who love).[17]

The commentary here uncannily rearticulates the sublime turn. First: An initial evocation of violence, of a body rent by forces of contradiction, is accomplished by Boileau's perhaps inadvertent alexandrine: "elle gèle, elle brûle, elle est folle, elle est sage." The paratactic strikes that syncopate this line resonate with his active evocation of the sublime in the preface as "ce merveilleux qui frappe dans le discours, et qui fait qu'un ouvrage enlève, ravit, transporte," and with what he will later call, in the *Réflexions critiques*, again apropos of a bodily disintegration and again celebrating the value of simplicity, "la petitesse énergique des paroles" (the forceful compactness of the words).[18] If that vibrant line epitomizes what is arresting in discourse, it is evidently because in the twelve syllables of the alexandrine we encounter in cascade seven l's and seven open e's, compressed in four grammatically complete propositions, with these cleanly separated mini-sentences being articulated in pairs that form elegant antitheses on each side of the caesura; if the line propels us toward the expressive or emotive register of what carries away, entrances, transports, it is because the play of contradictions it traces—from "freeze" to "burn," from "mad" to "wise"—arcs across the whole spectrum of mental and emotional experience and leads into the ultimate antithesis, an alternative that aptly contrasts and conflates the polar extremes of passion as it reverts from searing erotic intensity to the sealing passivity of death; and if the impact of artful and compelling simplicity is perceptible in the very vocables of the commentary, it is because the incantatory articulation driven by the four *elles* forces those ten little words into a kind of crystallization—a collusion-from-within-collision—that holds the antagonistic complements together inside the outreaching of the turbulent subject: it is as if the line runs together *gèle, brûle, folle,* and *sage* in the verbal body of this *elle* so as to condense all the tension and fragmentation that the ode evokes.

Second: From this dynamic recall of Sappho's feelings, the Longinian reading then makes its turn to the poet's self-restorative triumph. Under analysis, the sublime turn does not appear as a change of object since the four clauses are all intransitive and thus have no object other than to express the wrenching volatility of the invaded subject. Rather, the turn is merely a subtle shift in mode of representation, one that slides from a still active, experiencing subject—"elle est [encore]"—to a passive channel acceding to the subjectlessness of emotion—"elle est entièrement hors d'elle-même" or, precisely, to the pull of a living self-dispossession, a veritable death of the subject—"ou elle va mourir"—that the violence of love wreaks upon consciousness. Free and dauntless in its staging of affective movement, Boileau's flowing translation deposits a commutation from the impulses passing through the impassioned woman to the author's topographic representation of her soul as a meeting-place for the passions, a core of motivity somehow capable of housing and harmonizing all the emotions that well up within her. If the critic does more than reproduce the sublime turn of the poem, that extra contribution consists in specifying what is sublime about the poet's work: precisely its transcendent capacity directly and simply to express, not single passions one by one, not a select combination of emotions proper to love, but all the passions of the soul, the whole subjective order of pathos or emotivity. Sappho's poem articulates an integration, a fusion, an organic unity of passion as a ground or continuum or principle active through all the particular passions that no punctual analysis, no fixed topology, no instrumental account, no dispassionate idiom can ever hope to capture. Working from the translator's derivative position, Boileau seems to have expressed the most challenging implication of Longinus's move to situate the sublime turn inside the artist's inspiring experience of creative power. For on that Longinian account, no critical reading will rise to a reckoning with the sublime that does not itself reach, in writing, toward authorship of its own sublime effect. Interpretation anchored in the reader's experience alone bars itself from access to the sublime.

The Example of Demosthenes

In *On the Sublime*, Demosthenes's oratory, and notably his speech to the Athenians after their defeat at Chaeronea at the hands of Philip II of Macedonia, offers a second important occasion for probing the sublime author's performance. Boileau the translator could hardly have anticipated, in 1674, the pivotal role this example would assume in his dispute with Perrault in the 1690s. For Boileau, the polemical struggle on behalf of the Ancients, already under way in the 1670s, was destined to continue episodically until 1710, when he wrote the last three of his *Réflexions critiques sur quelques passages du rhéteur Longin*—which is to say that, like Perrault, he developed an abiding concern with positioning the art of his own time vis-à-vis the Greek and Roman classics and sustained it over the entirety of the end-of-the-century period. Through the 1680s and 1690s, moreover, Boileau and his colleague Racine had to be vitally concerned with the representation of Louis XIV and his century because they were serving together as the king's official *historiographes*. As for Perrault, his entrenchment in the camp of the Moderns was also firmly established at the start of the 1670s, long before "Le Siècle de Louis le Grand" provoked Boileau's ire.[19] The six years of polemics (which ended in a truce that Racine helped arrange) are crucially important for literary history because they occasioned the four volumes of the *Parallèle* (1688, 1690, 1692, 1697) and the *Réflexions critiques*.

In the first nine of these *Réflexions* (1694), Boileau laid out in copious detail his scornful corrections of the errors Perrault made in his defense of modernism in the *Parallèle*. If the disagreement that these two works document provides telling indications about the status of rhetoric at the end of the century, in large measure it is because Longinus's approach to rhetoric lies at the heart of the debate. In the first place, Boileau and Perrault are at odds over the evaluation of the Longinian exemplars of the sublime, Homer and Demosthenes. In the second place, the substantive issues that emerged during the quarrel are the very questions about the nature and value of rhetoric that Longinus confronted: the definitions of eloquence and of the sublime; the relationship between the sublime and technique, and between rhetoric and poetics; and the nature of genius and its role in artistic creation. Not only should the responses on these issues enable us to construct a sense of the transitional space toward which rhetoric gravitated at the end of the century; they should also reveal features of the rhetorical practices through which a sense of the century—if not of its ends—is elaborated. In particular, delving further into Viala's suggestion that the Perraldian retrospective does entail a vision of the century necessarily conditioned by a certain sense of its chronological end should make it possible to expand upon what is at stake in the Modernist's resistance to Boileau's classicist line on rhetoric. Over and beyond the lexical convergence of the two meanings of *siècle*, can we glimpse in Perrault's resistance to Boileau's position, which centers forcefully on the sublime, not merely a concept of progress proper to the beginning of a new century, but a century-ending rhetorical configuration? In order to pursue this line of inquiry, we must first flesh out the view of the sublime we have begun to extract from Boileau's end-of-century writings, then inquire into the fate of the sublime in the hands of Perrault.

Boileau's tenth Reflection returns to a particularly significant example of the sublime, the line from the creation story in Genesis, "And God said, Let there be light, and there was light." His very insistent commentary does not merely rearticulate the linkage between the sublime and simplicity;[20] it also positions the sublime within the communicative structure proper to the oratorical art of eloquence. Boileau offers this incisive comment on the conditions of its occurrence: "Pour bien juger du beau, du sublime, du merveilleux dans le discours, il ne faut pas simplement regarder la chose qu'on dit, mais la personne qui la dit, la manière dont on la dit, et l'occasion où on la dit; enfin . . . il faut regarder, non quid sit, sed quo loco sit" (to evaluate the beautiful, the sublime, the marvelous in discourse, one must not simply look at what is said, but at the person who says it, the manner in which it is said, and the occasion on which it is said; in sum . . . one must consider not the what, but the where and how).[21] In other words, Boileau ends up imagining something like a pragmatics of the sublime, an account of the sublime event's circumstantial singularity that cannot belong to style or rhetoric or grammar or any particular level of language structure because it has to arch over the entire process of enunciation and reception; such an account of discursive effects has to embrace the full range of expressive possibilities, the framework and strategy of rhetorical practice. No doubt Louis Marin is right to suggest that the seventeenth century's most profound attention to this process was engaged when Pascal, in analyses of perspective that anticipated the Romantic sublime theorized in Kant's third critique, extended the explanation of effects—"la raison des effets"—to the mind's humbling encounter with the two infinities.[22]

Pascal is not, however, a likely source of Boileau's enumeration of the features that make for a pragmatics of the sublime. It is more plausible to assume that he is restating an idea that appears, in perspicuous terms, in Chapter 16 of *On the Sublime*. There the object of inquiry is the famous example of Demosthenes's recourse to an oath sworn, not by a god or gods, but by the men who fought at Marathon. Here are two snippets from Boileau's translation that provide a sense of the pragmatics already at work in the treatise:[23]

Mais il n'y a pas grande finesse à jurer simplement. Il faut voir où, comment, en quelle occasion et pourquoi on le fait. . . .

Dans Démosthène, ce serment est fait directement pour rendre le courage aux Athéniens vaincus, et pour empêcher qu'ils ne regardassent dorénavant comme un malheur la bataille de Chéronée. De sorte que, comme j'ai déjà dit, dans cette seule figure, il leur prouve, par raison, qu'ils n'ont point failli, il leur en fournit un exemple, il le leur confirme par des serments, il fait leur éloge, et il les exhorte à la guerre contre Philippe.

But there is no great finesse in simply swearing an oath. One must see where, how, on what occasion, and why it is sworn. . . .

In Demosthenes, this oath is sworn directly for the purpose of rekindling the courage of the conquered Athenians, and of preventing them from henceforth considering the battle of Chaeronea to be an adversity. So that, as I have already said, in this single figure he uses reason to prove to them that they have by no means failed, he provides them with an example, he confirms it for them with the taking of oaths, he praises them, and he exhorts them to war against Philip.

Insight of such masterly comprehensiveness alone would suffice to justify Boileau's admiration for Longinus, who attends with equal precision to the logical and historical implications of the oath and then to three speech acts that it performs.

Just as impressively, in their general thrust the extended remarks on Demosthenes, formulated in Chapter 17, again take up the elusive relation between the sublime and topics of rhetoric such as those discussed in Chapters 16 and 17, images and figures. This problematic relation is queried from a familiar Platonic angle: does the use of figures not make the reader or listener suspicious of deceptive artifice or fallacious thinking, and thus contravene, rather than support, the search for the sublime? The general problem, in a word, is how literary language can work in the service of truth, while the particular question is how the sublime's irrecusable effects of authenticity and elevation can be preserved in language that is figurative and thus potentially deceptive. Unsurprisingly, Longinus repeats the traditional answer that we have seen Boileau, Fénelon, and others adopt in their turn: great art conceals its artifice. Thus, in Boileau's translation: "Il n'y a point de figure plus excellente que celle qui est tout à fait cachée et lorsqu'on ne reconnaît point que c'est une figure" (no figure is more excellent than the one that is entirely hidden and not recognized by anyone as a figure).[24]

But as Hertz's analysis shows, a lot more is going on in the passage. In talking about figurative speech that engenders suspicion, Longinus inexplicably focuses on the reaction of a particularly intolerant addressee—"un juge souverain, . . . surtout si ce juge est un grand seigneur, comme un tyran, un roi, ou un général d'armée" (a sovereign judge, . . . especially if this judge is a great lord, such as a tyrant, a king, or a general).[25] This sets up a situation in which the sublime turn, concealing the figure and thus allowing the subject speaking to the master to be persuasive, coincides with something like an Oedipal reversal. The crucial supplement to the conventional answer comes, however, in a pronounced appropriation of figurative language. Longinus asks how Demosthenes was able to hide the figure he used in the famous oath at Marathon. Here is the rather ample answer, again in Boileau's translation:

N'est-il pas aisé de reconnoître que c'est par l'éclat même de sa pensée? Car comme les moindres lumières s'évanouissent quand le soleil vient à éclairer, de même toutes ces subtilités de rhétorique disparoissent à la vue de cette grandeur qui les environne de tous côtés. La même chose à peu près arrive dans la peinture. En effet, que l'on colore plusieurs choses également tracées sur un même plan et qu'on y mette le jour et les ombres, il est certain que ce qui se présentera d'abord à la vue ce sera le lumineux, à cause de son grand éclat, qui fait qu'il semble sortir hors du tableau et s'approcher en quelque façon de nous. Ainsi le sublime et le pathétique, soit par une affinité naturelle qu'ils ont avec les mouvements de notre âme, soit à cause de leur brillant, paroissent davantage et semblent toucher de plus près notre esprit que les figures dont ils cachent l'art et qu'ils mettent comme à couvert.[26]

Is it not easy to see that it is by the very radiance of his thought? For just as lesser lights fade out when the light of the sun appears, so too do all the subtleties of rhetoric disappear in the light of this grandeur that surrounds them from all sides. Almost the same thing occurs in painting. For if we color certain things drawn on the same plane with equal relief and put in light and shadow, it is certain that what will first appear to sight will be the bright portion, owing to its brilliance, which makes it somehow seem to come out of the picture and move closer to us. Thus the sublime and the pathetic, whether by virtue of a natural affinity they have with the movements of our soul or because of their brilliance, stand out in greater relief and seem to touch our minds more directly than do the figures, hiding their art and, as it were, placing them under cover.

This Longinian account of the sublime covering the artful by saturating the field of vision marks insistently the affinity of the sublime with the "fiat lux": the sublime is an appearance to vision, and discourse on sublime figurality seems compelled to begin with the graphic (represented here by the analogy with painting), yet immediately to grasp the image initially evoked in the outbreaking power (*éclat*) of imaging—its bursting out of the picture upon the viewer—that makes for its assimilation to the order of the *pathétique*, to "les mouvements de notre âme." Hertz's close reading of Chapter 17 describes the rigor with which Longinus attends to the essential connection between the sublime and the process of figuration that casts language as art—the latter being named in the above passage (*rhétorique, peinture, art*), but more crucially figured for perception by the play of light against darkness (*éclat, lumières, soleil, éclairer, colore, jour, ombres, lumineux, brillant*). By its lighting effects, we might say, the sublime figure works like lightning: it reaches its listener or viewer in a flash, without mediation, and with enough force to drown in its brilliance any other figures that may accompany it. The sublime flood of illumination is thus a "limit figure" that obliterates the perceptible contours of figurativeness itself; insofar as the light overwhelming darkness is spatially undifferentiable or, as it were, total in the domination or saturation of its milieu, it figures that truth of immediate perception—*aletheia*—that erupts so powerfully in the event of its appearance as to admit only of a temporal demarcation, that is, of a narrativizing description like the Longinian account of the sublime as a crowning authorial experience. The sublime is the advent—coincident with its passing—of passion in poetic language; it embodies passion undecidably as fulfillment and as absolute expenditure, as the rush of life bursting forth and in the same breath passing away.[27]

The inward-bearing truth of this passion, no longer susceptible to being situated in the exteriority of pictorial representation ("il semble sortir hors du tableau et s'approcher en quelque façon de nous"), exerts an uplifting effect that is confined to the fulgurant, yet fleeting ecstasy—which, totally consuming, is not *ek-stasis*—of the momentous passage. The experience of the sublime thus presses its subject toward the delicate passivity that Michel Henry describes in linking the *cogito* to a radically interior self-sensing that Descartes evokes in certain passages of *Les Passions de l'âme*. As we noted in Chapter One, this imposing appearance of sublime truth, marked by unity, certainty, and full, undivided self-presence, makes for an evident complicity between the sublime and the equally compelling, singular, indubitable truth that the subject seizes in the *cogito*. Insofar as it positions the consummation of the sublime turn as the reversal of the Cartesian turn, and insofar as its revelatory cast and structuring impetus confer on it, for Longinus, the status of a fundamental ground, it adjoins great art to the work of cognition, to the search for truth in its deepest, most powerful principle. The *Parallèle*'s insensitivity to Longinus's view of a nobly philosophic Demosthenes, distinguished by the "éclat même de sa pensée," serves to identify Boileau's antagonist with respect to the sublime, not as the surface-level Perrault who espouses a somewhat facile anti-Cartesianism, but as the substantive Perrault whose deeper commitment is to the commanding value of visual representation.

The positioning of the sublime co-elaborated by Longinus and Boileau ends up embracing a rather complex cluster of coincident features and effects: elevation of thought, undefinability, simplicity of expression, dissimulation of the figurative, authenticity of sentiment, inspired authorship, articulation of passion in its principle, reintegration of the poetic subject, singularity of the speech event. Taken together, these traits do not quite strike the harmonious chord literary history has taught us to expect from Boileau. They would seem to confront the pillars of his neoclassical doctrine (*le rationnel et l'intelligible*) with a horizon of artistic experience (*le passionnel et le sensible*) that classicism is determined to respect, yet cannot assimilate fully to its predominant aesthetics of imitation and restraint. The sublime would be the special, almost magical achievement of the inspired artist; its faculty would be, in Kantian terms, the productive imagination; its tradition and its ultimately mysterious dynamics would be those of the *phantasia*, of visions or apparitions that spring, as it were, to the mind's eye, that embed poetic process in a prefigural order of fantasy, illusion, illumination, genius, spontaneity; and its effect, vis-à-vis a poetics of mimetic representation and reproductive imagination, would be one of questioning, resistance, and supplementation. It is as if the regulatory scheme enacted by *L'Art poétique* somehow had to acknowledge and reckon with a still separate and irrecuperable dimension of aesthetic experience disclosed analytically by the *Traité du sublime*. Since the sublime eclipses the very figurativeness that rhetoric purports to manipulate, it is as if the rhetoric of the sublime, envisaged as a pragmatics that treats discourse as action on an addressee, were subordinated to the "superrhetorical," to an elusive object beyond or outside its purview—thus, as if its aspiration were a level of eloquence that bespeaks the end of rhetoric.

Perrault's Penchant: Sublime Style

Although many points of dispute between Boileau and Perrault turned out to be largely inconsequential or resolvable in the light of the views and values they shared, their quarrel was sustained by one substantial opposition: the classicist Boileau steadfastly asserted this challenging and retorsionary sublime, whereas the modernist Perrault generally refused to truck with it and clung to the very oratorical standard for sublime style that Boileau, Rapin, and the partisans of the Ancients found suspect. In the second volume of the *Parallèle*, devoted to the crucial question of eloquence, Perrault's distaste for Boileau's line on the sublime is most trenchantly enunciated precisely with respect to Demosthenes (2: 158–90; 133–41). The representative of the Ancients in the dialogue, the Président, praises the orator's eloquence because, "sans figures et sans paroles inutiles elle plaise, elle charme, elle enlève, semblable à ces belles personnes qui sans fard & sans ajustemens superflus se font aimer de tout le monde par la seule force de leur beauté simple et naïve" (without figures and useless words it pleases, charms, carries away, not unlike beautiful people who, without makeup or superfluous finery, are liked by everyone as a result of their simple and naive beauty; 2: 163; 134). Here the dominant motif of forceful simplicity is perfectly in phase with Boileau's discourse on the sublime.

It should be noted that, for the most part, Perrault's spokesman, the Abbé, expresses values and measured judgments largely compatible with Boileau's classicism (whereas according to the preface of volume 1, his foil, the Chevalier, sometimes ventures naive or exaggerated views that should not be attributed to the author). The Abbé's retort here seems blunt and somewhat pretentious because he pursues the censorial practice, strenuously advocated by Perrault, of finding fault with specific passages in classical texts. While disapproving of excessive affectation or superfluous ornamentation, he condemns Demosthenes for the opposite vice, "qui est d'avoir manqué des ornemens essentiels à l'Eloquence" (which is to have lacked the ornaments essential to eloquence; 2: 165; 135).

A bit later, the Abbé proceeds to distinguish common simplicity from a fine, uplifting variety that condenses deep and far-reaching insights in economic formulations. Lest this good simplicity seem to correspond to Boileau's sublime, however, the Abbé quickly bars linking it with the ineffable:

Cette belle simplicité est à l'égard de l'autre ce que l'or est à l'égard du fer & du cuivre, car comme l'or contient en un petit volume la valeur d'une grande masse de ces autres metaux, de mesme le discours où se rencontre cette simplicité pretieuse renferme en peu de mots ce qu'un autre discours d'une simplicité commune ne pourroit égaler que par un grand nombre de paroles, ainsi le moyen le plus seur pour discerner la belle simplicité d'avec celle qui luy est opposée, c'est de voir si elle renferme beaucoup de sens & de bon sens sous peu d'expressions simples & ordinaires, & si elle peut estre expliquée par un plus grand nombre de paroles, qui toutes ensemble ne diroient pas davantage, & qui seroient en quelque façon la monnoye qu'on en auroit renduë. (2: 174–75; 137)

This fine simplicity is with respect to the other what gold is with respect to iron or copper, for just as a small amount of gold contains the value of a great mass of these other metals, discourse that has this precious simplicity puts in a few words what a discourse endowed with ordinary simplicity could only equal with a great many words; therefore the surest way to distinguish fine simplicity from the other kind is to see if it conveys a great deal of meaning and good sense with a few simple and ordinary expressions, and whether it can be explained in a much greater number of words that, taken together, say no more, and that can be regarded, as it were, as change being returned.

Now this extraordinary period calls for at least two comments. In the first place, as a statement of the critic's dual criterion for identifying good simplicity—quantitative/semiological ("beaucoup de sens) and qualitative/logical ("bon sens")—it reflects Perrault's confidence in method, in technical, analytic understanding. In the second place, it constitutes a remarkable emblem of a figural inclination—a fondness for comparison (implicit in the work's title) and analogy—that turns up repeatedly in the responses of the Abbé and the Chevalier. The uncannily Perraldian touch in the rhetorical flourish generated by "la simplicité pretieuse" lies not merely in its preciousness, but still more poignantly in the correspondence between the rhetoric of comparison and the analytic practice—comparing the words and meanings packed into a simple expression to those of a commentary elucidating it—that the Abbé recommends. The rhetorical gambit here is rooted in the commonplace metaphorics that represents discourse as money ("paroles . . . qui seroient en quelque façon la monnoye"). Longinus, as it happens, notes the affinity of metaphor and simile at the beginning of Chapter 37: "Les Paraboles et les Comparaisons approchent fort des Metaphores, et ne different d'elles qu'en un seul point."[28] His examples, moreover (from Plato's *Timaeus*), are elaborate constructions based on the geography of the human body that illustrate the overlapping of metaphor and analogy. Within the analogics or metaphorics developed by Perrault, the process of conversion that functions in translation or paraphrase is the key: in equating the value of a small quantity of valuable words to that of a large quantity of cheaper ones, the Abbé at once outlines and illustrates a linguistic economy of exchange that implies the essential equivalence—interchangeability or translatability—of compact and wordy messages.[29]

Thus the fine art of simplicity is not unfathomable and requires no appeal to the sublime; it is accessible to an analysis that enumerates and relates the components it configures through a rhetorical or poetic process of condensation. Hence the possibility of what Perrault's criterion effectively claims, namely, that the measure of good simplicity lies in fact in the complexity that informs and explains it. If inspiration or genius may enter into the achievement of such simplicity, the primary factor reflected in its production remains the orator's mastery of the linguistic economy. According to the Abbé, that mastery is missing from Demosthenes's speeches, which are marred by weak reasoning and loose organization. His vaunted simplicity is, then, usually of the common, mediocre kind. The Abbé insists, for example, that the occasion of an important speech to the people of Athens called for more than Demosthenes delivered:

Il falloit là du sublime et de l'heroïque, où pouvoit-il plus à propos deployer les grandes voiles de l'Eloquence, & employer ses plus nobles figures & ses plus beaux ornemens. La grande Eloquence a toujours esté comparée ou à un grand Fleuve ou à un Torrent, & jamais à un petit Ruisseau qui n'humecte qu'à peine son lit & ses rivages. (2: 180; 139)

What was required there was the sublime and the heroic, through which he could more properly unfurl the grand banners of eloquence and use its noblest figures and finest ornaments. Grand eloquence has always been compared either to a great river or a torrent, and never to a little stream that barely moistens its bed and banks.

This heavy-duty apology for the sublime style that Demosthenes lacks—for a heroic eloquence that Perrault emblematizes with the flow of water, in contrast to the inundating shower of light evoked by Longinus—prompts the Président to ask about another example: none other than that of the famous oath sworn by the soldiers killed at Marathon. Although the Abbé has some trouble with this undeniably fine passage, he manages to substitute for "l'esclat même de sa pensée" invoked by Longinus an intriguingly dismissive explanation: "Cependant cet endroit doit son plus grand esclat à l'impor

tance de la matiere & au peu d'élevation des autres choses qui l'en-
vironnent, car il n'est pas plus malaisé d'apostropher ny mesme de
faire parler les Morts que les Vivans dans une piece d'Eloquence"
(Yet this passage owes its greatest brilliance to the importance of the
subject and to the minimal elevation of the other matters that sur-
round it, for it is no harder to apostrophize or even to have the dead
rather than the living speak in eloquent discourse; 2: 182; 139).

The standpoint of this Perraldian rejoinder might seem unprob-
lematic.[30] Not only is its framework the very pragmatics of speech
events we have encountered in Boileau and Longinus, but in rhetor-
ical terms, as the phrase "l'importance de la matiere" indicates, the
sphere of *inventio* is paramount. The Abbé's stress on the subject
matter and context is consistent, moreover, with his inclination
throughout the chapter to emphasize logic and discursive structure
over style. What seems odd, only marginally appropriate, and far
from commensurate with the dense and subtle account of the dis-
cursive act in *Le Traité du sublime*, is the argument itself, by which the
Abbé clumsily draws back from what he has grudgingly admitted.
Suppose we grant that an apostrophe to the dead is a rhetorical
stratagem no more difficult than an apostrophe to the living in
an eloquent speech. Just what is the point of that comparison—
especially since the vital distinction in Longinus's commentary is
not between the living and the dead, but between men and the
gods?

We are apparently invited to infer that the enabling power of
eloquence—of "l'art de bien dire" (the art of well-wrought speech;
2: 185; 140)—suffices to explain Demosthenes's prowess. The rea-
soning would go something like this: since switching addressees is so
easy in oratory, the shift from the conventional formula for the oath
to one that validated the ancestral relations of the audience was not
really so extraordinary; therefore, contrary to Longinus's analysis
(according to which the apostrophe galvanizes its listeners by en-
abling them to turn away from defeat and identify with warriors of
the past on whom Demosthenes conferred divine status via the
performative force of his oath), we can take the oath lightly; far from
sublime, it is ordinary oratory. But even if this flimsy logic is not
what Perrault had in mind, the general point in the passage is clear
and will shortly be reinforced in a discussion of Cicero: the right
way to look at the discursive context and situate whatever effects

and meanings one detects is to privilege the techniques of rhetoric and style, is to withdraw the momentary allegiance to a pragmatics privileging the psychology of reception in favor of what the Abbé proceeds to define, in explaining his preference for Cicero over Demosthenes, as "la grande Eloquence, qui consiste, comme dit Ciceron, à parler avec abondance & avec ornement" (grand eloquence, which consists, as Cicero says, in speaking with abundance and ornament; 2: 183; 139).

The same preference for sublime style over the sublime surfaces in volume 3 of the *Parallèle*, devoted to poetry. The first half of this volume is dominated by a review of Homer and Virgil, with Perrault's preference going to the latter, if only because he is more modern. More insistently than its predecessors, the dialogue on poetry delineates a general horizon of historical progress in the arts in parallel with that of the sciences. In evoking the history of poetry, the participants in Perrault's dialogue take recourse to the arch-traditional biological metaphor. The issue is whether, given the analogy between the evolution of poetry and the growth of an organism, post-Homeric poetry continued to mature as other poets expanded and refined the art, or whether it could only diversify and decline in relation to an apogee of epic genius that could never again be reached. The Abbé states Perrault's progressive view as follows:

Comme rien ne peut arriver d'abord à sa perfection dernière; qu'Homère à notre égard a vécu dans l'enfance du monde . . . ; & qu'il est un des premiers qui s'est mêlé de Poësie, je n'auray pas de peine à faire voir que quelque grand génie qu'il ait recû de la Nature, car c'est peut-être le plus vaste & le plus bel esprit qui ait jamais été, il a néanmoins commis un tres-grand nombre de fautes, dont les Poëtes qui l'ont suivi, quoyqu'inférieurs en force de génie, se sont corrigés dans la suite des temps. (3: 32; 205)

Since nothing can immediately reach its ultimate perfection, since from our standpoint Homer lived during the world's infancy, . . . and since he was one of the pioneers in the sphere of poetry, I will have no trouble showing that, however great the genius he received from Nature—for his was perhaps the finest, most expansive spirit ever to exist—he nonetheless committed a very great number of errors, which the poets who followed him, although of lesser genius, learned to avoid as time passed.

The underlying claim that the Abbé goes on to flesh out is that poetry is ultimately a product of development and technique, and thus that contemporary poetry, exactly like science, advances in relation to its past because modern practitioners can build upon the great work of the past they have studied and learned to appreciate, while deploying superior instruments and more refined language materials that allow for greater complexity, subtlety, and control. Thanks to the theory and method provided by rhetoric and poetics, artistic quality cannot but rise as the body of poetry grows.

For the author of *Le Traité du sublime*, such technologistic optimism appears to have been quite unthinkable long before the partisans of the Ancients eschewed it. In the first place, when in his chapter on Plato (13) Longinus depicts imitation and emulation of the great historians and poets of the past as a path that leads to the sublime, the single sphere of imitation he invokes is by no means that of reproductive techniques or themes or textual mechanics; it is the sphere of inspiration and genius, presented, moreover, so that the relation of imitator to model, exemplified by Plato's mighty struggle to equal Homer, is itself caught up in the sublime turn:

Ces grandes beautés que nous remarquons dans les ouvrages des anciens sont comme autant de sources sacrées, d'où il s'élève des vapeurs heureuses qui se répandent dans l'âme de leurs imitateurs, et animent les esprits même naturellement les moins échauffés; si bien que dans ce moment il sont comme ravis et emportés de l'enthousiasme d'autrui.[31]

These grand beauties that we observe in the works of the ancients are akin to sacred sources out of which felicitous vapors rise and spread in the souls of their imitators, naturally animating even the most lethargic minds; so that it is as if, in that moment, they are enraptured and carried away with the enthusiasm of others.

For Plato, Homer is "une vive source, dont il a détourné un nombre infini de ruisseaux" (a vital wellspring from which he derived an infinite number of streams); and yet, Longinus says of Plato imitating Homer: "Jamais, à mon avis, il n'eût mêlé tant de si grandes choses dans ses traités de philosophie, passant . . . du simple discours à des expressions et à des matières poétiques, s'il ne fût venu, pour ainsi dire, comme un nouvel athlète, disputer de toute sa force le prix à Homère" (Never, in my opinion, would he have included so many great things in his philosophical treatises, ranging from simple speech to poetic subjects and expressions, if he had not put all of his energy, as a new athlete, so to speak, into struggling mightily against Homer for the prize).[32] So imitation is displaced into disputation, and its conversion into a battle of competing geniuses figures still another case of the authorial experience of inspiration. This time, it takes the form of a transfer of creative energy, with Plato turning his reading of Homer into his writing against Homer; and once again a movement from dispersion—"vapeurs heureuses qui se répandent dans l'âme"—into the poet's energetic rearticulation follows the sublime trajectory of the impassioned and enraptured soul as it rises powerfully to the challenge of the occasion. Thus the great author's practice of emulation is assimilated to the performance of the sublime; imitation itself dissolves figuratively, through a kind of psychic chemistry of vaporization or sublimation, into influence; and the neoclassical doctrine calling for imitation of the Ancients derives its most compelling rationale from the analytic of the sublime.

In the second place, the optimism about poetry in the hands of modern authors seems to break down where the incomplete text we have of the treatise breaks off. In Boileau's translation the substantial final chapter bears the title "Des causes de la décadence de l'esprit" (On the causes of spiritual decadence). The question there is why surpassing authorial genius and sublime works have disappeared, why there is decadence instead of progress:

D'où vient que dans notre siècle il se trouve assez d'orateurs qui savent manier un raisonnement et qui ont même le style oratoire; qu'il s'en voit, dis-je, plusieurs qui ont de la vivacité, de la netteté et surtout de l'agrément dans leurs discours; mais qu'il s'en rencontre si peu qui puissent s'élever fort haut dans le sublime, tant la stérilité maintenant est grande parmi les esprits!"[33]

So it happens that in our century there are plenty of orators who know how to conduct an argument and even to use oratorical style; that there are many whose speeches are lively, clear, and above all pleasing; but so great is the present sterility of mind that there are very few who can rise up to the heights of the sublime.

Far from guaranteeing or promoting sublime art, rhetoric and poetics thus have to recognize that they have failed to do so. Longinus readily admits (in Chapter 33) that there are flaws and infelicities in Homer that later generations were able to understand and shun. But whereas the sublime effects in Homer overrode the shortcomings and ensured their insignificance, technical prowess and correctness do not compensate for the absence of the sublime, do not enable modern poets to equal Homer. Thus the sublime work, even if it has technical flaws, far surpasses the formally perfected work that lacks the sublime; and Longinus's predominant concern with the processes of artistic genius and inspiration does tend to hold at bay the kind of formalist account that would construe poetry's decline as internal to its history or its structure. Instead, he looks to the history of culture at large for an explanation, and in that hardly unfamiliar perspective, his melancholy theme is the moral corruption of his society. Drained by unending wars, it has dissipated its creative energy and surrendered its noble values to lust for money and pleasure. In Perrault's discourse on his own century, we shall find hardly any attention to this Longinian pessimism. Only an occasional comment on domestic peace under Louis XIV suggests that he sees a need to confront it.[34]

Perrault's Reversal: Appropriating the Sublime

Such then are the general oppositions that give rise to the controversy in volume 3 of the *Parallèle*: the sublime versus sublime style, creative genius versus poetic workmanship, artistic progress versus cultural decadence. Now at the point where the Abbé takes up the challenge to criticize fine passages in Homer by proposing to examine those that Longinus considered the most sublime (3: 177; 313), Perrault's debating position toward Boileau turns out to be passably awkward. The Abbé's first example is a passage from chapter 7 of *Le Traité du sublime* that occurs right at a point where six pages of the manuscript are missing. As Boileau admits without noticeable embarrassment in the fourth of his *Réflexions critiques*, he is responsible, owing to the considerable translator's license he has taken, for some curious confusion here. In the original, the missing text falls between a fragment alluding to Alexander the Great's response to Parmenio, who had questioned his rejection of terms for peace offered by Darius, and a fragment alluding to a famous battle scene in Book 4 of the *Iliad* (4: 442), a passage in which Homer, in evoking the presence of the goddess of Strife among the Trojans, depicts her with her head above the clouds and her feet on the ground. In his translation, Boileau followed the lead of an early Latin translator, Gabriel de Petra, who sought to furnish a bridge between the two examples, Alexander's reply and the image of

Strife. From the context, it is clear that both are cases of the sublime. However, in the second case (Homer's image of Strife), the exact nature of the sublime is relatively elusive, since much of the context-setting text is missing; accordingly, the comparison Boileau allows in the bridge between the two examples is exceedingly vague.

It is clear that Perrault's commentary relies, as Boileau points out derisively, solely on the translation; the case is not isolated, moreover, since the Abbé, echoing Perrault's advocacy of translation, insists on using translations, in preference to the humanist's recourse to Greek and Latin originals, in his debates with the Président. The passage in question interprets the translation that ties together the truncated segments on the basis of Longinus's commentary on the next Homeric example, a few lines further on. This one refers to the vast distance the horses of the goddess Hera cover in a single leap (*Iliad*, 5: 770ff); it allows Longinus to reiterate his stress on Homer's high-minded vision and to remark upon the effect of cosmic grandeur the poet achieves through the use of a figure that seems particularly significant in *Le Traité du sublime*, hyperbole. In chapter 9, Longinus appends to his admiring comment on Homer's vision of cosmic grandeur via hyperbole his reservations about the Homeric theomachy, the sublimity of which recedes to the extent that it is built around a metaphoric representation of the gods as men. The invocation of divinity Longinus prefers paints it in its purity, "sans mélange des choses terrestres"[35]—as in the case of the god of the Jews, whose words are presented hyperbolically in the sense that they have the force of creation ("Dieu dit: Que la lumiere se fasse, et la lumiere se fit"), yet do not display a figurative quality in the manner of the elaborate metaphors of warfare that depict the Greek gods anthropomorphically.

Perrault has the Chevalier make fun of both Homeric examples by assimilating them to grotesque exaggeration: they would doubtless exemplify "bad" hyperbole. Then, significantly, the more sober and reasonable Abbé, whose wont is to tone down or recast the overdrawn views of his enthusiastic ally, this time elaborates approvingly on the opinion of the Chevalier. Here is their exchange, which begins with a Virgilian twist about which Boileau will chide Perrault (in *Réflexion* 4: 510): the Chevalier has substituted Fame for Strife, as Virgil did when he translated Homer's line and quite aptly applied it to Fame spreading the news of the union of Dido and Aeneas.

THE CHEVALIER: C'est que tant qu'on pourra voir la teste de la Renommée, sa teste ne sera point dans le ciel; & que si sa teste est dans le ciel, on ne sçait pas bien ce que l'on void. Pour l'autre hyperbole, elle n'a esté imitée que par ceux qui ont fait les contes de Peau-d'asne, où ils introduisent de certains hommes cruels, qu'on appelle des Ogres, qui sentent la chair fraische, & qui mangent les petits enfans; ils leur donnent ordinairement des bottes de sept lieuës, pour courir après ceux qui s'enfuyent. Il y a quelque esprit dans cette imagination. Car les enfans conçoivent ces bottes de sept lieuës, comme de grandes échasses avec lesquelles ces Ogres sont en moins de rien par tout où ils veulent: au lieu qu'on ne sçait comment s'imaginer que les chevaux des Dieux fassent d'un seul saut une si grande estenduë de pays. C'est à trouver de beaux & de grands sentimens que la grandeur d'esprit est necessaire, & se fait voir; & non pas à se former des corps d'une masse demesurée, ou des mouvemens d'une vitesse inconcevable.

THE ABBÉ: Monsieur le Chevalier a raison, & Longin ne l'a pas quand il compare en fait de sublime, cette description de la Discorde, avec la réponse que fit Alexandre à Parmenion. Darius proposoit à Alexandre de luy donner la moitié de son Royaume, & sa fille en mariage. Pour moy, dit Parmenion, si j'étois Alexandre, j'accepterois ces offres. Et moy aussi, repliqua ce Prince, si j'estois Parmenion. Il est certain qu'il faut avoir l'ame grande et l'esprit vif, comme l'avoit Alexandre, pour faire une telle réponse, mais il n'est point nécessaire d'avoir un grand esprit pour dire que la Discorde avoit la teste dans le Ciel, & les pieds sur la Terre. Il ne faut qu'avoir envie de faire une grande & estonnante hyperbole. (3: 119–21; 227)

THE CHEVALIER: As long as one can see the head of Fame, its head will not be in heaven; and if its head is in heaven, one cannot really know what one sees. As for the other hyperbole, it has been imitated only by those who fashion tales like that of the Ass's Skin, in which they introduce certain cruel men called ogres, who smell of fresh flesh and eat little children; they generally give them seven-league boots for running after those who flee. There is some spirit in this imaginary scene. For the children conceive of these seven-league boots as large stilts with which these ogres get wherever they wish to be in no time at all, whereas one does not know how to imagine the horses of the gods crossing such a great expanse in a single leap. For the purpose of finding beautiful and magnificent emotions, grandeur of spirit is necessary and does manifest itself; but it is not needed for envisioning bodies of outlandish size or movements of inconceivable speed.

THE ABBÉ: The good knight is right, and Longinus wrong when he compares, with respect to the sublime, this description of Strife with Alexander's answer to Parmenio. Darius proposed to Alexander to give him half of his kingdom and his daughter in marriage. For myself, said Parmenio, if I were Alexander, I would accept these offers. And so would I, that ruler answered, if I were Parmenio. One must undoubtedly have a great soul and a lively mind, as Alexander did, to make such a response, but it is not necessary to have a great mind to say that Strife had her head in heaven and her feet on earth. It suffices to want to make a grand and striking hyperbole.

Along with the curious mention of the "contes de Peau-d'asne" that we noted in Chapter One, what is unexpected here is the trenchant putdown of hyperbole at the end of both speeches and the precedence each speaker thereby gives to authorial greatness and spiritual elevation over stylistic invention. For what seems to be figured in this almost grotesquely forced interpretation is a chiasmatic inversion in which the censorial Moderns co-opt the posture favorable to the sublime and creative genius and hostile to rhetoric, while in the same breath shunting Longinus and Homer onto the terrain of sublime style and poetic workmanship. Perrault's stooges almost seem to take their critical cues right from Longinus, since they indict Homer's hyperboles for being the very kind that Longinus downgrades, namely, those that put their figurality on display instead of concealing it.

Perrault's flirtation with the sublime thus turns up in a critical context where his principal aim would appear to be polemical: he is turning the tables on his adversaries by using their sublime against them. But of course this unexpected twist is not quite so simple as our first glance may suggest. The Abbé, having criticized Longinus for a comparison he did not make, merely proceeds to distinguish the strong general condition imposed by the sublime on its author ("l'ame grande et l'esprit vif") from the weaker condition to be met be the writer of hyperboles ("envie de faire une grande & estonnante hyperbole"). As nearly as we can tell, he subscribes to the Chevalier's analysis of the objectionable hyperboles, although he has no specific comment on the example of the leaping horses. The analysis the Chevalier ventures has two parts. The first, devoted in his caricatural version to the exceedingly tall goddess, is the objection of a literal-minded observer. Displaying no scruples in applying his own standard of credibility to a work of the distant past, he fixes upon what is paradoxical or inconceivable about a head above the clouds. This is nothing more than a naive refusal to read the figurative dimension of the passage in the *Iliad*, or, as Boileau puts it in *Réflexion* 4, a failure to read the passage in Homer for what it is, an allegory connoting the universal spread of warfare. The refusal becomes more glaring when we compare it with the Longinian commentary on the star-trekking horses of Hera. Longinus, too, takes the hyperbolic extension of space to be implausible or unimaginable, but that, for him, is a cause for wonder rather than ridicule: it is what induces the straining mind to press beyond the parameters of ordinary representation.

The second part of the analysis, dealing directly with the long-striding horses, is quite another story. The Chevalier proceeds, as we might expect, by comparison and analogy. He deploys them so as to convey a sense of verisimilitude that depends, not on an understanding of literary convention and reading competence, which would allow for the appreciation of a hyperbole, but on familiar experience, which is the enemy of the hyperbolic. He finds only one analogue for those horses, the ogres with seven-league boots in "contes de Peau-d'asne," that is, in stories like "Le Petit Poucet" in Perrault's fairy tales—which is to say, in a developing collection of *contes merveilleux* in which the aspect of the marvelous is not a dimension one would ordinarily connect with Boileau's synonym for the sublime, *le merveilleux*.[36] But here the least one can say is that the context, a comparative inquisition into Homeric sublimity, forces a consideration of the difference between the ogre's magic boots, which the Chevalier defends, and Homer's divine steeds, which he derides. To the marvelous in the fairy tale, the Chevalier accords his assent: "Il y a quelque esprit dans cette imagination." But whereas the marvelous of the magic boots appears less unthinkable by virtue of the analogy with stilts, the horses of Homer's star wars are over-hyperbolic for want of such an analogy. Hence the Chevalier's dismissal of the marvelous illustrated by the supernatural coursers, his denial of the very imaginability of the imagined scene.

Thus a part of the Modernist's resistance to the sublime—precisely the resistance to that "je ne sais quoi" of the sublime that pushes the mind's conceptual powers to or beyond their limit—still informs the curious turning point in the commentary where a certain cagey adherence to the sublime, in tandem with a dismissive attitude toward venturesome style, surfaces in Perrault's contrived dialogue with the position of the Ancients. As we have just seen, the word casually used by the Chevalier to qualify this muted, less lofty sublime is *esprit* ("il y a quelque esprit dans cette imagination")— that is, the very same modulatory term that we have seen at work (in the final pages of Chapter One) in the allegorical elaboration of compromise formations in the *Histoire ou Contes du temps passé*. It is significant, moreover, that short stories—including Perrault's own "Le Miroir, ou la métamorphose d'Orante"—are precisely the example to which the Abbé appeals (2: 138–42; 128–29) in specifying the kind of allegory he prefers to the Greek model advanced by Boileau in his defense of Homer and rather convincingly recalled by the Président in his comment on the figure of Fame. The allusions to the *merveilleux* of the tales in the *Parallèle* thus contribute to the plausibility of reading tales such as "Le Petit Poucet" and "Riquet à la houppe" as allegories in which *esprit*—in its multiple connotations and dimensions—functions as the pivotal signifier around which Perrault's domestication of Boileau's strong sublime or *merveilleux* is reconstructed.[37]

In practice, then, Perrault's strategy vis-à-vis Boileau and the partisans of the Ancients in the 1690s is not so much to firm up the oppositions, conceptual and rhetorical, attendant to the dichotomy of the sublime and sublime style as to absorb the sublime, along with other neoclassical principles and values, into his own synthesis or compromise formation. In conceptual terms, the synthesis muffles the division between Ancients and Moderns, just as Boileau's work has already made the rift less transparent by juxtaposing the discourse on the sublime and genius with the prescriptive rationalism of his poetics; in rhetorical terms, it brings the hyperbolic under the rule of metaphor. This reversal of the priorities that prevail in Longinus lessens the tensions that the sublime engenders in Boileau's writing, without however eliminating them. If the compromise formation that tames or dilutes the sublime so as to make it appropriable is very significant, it is not so much that the identifying marks associated with the notion undergo a major transformation. Rather, Perrault's key adjustment corresponds to the move he makes vis-à-vis Descartes, shifting foundational truth away from the revelatory moment of the *cogito* onto the ground of the seeing subject, where it will be a function of adequate representation: it consists in displacing the sublime from the presiding position it holds for Boileau/Longinus. Whereas they treat the sublime as the ultimate artistic experience that, from (outside) the frontiers of rhetoric and poetics, governs their conception and reveals their limits, he positions it within a vision of eloquence and beauty, governed by reason and taste, that is prone to focus on the features and dynamics of the work itself. If the sublime drawn into the Perraldian orbit can retain its qualities of elevation and ineffability, it can no longer override the axiological priority of the natural and the beautiful; and if genius and passion may still enter into the account of its emergence, the status of rhetoric and poetics has been enhanced.[38] The inaccessibility of the sublime has given ground to the advance of technical understanding.

The Personified Century

Perrault's spokesman in the *Parallèle* makes his position of compromise and recuperation with respect to the sublime of Boileau/ Longinus appear as an extension of the rational outlook he brings to bear on the quarrel at large: the same critical attitude toward Ancients and Moderns, wholehearted admiration for both where it is due, but unwillingness to idolize either. Does this recuperative posture reappear in the discriminations and/or the operations we can perceive in his discourse about the seventeenth century? From *Les Hommes illustres*, one can extrapolate little more than what Viala noted on the basis of the work's full title and its conception: a collection of 100 eulogistic portraits belongs, as Perrault recognizes, to the tradition of panegyrics, of demonstrative rhetoric, and since his preface replays his standard theme attributing the concentration of great men in a *siècle* to great rulers such as Alexander, Augustus, and Louis XIV, praise for the century of Louis XIV seems to predominate over the evocation of the century at large. Yet the chronological century is clearly a factor in the design of the work, if only because a substantial number of the *hommes illustres* were born in the sixteenth century and died before 1630.

By far the most significant evocation of the century in Perrault's corpus actually lies in the formidably rich vein of reflection that these first two chapters have repeatedly tapped, the *Parallèle*. In a lengthy prelude (1: 50–79; 28–36) that includes a reference to "les hommes du neuviéme & du dixiéme siecle" (men of the ninth and tenth century; 1: 52; 29), the Perraldian metaphorics is deployed as a historical imagination. It represents human nature as a man with a childhood, adolescence, adulthood, and old age (1: 50; 28), and the arts and sciences as a great river that runs underground during times of barbarous ignorance, but returns to the surface during periods of internal peace and prosperity under great monarchs (1: 53; 29). The Abbé observes that there are also different ages within centuries, illustrating his point with a personified account of "le siecle où nous vivons" (the century we live in):

On peut regarder comme son enfance le temps qui s'est passé depuis la fin des guerres de la ligue jusqu'au commencement du Ministere du Cardinal de Richelieu, l'adolescence est venuë ensuite & a vû naistre l'Académie Françoise; l'âge viril a succedé, & peut-estre commençons-nous à entrer dans la vieillesse, comme semblent le donner à connoistre le dégoust qu'on a souvent pour les meilleures choses. (1: 54; 29)

We can regard the time between the end of the Wars of Religion until the beginning of Cardinal Richelieu's administration as its childhood; adolescence followed and saw the birth of the French Academy; then came the age of virility, and now, if the disgust people have for the finest things is indicative, perhaps we are entering into old age.

The Abbé proceeds to trace "par les mesmes degrez" (through the same stages; 1: 55; 30) the itinerary of sculpture, then eloquence and poetry, over "quatre-vingt ans de repos dans la France" (forty-eight years of tranquility in France, for, as he notes parenthetically, "les guerres estrangeres ne troublent point le repos des Arts & des Sciences," foreign wars do not disturb the tranquility of the arts and sciences; 1: 59; 31). In this biography of "la Republique des lettres," youth was a time of "jeux d'esprit"; adolescence brought a shift to "la mode des citations"; maturity under Louis XIV and Colbert ushered in the great age of reason and moderation; and to judge from the perfection then achieved and subsequently sustained in sculpture, further advances are not to be expected (1: 55–59; 60–61).

This mini-history also includes a sharp separation of the seventeenth from the sixteenth century (1: 66–69; 32–33), compelling remarks on printing and the abundance of books ("ce qu'on peut dire avoir en quelque sorte changé la face de la litterature"; we can say that this seemingly changed the face of literature; 1: 63; 32), and a claim that translations have enabled modern readers to develop a sound perspective on the Greeks and Romans (1: 65; 32). The Abbé insists that historical judgments have to be based on the comparison of particular works, not on the relative greatness of authors (1: 87–

88; 38), and as an image of the march of progress in his century ("du progrez prodigieux des Arts & des Sciences depuis cinquante ou soixante ans"; 1: 72; 34), he proposes, unsurprisingly, technological invention, symbolized by complex machinery that an operator uses but does not understand (1: 77; 35). In this vision, artists appear as the agents of styles, techniques, and positions; the movement of progress apparently leaves no role for authorial genius, no place for the sublime.

At first glance, the image of the century constructed by Perrault seems to be ordered through and through by his attachment to progress. As we have seen, the basis for his optimism—also, no doubt, the source of his resistance to the sublime—lies in his allegiance to the scientific spirit of Cartesian rationalism. His abiding confidence in the benefits of method and technical understanding in the arts and sciences makes the *Parallèle* a work anticipatory of some phases of the *siècle des lumières*. It is hardly accidental that the dialogues resort to a rhetoric of comparison and analogy, anchored in a metaphorics that privileges relations of equivalence and exchange. Clearly well suited to the elaboration of parallels between art and science that Perrault undertook, that rhetoric incorporates a conveniently amateurish view (doubtless befitting an all-out "modernist") of the French language as a perfected representational instrument.[39] It thus undergirds his views on the adequacy of translation and serves the technologic approach to poetry and eloquence, armed with the apparatus of rhetoric, poetics, grammar, and dictionary, that he consistently favored. Perrault would thus appear to be well positioned—able to draw on a stable, homogeneous set of interlocking tools, terms, and relations—for sketching a certain flattering portrait of the century.

Yet the unsurprising appeal to the biological metaphor modeling the life of a century upon that of a human being introduces a certain discomfiture that ends up putting Perrault's historicizing at risk. For if it is safely consistent in conforming to the metaphorics of anthropomorphism that Longinus found inferior to the purity of hyperbole, does the metaphor itself allow for preserving the progress and perfection of art against the threat of decadence that Longinus connected, not to technical deficiencies, but to a shortage of authorial greatness? Here Perrault's formulation concerning the old age of his personified century is already halting enough to give us pause: "peut-estre commençons-nous à entrer dans la vieillesse, comme semblent le donner à connoistre le dégoust qu'on a souvent pour les meilleures choses."[40] The banal problem with this figure of personification is of course the specter of mortality—which Longinus represents as a refuge and thus as an advantage men hold over the gods (9: 7)—and with it, not stable productivity in old age, but decline and death. Presumably, Perrault's position as a self-interested apologist for the century of Louis XIV underlies the glibly ironic modalization (effected by the multiple indices of the tentative: *peut-estre, commençons, entrer, semblent, donner à, souvent*) he weaves into his acknowledgment of old age and disgust, as if the perfection he exalts were not already a thing of the past, as if the peace and prosperity he vaunts as a condition of progress were still in place, as if progress were not at a standstill, awaiting the advent of the eighteenth century.

The more interesting problem with Perrault's personified schematic of the century, however, is the one brought into view when he actually begins to fill in the biographic structure of literary life that he has set up. What is the implication of the fact, not only that the space for old age is left empty, but that the representation of literary maturity—the age of Corneille, Pascal, Molière, Racine, La Fontaine, to mention only a few immortals whose portraits are included in *Les Hommes illustres*—is much less incisive than that of youth and adolescence?[41] Of Perrault's lame silence about the terminal period in his scheme, the least one can reckon is that it betrays his incapacity to portray the century *as a whole, coming to an end*. His considerable accomplishment is to have set in operation a rhetoric of the century; but the conditions are not ripe for an end-of-century rhetoric. As for the flattening of the period of high classicism into an age of reason, perhaps the Abbé's formulation is telling despite its concision: "Il en est arrivé de mesme [que dans l'Eloquence] dans la Poësie, où les pointes trop recherchées ont fait place au bon sens, & qui est parvenuë à satisfaire la raison la plus severe, & la plus exacte, aprés quoy il n'y a *rien à faire davantage*" (The same thing that happened in the sphere of eloquence occurred in poetry, where overrefined allusions gave way to common sense; poetry thus has met the standards of the most severe and exacting reason, after which there is nothing more to do; 1: 59; 31; my italics). This phrase can of course be read two ways. In the first place, it means that adherence to reason suffices to yield poetic perfection. But also, and quite compatibly, this achievement leaves nothing more to do: artistically, in accord with a model of rhetorical and poetic production that sweeps everything into the realm of intelligibility, leaving no residue, nothing beyond its limits, no higher or unknown level of achievement, no room for awe and inspiration, this perfection amounting to saturation is, in fact, already the end. If the period of maturity swallows up at least the last fifty to sixty years of Perrault's century, it is perhaps because, as he has begun gropingly to configure it, that extended adulthood has fully expended the century's resources, or as a critic sympathetic to Longinus might put it, carried out a sublimation of genius and passion. In any case, the uncanny coherence of his century-making rhetoric is only reinforced by this final twist: in the 1690s, Perrault can manage no end-of-century rhetoric since the century, as his Modernist discourse has imagined it, has already lived through its end.

3

The Preteritional Turn: Perrault Against Racine

C harles Perrault's stature in the history of French literature and culture rose dramatically during the 1970s and 1980s. Marc Soriano's prodigious erudition and analytic energy provided the crucial impetus for this development. In two weighty volumes—*Les Contes de Perrault: culture savante et traditions populaires* (1968) and *Le Dossier Charles Perrault* (1972)—Soriano presented an enormous compendium of biographical, historical, and textual material necessary for appreciating Perrault's extraordinary career as a man of letters. At the same time, he elaborated a remarkably adventurous, nontraditional interpretation of Perrault's writings, unapologetically drawing upon methods and insights of modern psychoanalysis and ethnography. On the one hand, his approach was psychobiographic: appealing to a classic Freudian model of family romance, he sought to determine the significance of Charles's position in the extraordinary Perrault clan. Not only did he occupy the position of the youngest among five remarkable brothers, but he had a twin brother who died in infancy. Soriano's research led him to be intrigued by the experience of the surviving twin, deprived of that special sibling rivalry while nonetheless enmeshed in competitive relations in the Perraldian fraternity. This family structure led him in turn to focus on various effects of coupling and doubling in Perrault's writing. On the other hand, as a reader of the Mother Goose tales, Soriano pursued a particular literary-historical interest in the folkloric material from which much of their narrative substance is derived. His painstaking exploration of the sources in popular literature and folklore has much in common with the ethnographic and

historical scholarship carried out by pioneering American investiga-
tors, notably Alan Dundes and Jack Zipes, whose comparative anal-
yses enable us to situate the fairy tales in a generic framework that
highlights the social functions of storytelling. If Soriano is able to
delve more deeply and pointedly into Perrault's use of folkloric
material and its implications than they, it is because of his dual focus
on the popular sources of the tales and on Perrault's personal cir-
cumstances and authorial concerns. By correlating these two di-
mensions, he is able not only to establish a narrative horizon against
which the tales can be read comparatively, but to pinpoint the
"modernizing" features that characterize Perrault's handling of the
material and make the *Contes* a work for a seventeenth-century
audience.

Although the aggressive integration of these psychoanalytic and
anthropological dimensions into literary scholarship puts Soriano's
Contes de Perrault and *Dossier* at odds with traditional academic crit-
icism, the antagonism has been mild and restricted. Without surren-
dering any reservations about Soriano's interpretation of Perrault,
established literary history in the 1970s benefited willingly from the
vast erudition and the elaborate case he made for re-viewing sev-
enteenth-century literature and culture through the lenses offered
by Perrault's writing and career. Two decades after the appearance
of these monumental—still engaging and controversial—works, the
Perraldian *dossier* underwent a further and quite formidable expan-
sion that should enhance the appropriation of Marc Soriano's work
on Perrault by traditional literary history. His recent (1989) edition
of the *Contes* offers an abundant, unconventionally structured schol-
arly apparatus, at the core of which is a splendidly capacious glossary
(120 pages of fine print in this 586-page volume) that functions as
the source of background information and editorial commentary.
By adding a bevy of illuminating texts—early tales and "antitales,"
fables, dialogues, poems, translations—to the corpus made available
in the popular editions of Gilbert Rouger (1967) and Jean-Pierre
Collinet (1981), Soriano has produced what must now be consid-
ered the one indispensable reference work for readers of Perrault's
literary writings. Even in cases where attribution or authorial status
remains debatable, these works and Soriano's probing introductions
and notes will have to be taken into account by serious students of
Perrault. A salient example is his presentation of the dialogue "La

Critique de l'Opéra," which sheds light on the conflict between Perrault and Jean Racine that will concern us in this chapter. Soriano situates the polemics of 1674 over Philippe Quinault's *Alceste* as an early round in the Quarrel of the Ancients and Moderns. The exchange is commonly remembered as the occasion of Racine's celebrated put-down of Perrault, in the preface to *Iphigénie*, for a gross misunderstanding of Euripides's characters, based on a faulty edition of the text.

In the light of this major, canon-revising scholarly and critical work, Soriano's little book *La Brosse à reluire sous Louis XIV* (1989), presenting Perrault's draft of a dedicatory letter from the members of the academy to the king for the *Dictionnaire de l'Académie française* (1694), with annotations attributed primarily to Jean Racine, will doubtless appear to be a minor, if revealing, *hors-d'oeuvre*. Quantitatively, Perrault's output in this epistle—restricted by the requirements of the occasional genre—had to be thin: something under 750 words in the draft, just over 600 words in the published version. By contrast, the annotations, nicely arranged on facing pages and keyed by number to the passages on which they comment, come to roughly 3,000 words. They are above all impressive for their unmitigated thoroughness and irascible vigilance: no proposition, indeed hardly a phrase, escapes critical attention.

This edition-cum-study does reproduce the version of Perrault's epistle actually published in the *Dictionnaire*; placed after some twenty pages of commentary on the draft letter and the annotations, and before the editor's explanatory notes on textual details, the definitive version serves, says Soriano, as a kind of terminal chapter to the book. The substantial composite of introduction, commentary, and notes makes the volume rather more a critical essay than an edition. It is noteworthy, moreover, that Soriano does not reckon with one of the most immediate, formal critical tasks made possible by the scholarly edition, a potentially fruitful direct comparison of the draft and published versions of Perrault's text. While weaving into his commentary a number of interesting remarks on what Perrault did and did not change, he has little to say about the two texts as ensembles, or about the effects of revision on the collective authorial voice and on the positioning of dictionarial "authorship" vis-à-vis the royal addressee. Pursuing this line of inquiry, which treats the published epistle as the compromise Perrault articulated in responding to the criticisms of his draft, is the second of the two tasks I shall take up in this chapter.

The first issue I shall attempt to address involves primarily the relationship between the editor/critic and academic literary scholarship. Although Soriano's treatment of this question covers background, especially concerning Racine's annotations, that is vital to a critical rereading of the epistle, its criticological emphasis might be regarded as marginal to the appreciation of Perrault's writerly career in general and to the textual confrontation between Racine and Perrault in particular. What is ultimately at stake in Soriano's theses, however, is the manner and the extent to which Perrault's writings call for judgments, ethical as well as historical, that eventually affect the scholarly reassessment of his place in literary and cultural history. In framing remarks at the start and finish of *La Brosse à reluire*, the author resurrects obliquely, but insistently, in the manner of a pamphleteer, the posture of an adversary: rather than grant that his work on Perrault has served to close the gap between traditional and modern critics, he bluntly reopens it, directing his complaint, moreover, against the representative par excellence of academic criticism, Raymond Picard (the editor and biographer of Racine who, in the 1960s, stridently protested against the interpretations of Racine's work ventured by Roland Barthes and other "moderns" of our time). But the wide relevance of this stricture becomes clear only in the light of the direct link Soriano makes between his criticism of Picard's critical language and his response to the discourses of flattery practiced by Perrault and Racine. The question is certainly not whether it is legitimate for the critic to express ethical judgments or to ask explicitly what lessons a thoughtful reader should draw from history. Rather, the issue has to do with the basis on which the critic's judgments on language use, implicit or explicit, should be formed and with the terms in which it is appropriate to formulate them.

By commenting on the questions of method Soriano raises before proceeding with my analysis of the dedicatory epistle, I position my reading, in effect, as an implicit attempt to refine or displace those questions. At this stage, it seems prudent to offer an explicit statement of my intent. I hope the reading will suggest, by pointing to the seriousness, subtlety, and intensity of concern at work in texts that many might dismiss as innocuous or insignificant, that ethically oriented reflection on the performance of a great writer such as Perrault needs to be anchored in a stern resistance to facility. Facing writings that summon the reader to a reckoning with moral issues, the critic must first wrestle with the need to bring to bear upon the text a range and depth of analytic and historical understanding sufficient to reveal the overdetermined difficulty, complexity, and elusiveness of a writer's choices. Patient pursuit of this task can yield a vital insight into the will or strategic determination that an interpreter has to muster if he or she is to cut through the retorsionary density of human dilemmas and arrive at informed judgments. Only through this labor in density and difficulty can the imperative to adopt an ethical standpoint and to pass judgments emerge—in critical language sensitive to the arbitrariness it has found inescapable and moved deliberately to assume—in a relation of commensurability with the object studied and judged.

The Specter of "Langues de Bois"

As the title—*La Brosse à reluire sous Louis XIV*—and subtitle—"L'Epître au Roi" de Perrault annotée par Racine et Boileau—suggest, Soriano's essay develops two distinct principal interests. In the first place, he makes his case—through a combination of external evidence and textual analysis—for the hypothesis specified by the subtitle: to wit, that Racine and Boileau, as partisans of the Ancients, collaborated in producing the annotations, with their stinging put-down of the archproponent of the Moderns. Although the evidence of Racine's involvement is fairly persuasive, what can be said about possible contributions by Boileau remains largely speculative. Soriano unmistakably leans toward regarding Racine as the main author ("le maître d'oeuvre et l'annotateur en chef")[1] and generally characterizes his stance as the prudent, analytically incisive one; this leaves, for ascription to Boileau, a few criticisms that Soriano deems ill-founded. The plausibility of such speculation rests on the assumption that Boileau's responses to Perrault tended to flow impulsively from personal spleen and to be either superficial or off the mark. But as the literary historian implicitly recognizes when he treats Racine as the primary author and criticizes Raymond Picard for omitting the annotations from the Pléiade edition of Racine's complete works, hard evidence for dual authorship re-

mains, in fact, in short supply. On the evidence at hand, it seems safe
enough to assume consultation and agreement between Racine and
Boileau, yet also necessary to respect in the annotations, as Picard
elected to do, the exasperating problem of a pointedly written but
unsigned text. Hence my preference for a hypothesis somewhat
more cautious than Soriano's, and less driven by a concern with the
issues surrounding authorship, according to which the annotations
offer an intriguing, perhaps privileged, but still muted access to the
discursive posture and critical insights of Racine. It makes sense
practically to treat most of the notes as Racine's work. They are not,
however, entirely comparable to the more than two dozen sets of
annotations that can be attributed categorically to Racine.[2]

Soriano elaborates on the title that designates his second major
interest in the essay's penultimate note: *La Brosse à reluire* is the
emblem of a grand publicity operation, devoted to the glorification
of the French crown, that is, to brushing (up, over, off) the surface of
stark social and political realities so as to maintain the appearance of
a shining finish during the second half of the Sun King's protracted
reign. Like most of their artistic compatriots, Perrault, Boileau, and
Racine perceived that their self-interest dictated cooperation with
the propaganda machine. Moreover, after Perrault's fall from grace
in the post-Colbertian era and the ascension into kingly favor of
Boileau and Racine as the royal *historiographes* (the term designates
officially appointed historians, whose status can be likened to that of
a poet laureate), the polemical oppositions of the Quarrel of the
Ancients and Moderns could hardly be detached from political ten-
sions, since Perrault did not disguise his concerted efforts to recover
the favor he had lost.

For the annotator(s) of Perrault's epistle, objection to his com-
ments on ancient languages and authors was doubtless made easier
by his infelicities of expression and by ill-conceived views on the
academy and its dictionary that exposed him to ready attack. How-
ever, as Soriano skillfully shows, Racine's task in criticizing Per-
rault's attempt to link Louis XIV's greatness with contemporary
French language and culture was a rather delicate one. Because his
objections had to remain faithful to the dominant discourse of rev-
erence with respect to the monarch, they could challenge the ap-
propriateness of Perrault's formulations but not the essential thrust
of his flattery. Soriano rightly stresses Racine's shrewd encomiastic

mastery. His portrait of the wily annotator using the *brosse à reluire* in designing and executing his censorious text for a royal reader provides an exemplary anticipation of the opportunistic, conniving, conformist artist at work depicted in Alain Viala's recent biography, *Racine: la stratégie du caméléon* (1990).

Retrospective Evaluation

Soriano's account of the subservient, flattering artist's situation is decisively distinguished from the more or less standard, essentially explanatory line we encounter in recent work on late-seventeenth-century French culture (notably in the many studies dealing with the representation of the king) by the forceful moralizing twist he introduces in the last two sections of his commentary. Referring in particular to Domenico D'Oria's study of the three great dictionaries of seventeenth-century French, Soriano very deliberately adopts an expression from the parlance of our own time, "la langue de bois," to characterize the special, ritualized languages required for sustaining the cultic celebration of the monarch. The wooden or fossilized language thus evoked is "composée de formules conventionnelles, inauthentiques, destinées à masquer la réalité plutôt qu'à l'exprimer" (composed of conventional, inauthentic formulas that function to mask reality rather than to express it).[3] The real problems such "langues dans la langue" masked under Louis XIV were "la misère populaire, les famines, les enrôlements forcés, les guerres interminables" (the suffering of the people, famines, compulsory conscription, interminable wars).[4] Not only does the annotated draft epistle allow us to distinguish the three languages of flattery practiced by Perrault ("il flatte gros"; his flattery is blatant), by Boileau (he made his adulation all the more telling by invoking his unsparing judgment as a satirist), and by Racine (his highly nuanced manner is the most scrupulous but still deceitful); placing the annotations alongside the draft also reveals, says Soriano, a Racine who exposes Perrault's *langue de bois* without questioning his own, and so enables us to appreciate the blinding hold of the monarch's cult over these great writers.

Defending the "sincerity" of Perrault, Racine, and Boileau, excusing the contradictions between criticizing flattery and practicing it, between dealing with the king as a human being in daily life and

deifying him in discourse, Soriano says of Racine's critical perfor-
mance in the annotations that "sa profonde adhésion au culte du
Roi l'empêche de voir qu'il travaille à remplacer une langue de bois
par une autre" (his deep adherence to the royal cult prevents him
from seeing that he is working at replacing one *langue de bois* with
another).[5] But in a penultimate chapter entitled "Et aujourd'hui?"
he goes on to suggest that we should not fail to draw lessons from
the artist's use of *la brosse à reluire* under Louis XIV, that the historian
should not shirk from comparing seventeenth-century forms of
propaganda with those of our own time: our task, he avers, is not to
judge the *langues de bois* of Boileau, Perrault, or Racine through
hindsight, but here and now to recognize and resist personality cults
and *langues de bois* in our own society and our own professional
practice. He returns to Raymond Picard's neglect of the annotations
as a case in point, asking if it might not be a symptom of a scholarly
langue de bois. The dubious logic that allows for excusing the dis-
simulatory language of the canonized author while blaming that of
the contemporary scholar serves merely to underscore the nature of
the excuse: it is transparently a denial that sustains the deprecatory
judgment it purports to set aside.

    Are there grounds for resisting the claim that Racine's insight—
his perception of the flaws in Perrault's flattery of Louis XIV—went
hand in hand with blindness to (or perhaps repression of) the objec-
tionable aspects of his own practice of flattery? Are there grounds on
which Soriano could deny that the noble sentiments of a liberal
humanist expressed in his little book are themselves caught up in the
hackneyed mechanisms of a certain *langue de bois*? The moralizing
turn in Soriano's handling of the annotated draft, even while it
solicits our approval of the ethical/historical questions he insists on
raising and our solidarity with the social enlightenment he espouses,
nonetheless confronts us with these difficult issues.

Racine's Critical Interest

    In a central chapter of *Les Contes de Perrault* entitled "Perrault
commis de Colbert," Soriano offers an account of Perrault's par-
ticipation in Colbert's "département de la gloire du Roi" (depart-
ment of kingly glorification), in which, debunking the altruism of
Perrault's *Mémoires*, he repeatedly attributes Perrault's dedication

to the propagandizing of the crown to his opportunistic sense of self-interest.[6] This view dovetails remarkably with Viala's take on Racine's career in *Racine: la stratégie du caméléon*. The irreverent author of this fascinating, often irritating, but always provocative book doggedly resists both ossified academic language and the cult of genius surrounding France's "greatest tragic dramatist." In his portraits of Racine, Viala never allows us to lose sight of the need to assume an intuitive or instinctive posture working so unerringly in tandem with self-interested calculation that attempting to sort out the deliberate from the instinctive is often futile: "Intelligence de Racine: intuitive ou calculée, elle est toujours là, visible; et cynique parfois" (Racine's intelligence, intuitive or calculated, is always there—visible and sometimes cynical).[7] But as Racine matures, his appreciation of his situation becomes ever more adept, and particularly in his writing, the calculative factor can hardly fail to be dominant. In reading Racine's texts closely, while keeping in mind a strong, integrally demystified account of his complex, intensely consequential, and by 1694 consummately sure sense of his aims, achievements, and self-interest, it becomes difficult to ascribe to their author anything other than a quite extraordinary strategic lucidity with respect to the self-promotional stakes he gauges in every facet of his writerly activity. "Racine était un animal amoral," Viala tells us. "Ses actes ne s'alimentaient donc pas à une raison évaluative; il n'avait de guide, conscient ou pas, que le calcul calculant" (Racine was an amoral animal. His actions were not nourished by an axiology; his only guide, whether conscious or not, was a calculating calculation).[8] Seen in this light, Racine's annotations can be read as a sign, not of his blindness to the full consequences of the personality cult surrounding Louis XIV or to the implications of his own concerted compliance with its demands, but of his necessarily studied and silent understanding and acceptance of them. What stance or concern will the reader who assumes such lucidity on Racine's part perceive in the annotations of Perrault's draft epistle?

The most prominent and persistent feature of the annotations is the extremely vigorous strict constructionism that they bring to bear on the issue of proper language use. Of the thirty-one segments numbered by Soriano, no fewer than twenty-six—including the few complaints that he considers insubstantial—touch upon the quality,

aptness, or propriety of Perrault's expression.[9] The annotator re-
peatedly condemns the epistle writer for failing to say what he
means, often indicating the right way to say it; points out terms and
phrases that are inaccurate or inappropriate; decries redundancies
and constructions that are grammatically unsound because of inat-
tention to antecedents, the sequence of tenses, and semantic rela-
tions between clauses; and tirelessly ferrets out the connections be-
tween sloppy, imprecise language and implausible or contradictory
ideas. As for the dictionary project and the status of modern French,
the annotations are interesting precisely because of their reasoned
response to Perrault's apparent attempt to score points for the Mod-
erns against the Ancients. Racine insists on making the references to
the dictionary circumstantially apt and conceptually sound; reject-
ing hyperbolic claims about the king's relation to the project, he
holds out for observations that readers of the published epistle—
Louis XIV foremost among them—will find reasonable and histor-
ically defensible. In segment 11, he dismisses Perrault's view that
French could be put on a par with Greek and Latin on the basis of
their common weakness (namely, an inability to express Louis's
deeds in words), qualifying Perrault's facile retreat into the idea of
inexpressibility as unworthy of the academy. In calling, in segments
29 and 30, for a reformulation that will mute both the claims about
the importance of the king's role in the dictionary project and the
dictionary's relation to the future of French, Racine's aim is clearly
not to dispute, but to strengthen the conclusion situating the reign
of Louis XIV for posterity "dans le temps de la pureté du langage et
dans le beau siécle de la France" (in the time of linguistic purity and
in France's splendid century).[10]

The immediate thrust of the annotations is clear: they are a call
for revisions that would make the draft epistle a text to which Ra-
cine, Boileau, and like-minded academicians could comfortably
subscribe. For Racine—as an unerringly stringent reader, a long-
term member of the academy, and an official participant in the
king's entourage—could not fail to be sensitive either to his personal
stake in the dictionary or to his implication in the collective subject
of the dedication addressed to the king.[11] It is hardly surprising that a
historiographer, after some fifteen years of labor in the service of the
monarchy, would disallow condescending views on the French lan-
guage recorded and sanctioned by the dictionary or on writings

about the king's greatness in that language; likewise, that he would
allow instead for a pure, highly perfected classical French capable of
representing the age of Louis XIV in its splendor. Rather, such
views are noteworthy only to the extent that they could well be
those of a *modern*, that is, as Viala would be quick to note, of a *modern
classic*—of an active, ambitious artist, anxious to guarantee the future
glory of his own work and epoch, who is jealously preserving his
privileged position at court and his overarching prestige in the
world of letters. On this account of Racine's posture, his capacity to
straddle the fence between the pro-Ancient and the pro-Modern
perspectives in his response to the draft epistle might well be articu-
lated with the rather devious role he was to play, again in 1694, as the
engineer of the public reconciliation of Perrault and Boileau.[12]

In any case, in their meticulous dissective precision and correc-
tive acerbity, the annotations demonstrate an intense commitment
to a rigorous classicism—marked by an exacting, strictly controlled,
yet confidently artful use of the French language—that Racine also
invokes via reference to such positive values as "la justesse de la
construction" (well-wrought construction; segment 9), "la bien-
séance" (propriety; 10), and "l'exactitude et la pureté du style (stylis-
tic precision and purity; 12). In one passage in particular, he seems
intent on asserting the great author's capacity to use language subtly
and creatively. Having quite adequately rectified Perrault's inflated
version of the academician's role by noting what compilers of dic-
tionaries really do, he nonetheless chooses to reinforce the point by
contrasting the lexicographer's work to that of the writer: "On
orne, on embellit une langue par des ouvrages en prose ou en vers,
écrits avec un grand sens, un grand goût, une grande pureté, une
grande exactitude, un grand choix de pensées et d'expressions" (one
adorns or embellishes a language through works in prose or verse,
written with a fine sense, a fine taste, a fine purity, a fine precision, a
fine choice of thoughts and expressions; 26). This constrictive un-
derstanding of ornament or embellishment incorporates the *classic*
author's conservative view of linguistic invention: to generate new
meanings or to express deepened insights, the writer relies, not on
expanding or altering the lexicon, but on adroit syntactic combina-
tions. The annotations display one such syntactic resource when
they evoke greatness and refinement via the cascade of "grands."
When we weigh these qualifiers alongside Racine's protest against

situating the work of the academicians in the quite distinct orbit of royal action and his refusal to treat the king's speech as a model of eloquence, it is nearly impossible not to perceive the *modern* author's interest in defending the integrity and significance of his own great work. Hence the judgment that the driving force behind Racine's manipulation of critical language in the annotations is rather more his irrepressible pursuit of his own cause and career than a whole-hearted adherence to the monarchic cult. But is it a blinding force? Given the extraordinary acuity of his insights into language and language use in this text, it is perhaps less plausible to suppose that his self-interest prevents him from perceiving the reality-masking effects of ritualized flattery than to assume that it constrains him to recognize, accept, and strive to control them.

By urging his readers to draw the lessons of history, Soriano asserts an unexceptionable commitment to intellectual responsibility. Yet his conclusion also raises a difficult question about the terms and contexts of historical judgment. Racine's incisive use of and insight into the workings of French also incline me to doubt the wisdom of treating the complicity of his critique of Perrault with the less vigilant idiom of homage that it seeks to upgrade as sufficient reason for associating it with the suggestive but elastic category of *langues de bois*. This stigmatizing term, deliberately highlighted by Soriano and used as a kind of focalizing supplement to more traditional pejoratives such as propaganda, hardly befits the conception and the practice of language we encounter elsewhere in the work of Racine—a corpus containing a large number of eulogistic texts in which an unmistakable, generically determined intent to flatter by no means prevents the author from sustaining an extraordinarily meticulous, cogent, inventive practice of French discourse. It is a corpus, moreover, in which Soriano, sensitive to the verve and acuity of the annotations, insists that these unsigned comments should be included. In short, Racine's practice of flattery is, in a sense, too deliberate, too skillful, too intricately and overtly self-controlled, to be regarded as the inane, mechanical, or artificial exercise of a *langue de bois*.

Critical Language or Ideological Bias?

A further difficulty with the expression *langue de bois* needs to be noted in response to the penultimate chapter of *La Brosse à reluire*.

Soriano's aim at that point is to warn us about terms in the institutionalized, "party line" languages of our own time that, no less than panegyrics designed to deify the king of France, serve to gloss over disagreeable realities. Among present-day intellectuals concerned with facing up to the lessons of history, Soriano is hardly alone in adopting nontechnical, commensensical terms or figures, such as *langue de bois* or "jargon," to designate and condemn discourses deemed inauthentic, obfuscatory, or delusionary. One factor in this recourse to "straight talk" is perhaps the disfavor into which the more complex and theoretically loaded concept of ideology, discredited in the eyes of some by the political decline of western Marxism, has recently fallen. But this manifestly important shift in intellectual climate by no means relieves the historian or critic of reckoning with a difficulty that ideology, as a critical concept disallowing facile suppositions of neutrality or disinterestedness, makes it necessary to confront analytically—namely, that no use of language pretending to represent social and human reality in its historical complexity can escape from its own entrenchment in ideology. This amounts to saying, if we leave aside the notion of ideology, that no discourse can escape either from its complicity with a value system and an institutional framework or from the structural necessity of occluding some facets of reality in order to expose and thereby valorize others. If reality-masking and compliance with a set of linguistic conventions are to be the only criteria used for identifying a *langue de bois*, the discourses of the humanities and social sciences would all have to fall gradually into the "wooden" category in the process of emerging as the expressive vehicles of a discipline or position.

Moreover, owing to the long history of critical objections to discourses deemed "inauthentic," the notion of inauthenticity is universally available as a theme, a commonplace target of criticism. Yet its very popularity has made the notion liable to abuse, to unthinking usage that is vague and trite.[13] To resurrect the call for authentic language in a meaningful way thus requires a considerable elaboration of context and argument, sufficient to reenergize a deadened, hackneyed notion and to sustain a continuing commitment to linguistic rigor. If we can readily see how just such a studied and durable linguistic awareness would be generated and sustained by a body of principles such as Racine's classicism, it seems idle to imagine that a single familiar precept or tenet, however apt or poi-

gnant it may be, could have that effect. Given only the tools and
perspectives that inform the criticism of *langues de bois* in *La Brosse à
reluire*, there would be no reason to consider Marc Soriano any less
vulnerable than Raymond Picard or other great scholars to the vice
he calls to our attention.

In the case at hand, Picard's account of his own editorial deci-
sion-making may well give pause when examined in its formulative
detail. However, it first deserves to be appreciated in a larger context
to which Soriano pays short shrift. Picard rightly takes credit for
including in his edition far more of Racine's texts than his major
predecessors did. His reasons for those inclusions are sound and, for
the most part, well explained. The real difficulty with which he is
struggling in the passage that Soriano quotes disapprovingly is the
standard one raised by hybrid texts produced under conditions of
collaboration about which we are not well informed: where, and on
the basis of what criteria, should one draw the line when deciding
what to include in an author's oeuvre? Picard's judgment on this
question is an independent, relatively liberal, unfailingly scrupulous
one that reflects his wish to give informed, dedicated readers of
Racine an ample store of material to explore. Unfortunately, in the
introduction to the "travaux officiels" (official works) from which
Soriano quotes, Picard lapses into terms that obscure the issue:
"Sauf . . . dans le cas de certains travaux historiques en collaboration
avec Boileau, je devais me contenter des textes qui appartiennent en
propre à Racine; sinon il n'y avait aucune raison de s'arrêter, et il
fallait reproduire entièrement *le Dictionnaire de l'académie* de 1694 à la
rédaction duquel Racine a collaboré pendant vingt ans" (Except in
the case of certain historical works done in collaboration with Boi-
leau, I had to be satisfied with texts properly belonging to Racine;
otherwise there would have been no reason to stop, and it would
have been necessary to reproduce the entire *Dictionary of the Academy*
of 1694, in the preparation of which Racine collaborated for twenty
years).[14] The exception noted here, the historiographers' collabora-
tion, is well justified by Picard, who sought to convey a sense of how
the design of an ongoing royal history was executed. But in arguing
against making exceptions other than this one, Picard offers a ra-
tionale (including the farfetched, albeit instructive, claim that logic
would then have required incorporating the whole of the diction-
ary) that serves to show why the phrase "appartiennent en propre

à Racine" (properly belonging to Racine) embodies a problem, rather than a viable criterion.

If exploring Racine's complete works in the light of Picard's account of their production in *La Carrière de Jean Racine* has one lasting effect, it is surely to make highly problematic the notion of works "belonging properly/exclusively to Racine." The concept turns out never to be simple: it is elusive—even in the narrow sense that Picard abandoned in doing his expansive edition—because of the consultative approach Racine took in composing many of his most important works and because of the unstable social and legal status of texts and authorship under Louis XIV. Once one takes Picard's editorial stance, which is to sin on the side of giving the reader access to a variety of texts in which Racine had a hand, as it were (whether or not they were intended for publication or for any reader other than Jean Racine himself), the individualist notions of authorial production and possession have to give way to an institutional framework, that of the corpus of works constituted after the fact by dedicated readers and scholars. It is clear that much collaborative work, since it is exemplary of a particular, historically important form of writerly activity, deserves to be included in such a corpus, just as collaborative efforts should be noted in a curriculum vitae; it is just as clear that, in every case of collaborative work, as in all cases of unpublished and unsigned material that can be characterized as incidental or of questionable attribution, the editor cannot rely on the mechanical application of a straightforward principle or concept but must make an ad hoc judgment; and it is clear, finally, that available knowledge about the actual production of a text enters into that judgment. Furthermore, as Picard indicates, in selecting texts he was bound not only by scruples concerning the status of the texts, but by material limits on the size of his edition. In the case of the annotations of Perrault's draft epistle, Picard implicitly admits that his judgment is subject to debate, and elsewhere his commentaries acknowledge that he can also be faulted for including many notes and fragments of texts, indubitably produced by Racine, that turn out to be so incidental, so marginal in significance, that they might well have been omitted from the corpus of his writings.

Reviewing the larger context thus leaves us with a fairly simple question: does Picard fall prey to an inauthentic "langue de bois de professeur" when he refers to texts that belong strictly or proprietarily to Racine? Or is this merely an uncharacteristic moment of formulative haste in which Picard falls back on a conventional notion, privileging an individualist model of authorial production, that does not quite fit the real difficulty with which he generally reckons in a thoughtful, objective manner? The crucial point here concerns the relationship between the studied judgments that Picard makes constantly in the introductions and notes of his edition and the language in which he conducts and presents them. No doubt those judgments are informed by the outlook of traditional scholarship. In certain instances, such as Picard's instinctive and perhaps unwitting reference to the model of authorial production, they may reflect a questionable bias. But far from depending on the prejudicial terms, phrases, and conventions of a prescribed, distortive language, they are grounded in the analysis of facts and in reasoned arguments. As such, they embody the same alert use of language—oriented by the search for clear meaning and appropriate expression—that Racine's annotations describe and enact. It would therefore seem immoderate to treat Picard's discourse as "wooden," as other than authentic. Hence, with respect to the conclusion of *La Brosse à reluire*, this counter-hypothesis: the differences that separate Marc Soriano's modernist stance from Raymond Picard's traditionalism are not linguistic but ideological; that is, their divergences have less to do with language use than with the way in which they situate their aims, values, and interpretive models within a larger intellectual-and-discursive formation that, by and large, they share. Might we then doubt that their intra-ideological differences are as momentous as Soriano has imagined? Far from objecting in principle to the criterion invoked by the phrase "textes qui appartiennent en propre à Racine," he appears content with it, blaming Picard for failing to agree that Racine was indeed an author of the annotations. The outcome is tinged with ironies. For insofar as the dispute comes down to a disagreement over attribution, one can easily hold both scholars blameless.

Now a reader sympathetic to Soriano's central admonition—to guard against the intellectual sclerosis and moral abdication that result from ritually repeating the code words, clichés, and truisms of an acquired idiom—would protest that, in pointing out instances of *langues de bois*, he did in fact bring to bear other criteria. We can assess their adequacy only insofar as they can be made explicit. An implicit sense of Soriano's ethical concern emerges in his remark that the pervasive personality cult around Louis XIV did not prevent certain courageous thinkers—Fénelon is the notable and very compelling example he mentions—from making strong statements about social ills. At issue here is the basis on which (and in a scrupulous discussion the question would of course extend to the method by which) the critic goes about determining the realities that a given discourse serves to mask. From the few examples Soriano sketchily presents in *La Brosse à reluire*, I surmise that the test he applies to texts stems from a set of modern liberal, humanitarian values anchored in the Enlightenment's reflection on human equality and individual freedom. This subject-centered axiology predicates its development and preservation on attention to the lot of men and women in society at large, to universal moral principles and public welfare. The intellectual's task is to protest when post-Enlightenment political and academic discourses fail to address social issues fully and honestly. Does the key to carrying out this responsibility lie in vigilant resistance to *langues de bois*, in the hope that this critical practice will somehow support "des hommes politiques courageux [qui] se donnent comme objectif la 'transparence' ou le 'parler-vrai'" (courageous public servants who take "openness" or "truthfulness" to be their objective)?[15] Should it also entail, as the one feature of Soriano's critical performance in this essay that clearly distinguishes him from Picard suggests, forcefully voicing concerns about the moral significance of history that traditional criticism would normally omit or, at most, state with cautious discretion?

It would be comforting to be able to think so. It would be invigorating to be able to count on the sociomoral efficacy of truthful speech ("le parler-vrai"), just as it would be uplifting to be able to justify the work of enlightened, historically observant, and morally responsible academic criticism as a struggle—appropriately confined to the sphere of ideas and language—against discourses that are false or insensitive to human needs, rather than understand it as an uneasy and largely ineffectual compromise with them. Alas, as an enactment of critical principle, the conclusion of *La Brosse à reluire* instantly obtunds the very posture of linguistic vigilance and ethical integrity that it espouses because it so blatantly reverts to a perfectly comfortable, indisputable mainstream position. In its substance (i.e., without regard for the neologistic term), its central proposition

about combating *langues de bois* echoes a pious truism and is per-
fectly at home in the complacent discourse of traditional scholarship
that Soriano purports to contest. That is, it would itself fit nicely
into the "langue de bois pour les professeurs et critiques 'tradition-
nels' de notre époque" (a wooden language for the professors and
traditional critics of our time) that he evokes as he turns from "Et
aujourd'hui?" to present the published epistle.[16] To appreciate Sori-
ano's central theme fairly, to understand why its importance and
relevance are, paradoxically, heightened by the depressing realiza-
tion that he falls prey to stale, cliché-ridden discourse in the process
of condemning it, we are constrained to recognize that his warning
against *langues de bois* hardly puts him at odds with Raymond Picard
or traditional criticism: no one, ancient or modern, conservative or
liberal, can disagree with it; no one can deny the importance of
autocritical reflection and revision; nor can anyone doubt that re-
sisting the loose and empty discourse that is flooding our culture
needs to be a vital preoccupation of today's intellectual.

Lessons of History

Tzvetan Todorov outlines such a mainstream view of intellec-
tual activity—but a version that is sharpened conceptually and more
nuanced historically—in the conclusion of his collection of essays,
Les Morales de l'histoire. As the title suggests, Todorov's concern is
precisely to respond to the call Soriano addresses to scholars and
intellectuals of our time: to draw the lessons of history. Here and in
other recent books, Todorov explores the possibility of using ordi-
nary language and a relatively straightforward, matter-of-fact ap-
proach to intellectual history to identify and probe issues of ethics
and political theory such as those that Soriano mentions in passing.
If Todorov can serve as a useful contrast and palliative vis-à-vis the
moral view of history that Soriano commends, it is because, by and
large, their respective stances are congenial.

The essays of *Morales de l'histoire* are diverse, uneven, and at
times exasperatingly reductive. Their successes depend on the con-
struction of a historical context or framework in which the choices
open to individuals and groups can be grasped in their human den-
sity, and in which the consequences of those choices can be deline-
ated in specific and practical terms. Todorov's vision of the intel-

lectual's role deserves to be counted among those successes, not because the position adopted is a satisfactory one, but because it respects the complexity and difficulty of the inquiring scholar's presumed detachment while nonetheless outlining with orderly precision the interests at stake, the choices available, and the compromises that come into play. On Todorov's account, the intellectual is neither an activist nor a recluse, is rather an artist or scholar whose enterprise bridges the gap between thought and action: "révéler et, éventuellement, modifier le complexe de valeurs qui servent de principe régulateur à la vie d'un groupe culturel" (to reveal and potentially to modify that complex of values that serve as a regulatory principle in the life of a cultural group).[17] In part, this role may indeed derive from affiliation with a class or social group and self-serving adherence to its presumably bourgeois interests; in part, the function of intellectuals in society may well be to serve as tools of the state or a dominant ideology. Yet these partial insights have to be situated in the light of the constitutive values of democracy, freedom and equality of opportunity, of which intellectuals are *obliged* by the history and structure of modern society to be the guardians. On the basis of these values, the critical intellectual's duty remains what it was for the exemplary gadfly Socrates: to act upon society ("il agit sur elle") through participation in public debate, to provide groups and institutions with a conscience. The gadfly will hold, Todorov insists in an earlier essay, to an unshakable but difficult and demanding commitment to truth—difficult because the truth in question cannot be limited either to the act of representation (accurate, objective, honest observation) or to the deeper, denser insight that is revealed in analysis, discovery, and interpretation but must partake of and integrate each of these two indispensable modes of appearance, representation and revelation.[18]

Todorov's reversion to the time-worn image of the gadfly is helpful—and far less problematic than the lesson about *langues de bois* that Soriano draws from his reading of history—to the extent that it eschews the comfort of ivory-tower wisdom and introduces the prospect that intellectual integrity will require, as it did for Socrates, grave personal sacrifice. Moreover, in acknowledging that intellectuals not only must make and convey an analytic and strategic judgment about the needs and problems of society, but also have to reckon with their actual and potential complicities (self-interest, identification with an institution or class, co-optation by centers of power) in rationalizing their role, he offers a contextualization that embraces the full range of the responsible citizen's dilemma. The consistency of Todorov's heuristic practice in *Morales de l'histoire* is such as to confer upon the irrepressibility of context the status of a further exigency, a corollary of the intellectual's obligation as the guardian of values: a burden of historical awareness. Yet it is precisely the macro-history that Todorov recounts in broad strokes that interferes with the invocation of Socrates and makes the engaged philosopher's moving struggle, recalled in the book's final paragraphs, appear incommensurable with the dilemma of the modern intellectual. Asking what a Socrates might do now, facing an over-populated planet, an intensifying struggle in most of its societies between haves and have-nots, and unfathomable cultural transformations wrought by modern technology and media, makes transparent the difficulty of imagining precisely what intellectuals can or should do in order to make the values for which they stand viable for communities or for society at large. In particular, by what standard should one measure the personal sacrifice that the individual committed to a given set of social or political values is called to undertake? If Todorov's stance—in the end a passably comfortable, unchallenging one—leaves many questions begging for (perhaps impossible) answers, it nonetheless has the signal virtue of raising for intellectuals questions worthy of the adjective *authentic*, and of reminding them that the scholar's duty lies not so much in evaluating the authenticity of language and ideas as in understanding and taking responsibility for their connection to action.

From Draft to Finished Text

In relation to manifestly important liminary texts, such as the preface to the *Dictionnaire de l'Académie* or the prefaces Racine wrote to introduce his plays, the status of a *preliminary accompaniment such as the dedicatory epistle (or the *dédicaces* Racine attached to the first five of his tragedies) is presumably that of a minor framing device. Very schematically, we can place both preface and dedication in the domain of rhetoric, since both entail the writer's attempt, analogous to that of an orator, to carry out an act of persuasion in the real world. (By contrast, the literary work, while reproducing the author's effort to act upon an audience, converts the process from direct to indirect communication: the work typically represents within itself human relations that mediate between author and audience.)

From the standpoint of the classical rhetoric that presided over the seventeenth-century writer's understanding of the author-text-reader relationship, the typical preface can be associated with the deliberative genre of oratory, since it is given over to the attempt to convince the reading public of the truth or aptness of the author's position.[19] The dedication, on the other hand, would have to be placed alongside the least well defined of the persuasive arts, the epideictic or demonstrative genre. Here the distance between writer and reader declines, shifting from the impersonal mode of instruction (pursued via argument, narration, description) to a mode of personal address aimed at provoking pleasure (typically via praise): the goal is to reinforce a judgment or sentiment to which the addressee is already a party. Given the tacit accord on the substance of the message, shaping it into a pleasing artifact becomes paramount. For both the practitioner and the recipient, eulogistic discourse thus tends to place a premium on rhetorical artistry. In reckoning with the imperative to please, the author of the dedicatory letter whose addressee is the sated yet demanding Louis XIV is obliged to displace the context-setting problem we have encountered previously (what can one say *about* the king and his reign?) into a more confining discursive framework: what can the academicians appropriately write *to* the king?

As we saw in Chapter Two, the critical reflection on rhetoric that Descartes inaugurated, that the logicians of Port-Royal pursued, and that Boileau's classicism consolidated furnishes the predominant horizon on which Boileau and Perrault came into substantive conflict in the Quarrel of the Ancients and Moderns.[20] However, even within this sphere, where the lines of opposition separating Boileau—the defender of a strong sublime associated with the value of simplicity—from Perrault—the advocate of sublime style, associated with elaborate rhetoric—seem sharply drawn, Perrault's propensity for co-opting aspects of the classicist outlook and blending them into his own at times makes it hard to detect principled disagreement (as opposed to personal rivalry or enmity) between the adversaries. A case in point turns up in his preface to volume 1 of *Les Hommes illustres* (1696), which the author places squarely in the lineage of "les Recueils d'éloges" (collections of praise). Here we find him chiming in with his own endorsement of simplicity and forceful depreciation of rhetorical inflation:

> La simplicité du stile de ces éloges pourra n'agréer pas à ceux qui ne veulent voir dans ces sortes d'Ouvrages que des loüanges ingenieusement tournées & énoncées d'une maniere majestueuse. . . . Car s'il est vray qu'on doit avoir pour but de faire bien connoistre le veritable caractere de celuy dont on parle, il n'est pas moins vray que rien n'est plus propre pour y parvenir que le simple recit de ses actions. (iii)

> The simplicity of style in these eulogistic speeches may not please those who wish to see in such works only praises that are ingeniously crafted and articulated in majestic fashion. . . . For if it is true that our goal should be to reveal the true character of the person of whom we speak, it is no less true that nothing is better suited to reaching that goal than the simple narrative of that person's actions.

The action-speaks-more-loudly-than-words motif, if not entirely consistent with the author's views on eloquence in the *Parallèle*, is a commonplace of the period. Perrault sought to work variants on the theme into his praise of Louis XIV, as we see in these snippets from the draft epistle:

> Tout ce que nous voyons de brillant et de sublime dans leurs [des Grecs et Romains] plus fameux Panégyriques, n'auroit ni assez de force ni assez d'éclat pour soutenir le simple recit de vos Victoires. (segment 13).
>
> L'éloquence où nous aspirons par nos veilles, et qui est en vous un don du ciel, que ne doit-elle point à vos actions héroïques! (23)
>
> Mais ce sont les grands événements qui font les poètes et les orateurs. (24)

> Everything brilliant and sublime in the most famous panegyrics of the Greeks and Romans would have neither enough force nor enough radiance to sustain the simple narrative of your victories. . . . The eloquence we seek through toil, which you possess as a divine gift, owes everything to your heroic actions! . . . But great events are the producers of poets and orators.

Although present-day scholars and critics are less prone than seventeenth-century writers to employ the conceptual frames of rhetoric in thinking about discourse, they generally subscribe to French neoclassicism's critical bias when dealing with preliminary texts such as the dedicatory epistle. As a result, such texts are for the most part treated dismissively today. In understandable sympathy with the simple language of facts and with the suspicion of overtly rhetorical speech, contemporary scholars attend only to those aspects that may appear significant notwithstanding the dedication's contingent, convention-bound nature. Predominant among these factors are the choice of addressee, information about the circumstances in which the work was composed or received, and references to themes. We assume, in other words, that a dedication invariably has an external, real-world function (expressing gratitude, defending publication, marking allegiances, seeking favor, and so forth), and that its contents may include certain indications, probably slight and superficial, about the historical and/or thematic context in which the work was meant to be read. On the other hand, the form of such a text—its style, its argumentative structure, the intersubjective relations and act of communication that it articulates—is rhetorically overdetermined and of little interest. Taking a closer look at the draft and final versions of Perrault's *épître dédicatoire* will not necessarily challenge the well-anchored logic of the standard, dismissive view, but should at least serve to sharpen our appreciation of it.

A Draft with Problems

The typographic presentation of Perrault's draft epistle in *La Brosse à reluire* divides it into three paragraphs of comparable length. Both discursive and thematic features justify this division. Paragraph 1 takes as its point of departure the work of the academicians on the dictionary and their discovery that French is inadequate to capture the brilliant spectacle of the king's power over all of Europe. But, opines Perrault, they take solace in the comparable weakness of Greek and Latin. In paragraph 2, the focus shifts from the academicians and their use of French for praising Louis to the portrayal of the king himself: a model of eloquence, as well as the sustaining patron of the arts and sciences, he is the fountain of inspiration fecundating the flood of great artists and works in France. Paragraph 3, with notable thematic redundancies, situates the lexicographic work of the academicians as complementary, albeit subordinate, to Louis' political feats, which are imposing French as the international language.

Starting with the simple communicative structure of a letter addressed in the first person plural from the academicians (*nous*) to the king (*vous*), we can obtain one measure of discursive emphasis by studying (a) the frequency of references to the respective parties, (b) the frequency of first- and second-person indices (pronouns, possessives, titles [*sire*], and (c) the distribution of clauses and phrases in the first, second, and third persons. Comparing the results from category to category, and in particular the totals of (a) and (b), yields a clear-cut picture: notwithstanding the intention (explicitly stated in the second and third sentences) to heap praise on the addressee, in the first paragraph the emphasis on the writing subject—and thematically on the academicians' privileged, proprietary relationship to the French language—is very pronounced; in paragraph 2, this situation is decisively reversed by the highlighting of the king; and in the last, the play between the sending and receiving parties is almost evenly balanced, allowing for only a slight preponderance of emphasis on the king.

Although the draft epistle does not present itself as an argumentative progression, its three parts do, in fact, evince a continuous preoccupation with a relationship: on the one side, the king of France; and on the other, the academy, whose members are servants of the crown and whose duties include not only the custodianship of the French language that their preparation of an official dictionary entails, but also the task of celebrating the French monarchy that Jean Racine had described in 1678 as "le dessein que nous nous sommes tous proposé de travailler à immortaliser les grandes actions de notre auguste protecteur" (the project we all took on to work at immortalizing the great actions of our august protector).[21] Perrault's draft none too subtly slants the express purpose of the collective subject of enunciation toward self-interest: the project is to depict the dependency of the academy and the dictionary on Louis in flattering terms that allow them to partake of his greatness.

Implementing this self-serving operation is not, however, devoid of awkwardness. The problem is not limited to Perraldian touches apt to strike Racine or Boileau as malapropos (such as mentioning the dictionary's long-delayed publication and evoking the Quarrel); it also has to do with argumentative design and rhetorical tactics. Upon reducing his draft text to a series of propositions about the language recorded in the dictionary and its connection with the king, we confront the following sequence, section by section:

1: *The French language is not adequate to express the greatness of Louis.*

2: *Louis's impeccable and powerful eloquence in French, born of his heroic achievements, is an exemplary reflection of his sovereign perfection.*

3: *The French language, as perfected under Louis and recorded by the dictionary, deserves to rise to international domination and to be recognized as definitive— "la Langue pour toujours."*

The glaring difficulty here stems from the insistence with which Perrault develops the first of these propositions. In its logic, it could of course work as it does for Racine in the passage from his reception speech for l'abbé Colbert cited above, which continues with this rhetorical question and comment: "Qui pouvait mieux nous aider à célébrer ce prodigieux nombre d'exploits dont la grandeur nous accable pour ainsi dire, et nous met dans l'impuissance de les exprimer? Il nous faut des années entières pour écrire dignement une seule de ses actions" (Who could better help us celebrate this prodigious number of exploits whose quantity overwhelms us, as it were, and leaves us powerless to express them? We would need whole years to produce a worthy account of a single one of his actions). Pretending that the academicians are powerless to carry out the celebratory writing that he nonetheless ascribes to them, Racine is adroitly using the "figure d'expression" that Fontanier terms *la prétérition* or *la prétermission*. This figure "consiste à feindre de ne pas vouloir dire ce que néanmoins on dit très-clairement, et souvent même avec force" (consists in feigning not to mean what one nonetheless means very clearly, indeed often insistently).[22] Indeed, in the wake of his rhetorical question (in Fontanier's usage, a "figure of style" called *l'interrogation*, and linked by its capacity to say what it does not say directly with the "figure of expression" Fontanier juxtaposes to *la prétérition*, namely, irony), Racine's clarifying afterthought imposes awareness of the preteritional turn: he implicitly acknowledges that the reference to expressive impotence is somewhat hyperbolic, and thus that the meaning of the proposition lies, not in what it says literally about the effects of kingly grandeur, but in the interpretation required of the listener, who correctly answers his question affirmatively.

Properly construed, the preterition gives all concerned—l'abbé Colbert, the audience of academicians, eventually the king and his court—to understand not only that the powerlessness in question is relative and surmountable, but that Racine's text is itself already caught up in and working with a conventional paradox: one of its basic stratagems for overcoming its expressive subjection to Louis's unspeakable greatness consists in evoking that greatness, in noting the undescribable aspect of what is being described. The reference to the unfathomable or the inexpressible can thus be integrated into the flattering portrait as a reinforcing commentary on its necessarily evocative thrust. Although the key example of preterition that takes the king as the object of figuration brings into play an overt thematic kinship with the (lofty, brilliant, inexpressible) traits of the sublime, one can imagine that Perrault would be favorably disposed toward the rhetorical function of the preteritional turn. For its effect is not to engage, but to block the sublime turn. Whereas the sublime turn would release the movement of psychic saturation evoked by "la grandeur nous accable" into unbridled expression and allow the swell of hyperbole to run its poetic course, to achieve its full, enrapturing impact, the preteritional turn shunts in the negative, interrogative, or conditional mode so as to hold the phrasing that sets its object off in relief under the control of a preliminary molding. Figural discourse is thus accompanied by a kind of discursive counterpoint or modulation that mutes or modalizes the descriptive statement as it is articulated. Insofar as the qualifiers or modalizers on which preterition relies serve to acknowledge, if not to excuse, the inadequacy of representation, they remind the capacious reader of the need to interpret, to forge the kind of access to the forbidding reality under description that can be gained only through strong, imaginative reading.

Perrault's draft epistle expands remarkably on the theme of linguistic indigence, connecting it to the work of the authors of the dictionary, then recounting examples of their failures, then unleashing his rambling, unsparing comparison of French to Greek and Latin. The trouble with this tactic is that it confers on the central proposition in paragraph 1 a force and seriousness that undermine the potential for a preteritional turn (such a turn would allow paragraphs 2 and 3 to proceed with saying what has been conditionally termed inexpressible). The whole of paragraph 1 reads as the introduction to a crucial image setting off the vision of Louis's incomparable supremacy—"toute l'Europe armée contre vous, et toute l'Europe trop foible"—against "le simple recit de vos Victoires" ("all of Europe armed against you, and all of Europe too weak" against "the simple narrative of your victories"): the brilliant Greek and Latin panegyrists could not even bring off the latter, never mind the former. The result is that the paragraph, ending conclusively, seems to close off the possibility of resolving the apparent contradiction between the premise it develops and the central propositions of paragraphs 2 and 3. The academicians are not far from suggesting to the king that, despite his linguistic prowess, he would be unable to express the brilliance of his own achievements; that the language he speaks with such mastery, while deserving to be established inviolably and for all time, remains to be perfected. It is doubtless a sign of the intensity with which Racine's word-by-word and line-by-line scrutiny was devoted to expressive detail and propositional rigor, of the degree to which it was microscopic rather than macroscopic, that the annotations do not make Perrault's failure to smooth over this argumentative muddle the object of a spiteful stricture.

A secondary conceptual knot, which the Racinian annotations do untie with consummate acumen, comes to the surface in the second proposition and its relation to the third and final one. Syntactically, Perrault's assertions about language and action either take or readily reduce to the form of simple transitive relations:

2a: *Vos discours . . . vous rendent . . . maître de toute l'âme de ceux qui vous écoutent→vos discours maîtrisent vos interlocuteurs;*

2b: *L'Éloquence doit [beaucoup] à vos actions héroïques→vos actions [font] l'éloquence;*

2c: *Les Grands Événements font les Poètes et les Orateurs.*

The logical ground of these claims is the idea that action, appearing as the object to be expressed in discourse, is the origin of eloquence. According to the full sentence constructed around clause 2b (cited above, p. 100), the premise is enacted exemplarily by the king himself, whom the academicians wish to emulate. Since the same heroic actions that make the king's speech so powerful underlie the production of the artists who celebrate them, one can imagine—thanks to the royal model and the associations Perrault is developing between political and cultural greatness—that the king's effect on the artists he produces is to induce a transfer to them not merely of his will, but of his eloquence. Racine flatly rejects this scenario and the submergence of the cultural in the political that it implies.

Yet as Perrault presents them, the dynamics of this process are somewhat contorted: he perceives no need to explain how the same eloquence that derives from Louis's actions and instills his will in others is initially an innate gift ("Vous êtes, SIRE, naturellement . . ."), and subsequently "un don du Ciel." The twenty-third annotation offers a merciless rejoinder: "C'est dire précisément que le don du ciel, qui est en lui, doit beaucoup à ses actions" (that is to say precisely that the divine talent he bears within him owes much to his actions). Moreover, the link between monarchic eloquence and the sphere of action and events is so integral, so fluid, that in the person of the king the difference between action and speech seems to collapse into an identity: his speech (see 2a) immediately functions as a domineering force exerted upon his listener. The royal example thereby provides for the convertibility of speech and action: the king's actions already have an inescapable meaning that informs his speech; since his discourse emerges from a "natural" relation of continuity with his action, they are together constitutive of his eloquence and together occasion eloquence in others. In the case of the ruling subject, then, action speaks eloquently and speech acts efficaciously. But for other subjects, is this process of conversion, internal to royal language use and productive of the speech-action equivalency, at all accessible? Do the royal *performances*—heroic feats and speech acts—communicate their effects with a force that extends into and shapes the language used to describe them? And if the annotations are right in countering that the relation one has to posit here entails influence or inspiration, but not full determinacy, how far does it reach? To what extent does it account for writing about the king?

This question is of course central to Perrault's overriding concern with the relationship between the academicians and their august protector. No doubt by appealing to the context one can translate 2c—"les Grands Événements font les Poètes et les Orateurs"—into an implied assertion that eloquence in a given era results from the actions of great men. As the annotations insist, that sweeping, baldly elliptical claim still begs the question. It thus has to be supplemented by the argument of the third paragraph: if the plethora of eloquent artists in France is an inevitable outgrowth of Louis's greatness, that does not put them on an equal footing with him; rather, it furnishes them their subject matter, their stimulus, their obligation to find the words required to express his greatness—without, however, endowing them with the efficacious eloquence that the king incarnates, and without masking the wide gaps between him and them (gaps that are vigorously reacknowledged in the first half of paragraph 3, which builds an impressive antithesis with three sets of paired clauses opposing *vous* to *nous*) and between language and action. The annotation of segment 24, while ignoring Perrault's subsequent development of the very point it makes, is apposite and emphatic in its rejection of 2c: "Tout ce qu'ils [les grands événements] font, c'est de leur fournir des sujets propres à les exciter et à les soutenir" (All the great events do is furnish subjects suitable for stimulating or sustaining them).

Thus, in responding to the succession of forceful transitives strung together in the middle paragraph so as to magnify Louis's capacity to produce eloquence, to bring (the French) language under the expressive sway of his thought and action, the proposition developed in paragraph 3 applies restrictive and revisionary backpressure: the passage is not allowed to achieve the associative assimilation or transfer literally; it grafts the king's model of eloquence onto the practice of his inspired subjects (poets, orators, academicians), which it adumbrates figuratively. Paragraph 3 appears, in fact, to end with a balanced view that corrects the extremes of paragraph 1, with its accent on the academicians' experience of expressive deficiency, and paragraph 2, with its contrasting vision of the royal speaking subject's phenomenal proficiency. In handling the king-to-subject relationship that Perrault has sought to turn to the academicians' advantage, this passage returns Louis XIV to the position of privileged object for writers and locates the perfection of the language not in monarchic discourse but in writing about the king. It is as if, after two tendentious ventures into conceptual quicksand, Perrault finally came up with a reasonably appropriate framework both for praising the king and for portraying the academy in a favorable light. It happens, moreover, that paragraph 3, the compromise internal to the draft, contains the gist of a compromise with Racine that Perrault will effectively work out in the process of rewriting the central part of the draft for publication.

In Pursuit of Revisions

The definitive version of Perrault's epistle is roughly one-third shorter than the draft. As Soriano indicates, Perrault eliminated numerous infelicities to which Racine had objected, but he also retained a significant number of the criticized formulations. A first, superficial comparison of the two versions yields the impression that, despite the many differences between them, the published text is still built on a dominant base of resemblances to the original. This impression, derived largely from the repetition of themes and phrases, has to be tested analytically. For several reasons, it is difficult to account for the diverse adjustments Perrault made, or to measure his specific reactions to the annotations with numerical exactitude: some of the annotations contain more than one objection, but they are so interwoven that sorting them out into discrete points becomes a delicate and approximate operation; some of Perrault's changes clearly repair problems that the annotations point out, but in a majority of cases the flawed expression or passage has simply been omitted from the final version; and the recasting of the draft includes a more thoroughgoing overhaul of its argumentative and discursive superstructure than first meets the eye, so that many of the problems observed by Racine are resolved, not by direct attention and correction, but as a result of the process of reconception.

Recognizing these complications, we can still conduct a text-to-text comparison that yields at least one unmistakably significant datum. In the thirty-one segments identified by the cross-referencing of the annotations with the draft, there are some forty specific objections that can be checked one by one in comparing the draft to the published epistle. Perrault retained his original wording with little or no change in about one-fourth of these cases. Among the ten retentions, no fewer than eight are concentrated in the relatively similar opening paragraphs of each version. Hence this inescapable two-pronged hypothesis: first, that Perrault began with a demonstration of his strength—his capacity to resist carping and impose his authority—by pointedly retaining an ample cluster of criticized terms from paragraph 1; second, that he painstakingly redesigned and composed the rest of the letter so as to overcome some of the unsettling conceptual problems that plagued paragraph 2. Although these claims are not subject to decisive proof or disproof, their relative plausibility is confirmed by an examination of the published epistle that persists in considering the dedicatory text as a discursive and argumentative ensemble.

Perrault's draft opens with a compound sentence, switching somewhat lamely to the first-person plural and direct address in the second clause: "et nous avons osé mettre à la tête de notre ouvrage le nom auguste du plus grand des Rois" (and we have dared to place our work under the heading of the august name of the greatest of kings). Whereas this opening puts the academicians and their work in high profile, the more succinct overture of the final version inaugurates a very decisive shift away from this first-person orientation: "SIRE, l'Académie Françoise ne peut se refuser la gloire de publier son Dictionnaire sous les auspices de son auguste Protecteur" (Sire, the French Academy cannot forgo the honor of publishing its dictionary under the auspices of its august protector). The remainder of paragraph 1, taking up nearly half the epistle, contains only one proposition with *nous* as its subject (as opposed to seven in the shorter first paragraph of the draft), and the heavy preponderance of references to the academicians (14) over the king (7) has been reversed (6 to 14). The change in emphasis is made all the more pronounced by the material that elongates the paragraph in the final version: its last three sentences construct a veritable mini-portrait thematizing this emphasis as uniqueness, as the king's historical incomparability. In weaving this portrait, moreover, Perrault deploys, within a multitiered rhetorical question that is the modalizing vehicle of an extended preteritional turn, a subtly powerful evocative and relational technique. This interrogation, followed by a meld of the imperative and the negative in an exclamation that extends the modalizing procedure of preterition, effectively channels the focalization that is being carried across the final movement of the paragraph toward a dramatic projection of royal cynosure:

Comment exprimer cet air de grandeur marqué sur vostre front, et respandu sur toute vostre Personne, cette fermeté d'âme que rien n'est capable d'ébranler, cette tendresse pour le peuple, vertu si rare sur le thrône, et ce qui doit toucher particulierement des gens de lettres, cette eloquence née avec vous, qui tousjours soustenuë d'expressions nobles et précises, vous rend Maistre de tous ceux qui vous escoutent, et ne leur laisse d'autre volonté que la vostre. Mais où trouver des termes pour raconter les merveilles de vostre Regne? Que l'on remonte de siecle en siecle, on ne trouvera rien de comparable au spectacle qui fait aujourd'huy l'attention de l'Univers: toute l'Europe armée contre vous, et toute l'Europe trop foible.

How is this air of grandeur that marks your brow and extends to your entire person, this firmness of soul that nothing can shake, this affection for the people, such a rare sovereign virtue, and one that must be particularly endearing for men of letters, this innate eloquence that, always sustained by noble and precise expression, makes you the master of all those who listen to you and leaves them no will other than your own, to be expressed? Where are terms for recounting the marvels of your reign to be found? If we go back through the centuries, we will find nothing comparable to the spectacle that today draws the attention of the universe: all of Europe armed against you, and all of Europe too weak.

A Poetic Portrait

In the opening sentence of this portrait, the ellipsis built into the conventional interrogative/exclamatory form, "comment exprimer," which omits the specification of the infinitive's subject, is compounded by the initial demonstrative, "cet," technically a rhetorical shifter that "dangles" until the deictic movement linking the "cet" to the possessive "votre" is in place. This structure of forward referencing produces of course an evocative effect of intimation, of rapprochement, bringing the enunciating subject and addressed object—in this case, as the explicit apposition indicates, "toute vostre Personne," the perceptible being of the addressee in its expansive (cf. "respandu sur") fullness—into a relation of immediacy or "presence-to"; it is as if the exclaiming viewer were gazing at or gesturing toward the depicted addressee in a face-to-face (cf. "vostre front") that is, as it were, insinuated by the proximity of the demonstrative to the facial object it sets into relief; as if the "cet," conjoined by elision with the noun it brings forth, were calling or conjuring or pulling this exuding, spreading "air" out of the air into the here-and-now of visibility, of sensible presence, in the act of designating it via a poetic flourish.

The series of four demonstratives debouches, in the definitive epistle, in a characterization of royal eloquence as performative mastery that uses terms nearly identical to those used in the draft. But here this eloquence is conspicuously not a model. Insofar as its order is still, as in the draft, a kind of psychological dominance ("cette éloquence . . . vous rend Maistre de tous ceux qui vous escoutent, et ne leur laisse d'autre volonté que la vostre"), it is an extension of the king's mastery, his overarching, pervasive, indeed invasive presence *to* his interlocutors that the imposing period, gradually built up by the swelling compound object and held in combination by the chain of four demonstratives, has been working to adduce. As the last, most insistent and most directly transmissive of the four royal features making up this chain, monarchic discourse bears the impress of kingly presence on his subjects with consummate efficiency. Infusing all who hear it with the king's will, it imposes an in-fluence or inter-ference that pushes the relation of immediacy between master and subject toward a veritable transfer of desire. Insofar as the king, via the imbrication of wills, imparts the informing principle of his own identity to his listener, "presentification" turns into identification.

As the portrait develops, the formidable expansion of Louis's presentification extends far beyond his own court or people. For his radiating and permeating presence carries over into the international sphere of political and military action. As the ensuing, parallel rhetorical question ("où trouver des termes?" | | "comment exprimer?") suggests, by virtue of their inexpressibility, the king's observable character and eloquence are comparable to his marvelous deeds; they can now be understood to be part and parcel of the marvels of his reign, caught up in a relation of continuity between his virtuous being and his heroic action. When the grounding constituents of royal identity are brought together in the grandiose evocation that completes the mini-portrait—the riveting "spectacle qui fait aujourd'huy l'attention de l'Univers: toute l'Europe armée contre vous, et toute l'Europe trop foible"—the composite image reflects the simultaneously centrifugal and centripetal force of presentification. This crowning representation, positioned in the draft as the ultimate example of the king's incomparable, inexpressible being and action, has become the articulatory center of the king's poetic portrayal in the published letter. In a formal sense, the combined effect results from the process of apposition that makes the spectacle the end of a series of components forming the royal portrait; in a more incisive thematic sense, the image is a culminatory and annunciatory rearticulation, resuming and recasting the relation of pervasive presence that the developing portrait has brought to the fore. Here the poetic function in Perrault's prose serves, in accord with Roman Jakobson's famous definition, to form a network of equivalences within the linkage between the term "spectacle" and the person of the king. The transparent connections posited by the final proposition itself embrace, in their syntactic order, the following terms: *rien de comparable/spectacle/l'attention de l'Univers/l'Europe armée/l'Europe trop foible*. Within this series, the connective junction on which the realization of equivalences relies is supplied by the phrase "spectacle qui fait aujourd'huy l'attention de l'Univers."

Read prosaically (with "fait l'attention de" simply asserting an identity between the spectacle and the object seen), the phrase situates the scene—Louis vis-à-vis Europe—as the image on which a universal gaze is fixed. But a strong, poetic reading that takes "fait l'attention" literally grasps here a second assertion, compatible and consequential, according to which the spectacle constitutes the attention—the gazing—of all who can see, positioning them in and through their visible relation to the overarching king as effects of his ubiquitous presence. On this reading of the epistle's Eurocentric discourse, then, the relation between the king and the population of all viewers designated by "l'Univers" and including those of "l'Europe" parallels his relation to his immediate subjects (the authors, the "gens de lettres," "le peuple," "tous ceux qui vous escoutent"). The image is again that of the king's *presence to*—contact that brings him up against—the people of Europe. The sense of presence extending through the whole universe is conveyed by the word "attention" (*tendere + ad*, "stretch toward"), with its connotations of tension and directionality, of focused observation. In the tense, self-extending encounter of Louis with the whole of Europe, it is the mutual at-tending of the opposed parties to one another that structures the universe as the unique, incomparable unfolding of the present ("aujourd'huy") in a historical tableau, a spectacular vision of Louis's relation to his world.

The spectacle [Lat. *spectaculum*] itself, moreover, as it is specified by the iconic formation of the two European wholes set off against Louis and against each other, embraces precisely the specularity—the contrastive fold or flexing within reflection—that the term subsumes (*spectaculum* contains *speculum*, "mirror"). The folding-back of the image—the spectacle *of attention*—on or into itself allows not

only for the reciprocating play of reflexivity, but also for the order-
ing of an all-pervasive *perspective*. For as soon as the specular struc-
ture surfaces in the tableau of Europe and Louis apprehending
themselves in their relation to each other ("l'Europe . . . contre
vous"), it is settled into the dominant framework delineated by the
no less contrastive than duplicative doubling of "toute l'Europe"/
"toute l'Europe": the integrative picture pairing Europe with Louis
in the immediacy and reciprocity of their attention to each other
nonetheless represents Louis in his position of enlightening strength.
As the unified image of Europe registers the paradoxical movement
of sequential simultaneity (from "armée contre vous" to "trop foi-
ble") that inheres in perception and reflection, it restores to the
monarch who had once been emblematized as the Sun King an
overshadowing presence that relegates his adversaries to their posi-
tion of relative weakness. Specularity and domination, identifica-
tion and subordination, thus appear to go hand in hand in the
spectacle of royal presence.[23]

The plausibility of this intensive reading depends on the various
continuities in the portrait: its purview widens from the sphere of
French subjects to the larger European population of all viewers in
which the former are included; within this metonymic structure,
the parallel constructs in the two geographic spheres are caught up
in the preteritional turn that extends across the entire portrayal of
Louis's greatness; the thematics of the inexpressible and incompar-
able recur in each proposition; and the crowning image of the king
under the gaze of the universe sums up the portrait that it completes.
The outcome of this expansive movement positions the king as a
kind of outreaching magnet, drawing the components of his world
into face-to-face contact (indicated by the two "contre"s) with him;
the centering, attention-captivating thrust of his spreading influ-
ence thus corresponds to that of the imposition of communicative
intimacy connoted by the series of demonstratives in the opening
interrogation. Because the exercise of this domineering force would
produce, at the limits traced first by the imbrication of wills (de-
scribed above in the commentary on the king's eloquence) and the
formation of the collective gaze traced by the gloss on the word
"spectacle," nothing less than the assimilation of each subject by and
into the overriding royal mastery that determines what all subjects
desire and see, the relational process fundamentally at stake here

ensconces the king at the center and origin of a scenario in which he constitutes his world in subjection to him by imposing his identity on it. So the integration of all the objects that make up the spectacle of royal sovereignty issues out of the absorbing and informing impact of the king's all-embracing omnipresence. At bottom, this ongoing process of determination effects the identification of his subjects in, through, and to the king. Louis's presence provides, in sum, the essential bond of equivalence that permeates the entire spectacle and fuses all of its components into a larger-than-life representation of the king in his unbounded power of self-imposition and self-aggrandizement. To write to the king of this universe, of Europe, is to write to him of himself, of his personal hegemony.

Like so many representations of Louis XIV that historians and critics have studied in the wake of E. H. Kantorowicz's *The King's Two Bodies* (1965), the purport of the portrait around which Perrault constructed the final version of the epistle extends well beyond the mythology of enlightened monarchy. Ultimately, it ventures a portrayal of absolutism as political power. If the mastery ascribed to the king by the three propositions of the portrait is, in its essence, absolute, its form is not that of a total domination that reduces the subject to abject bondage; rather, it is the position of power that is omnipresent and unique, power that cannot be circumscribed because it is circumscribing, because it derives from an independent, self-determining origin and center. In relation to the free and defining agency at the center of power, all people and places gathered around it are dependent and subordinate, even as they appear in opposition to it. Having observed this manifestation of absolute power in the three propositions of the decisive mini-portrait, we have only begun to grasp the implications of the portrait for the epistle as a whole. In order to do so, we must return to the comparative analysis of the letter's rhetorical configuration and see how the dramatically highlighted central image of Louis's confrontation with Europe, set off no less as a conclusion of the first paragraph than as an introduction to the rest of the text, fits into the overall epistolary structure.

Preterition with Hypotyposis

The image of military supremacy embeds the close-up portrait formed by a vision of Louis's personal qualities in the sweeping perspective of a vast panorama, a dramatic setting in which the king's dominance of the field of visibility remains the focal point. The swift diachronic, then synchronic survey realized by the last two sentences of the passage infuses the transformation from close-up portrait into majestic tableau with the form and force of a full-blown hypotyposis: "Mais où trouver des termes pour raconter les merveilles de vostre Regne? Que l'on remonte de siecle en siecle, on ne trouvera rien de comparable au spectacle qui fait aujourd'huy l'attention de l'Univers: toute l'Europe armée contre vous, et toute l'Europe trop foible."[24]

The interest of this process of figuration is as much semantic as it is stylistic. For one must weigh the sense of the boldly highlighted stasis that is at once expressed and enacted by the symmetrical redundancy of the curt paratactic closure ("toute l'Europe . . . toute l'Europe"), and that itself reinforces the drive toward totalizing or absolutizing connotation expressed in the apposed "*tout* l'Univers" and the earlier "*toute* vostre Personne" (as well as by the negative superlatives "rien n'est capable" and "rien de comparable," and less forcefully by "tous ceux" and "tousjours"). On first reading, the semantically similar parallel rhetorical questions introduced by an interrogative adverb plus infinitive, "comment exprimer" and "où trouver des termes," clearly come across with the paradoxical force of exclamations that the climactic freeze on the image of Europe echoes and completes. Consistent with each other, conforming to the model (with the "figure de style" of *l'interrogation*) we saw illustrated earlier in Racine's tribute to l'abbé Colbert, they express the uniqueness of Louis's qualities and feats even as they term them inexpressible. In other words, the questions suggest that the evocative crescendo leading up from Louis's initial presentification to the spectacle of his dominance supplies the preteritional turn that was missing from the draft—in a preterition that is, moreover, powerfully articulated and masterfully extended across the full exclamatory upsurge of the hypotyposis. Might it be legitimate, nonetheless, in an elaboration of our first reading that attends to the connection between the epistle's two main paragraphs, to grasp in these *interrogations* the embryonic form of an authentic question about language, meaning, and even rhetoric that the letter as a whole attempts to address?

In addition to the introduction of the portrait, a second salient feature distinguishes the first paragraph in Perrault's published epis-

tle from its draft predecessor: a general tightening, formal and the-
matic, of contextual linkage. Preceding the portrait is a reflection on
a single, central theme, carried over from the draft in a slightly
condensed, subtly tempered form: the unavailability in the French
of the *Dictionnaire* or in any language of terms adequate to express
the king's greatness. Both the sphere of action and the sphere of
wisdom and personal virtue are in question throughout. The tem-
pering stems from several small adjustments: (1) the draft's reference
to "le défaut et la foiblesse" of French is clipped to "la foiblesse"
alone; (2) the final version softens the flat assertion that the terms
prévoyance, prudence, and *sagesse* "ne répondoient pas à nos idées"
with a restrictive, "ne répondoient qu'imparfaitement à nos idées";
(3) the draft's remark on the inapplicability of the word Providence,
"qui n'appartient qu'à Dieu seul," is dropped, as is (4) the vehe-
mently hyperbolic disparagement of Greek and Roman panegyrics,
which brings the draft's reflections on laudatory language to a close
in a declaration of inevitable defeat. The comment that replaces (4)
characterizes the terms for virtue as "trop foibles"; the substitute for
(5) remakes this same point, casting the virtues of great men as more
sublime than the expressions for them, as it leads into the portrait.
The uniform drift of these adjustments is to tone down the draft's
accent on outright expressive incapacity and to place the focus on
weakness, on gaps between terms and their referents. If the inade-
quacies and expressive shortfalls to be overcome make the academi-
cians' task of praising the king a forbidding one, the underlying
assumption remains that it must be—is being—pursued with the
terms and expressions that are available. In short, the opening pas-
sage of the final version, notwithstanding its close resemblance to
the draft, has begun shifting the conceptual horizon of the reflection
on language away from radical disability—the mode of impotence,
of impossibility—toward that of relative inadequacy—the mode of
imperfection and limitation, of need and difficulty.

While the portrait brings into play a decisive discursive shift and
a new motif, its main propositions continue to be articulated upon
the concern with words and expression. It thus emerges in a relation
of direct logical continuity with the five substantial propositions that
precede it and form the central core of the paragraph. Its immediate
rhetorical effect is, as we have seen, to infuse the hypotyposis it
inaugurates with the very preteritional turn that the draft fails to

exploit. As we noted above, the proposition immediately prior to the portrait proclaims the incommensurability of human language with certain sublime virtues. In this light, "comment exprimer" has the force of a logical follow-up: how then, given the infirmity of words, are we to express *your* sublime virtues? This is hardly just a rhetorical question. As a real, historically charged query about the representation of royalty, it is doubtless the key century-specific question that at once propels and limits the debate over the sublime during the age of Louis XIV. Yet in its preteritional thrust the question already foreshadows an eminently Perraldian answer that will displace the unspeakable, sub-liminable (i.e., contourless, un-circumscribable) essence of the sublime toward the realm of the expressible and figurable. For inherent to rhetorical questions is a paradoxical twist or artifice that makes them particularly suitable for implementing the preteritional turn: since they typically contain or determine the answers to the questions they ask, they function as barely disguised assertions. Interestingly, however, the second of the two in this passage—"Mais où trouver des termes"—lacks the transparency with which the first one provides, through rhetorical manipulation, an answer to the question it is simultaneously declaring unanswerable: the contrast or heightened insistence, marked by the connective *mais*,[25] makes it easier for us to read it as a real question; and its brevity and directness, coupled with the oratorical imperative marking a modal disjunction and a relaunch of forceful assertion at the start of the next sentence ("Que l'on remonte"), make it construable as the clinching, summational prelude to what will finally be the academicians' positive response to their general question about how to capture royal grandeur.

In short, it is possible to follow in this passage an accomplished intertwining of figural and conceptual structure.[26] Its locus is the endpoint of the extended preterition bringing the inexpressible and the incomparable into the forcefully articulated focus provided by the crowning image of Louis in a face-off against the European world. The coalescence occurs to the precise extent that this image, set off in relief as a linguistic and visible *spectacle*, appears as the text's answer to a real question about language that it has been bringing to a head. The answer harks back to the Perrault we discovered in Chapter One, whose allegiance to the Cartesian turn goes hand in hand with his propensity to treat the graphic image as the essence of poetry. Artfully constructed, it is the graphic image of the king that will compensate for the deficiency of words. In language, to be sure, this means that the imaging capacity of the words used in combination to construct a portrait makes it possible to bring the special, culturally central sublime attendant to the virtue and power of the king into the sphere of representation. In this passage, the preteritional turn comes to coincide with the Cartesian turn in the reintegration—via re-presentation—of the sublime. For the articulation accomplished by the preteritional turn carries what first appears as the irreducibly immediate, absorbing presence of the king, the force of indivisible self-imposition bathing his world in relations of identity, into the differential order of the well-delineated image—that is, precisely, into the *ek-stasis* that results from the Cartesian turn.

From Image to Narrative

Now that the epistle's rhetorical structure has, as it were, vaulted this vividly assertive image into the order of representation, much remains to be read in its contours as the rest of the text unfolds. To grasp the essential point, we need to finish looking at the published letter comparatively—as an ensemble that differs in important respects from the draft. In lieu of a three-part organization, the final version really has only two, to which it appends a brief coda, a highly modalized, protracted and effusive period appropriately set off from the rest since it shifts to the vantage point of posterity looking back on the glorious age of Louis XIV. Thematically, the second main paragraph closely parallels paragraph 3 of the draft (much of the draft's problematic middle section has simply been jettisoned), but argumentatively, it is rather more homogeneous. It turns upon the king's relationship to French—the language of the academicians and their works ("vostre Gloire . . . fera vivre nos Ouvrages"; your glory will cause our works to endure), and that of the nation, spreading across Europe and rising toward "le premier rang entre les Langues vivantes" (the first rank among living languages). The claim registered here is precisely the one gropingly reached in the draft and lucidly recognized in annotations 18, 23, and 24: the durable glory of the French language and the work of French artists and men of letters will depend on the unforgettable achievements of Louis XIV. In developing this all too obvious thesis, paragraph 2 maintains the proportional emphasis of paragraph 1, and thus of the whole published epistle, on the king (12 references to the king, 7 to the academicians). In the one somewhat belabored passage it carries over from the original (as annotation 25 rightly complains, it is "une période d'une extrême longueur, et qui n'en a nulle proportion avec les autres"; a period that is extremely long and out of proportion with the others), Perrault drops the draft's ill-conceived reference to ornaments that the academicians add to the language and adds two remarks in the third person on French's diplomatic hegemony. It is doubtless more significant, however, that throughout the paragraph the newly unified argumentative thrust is to expand upon the representation of the king's conquests and political power. In other words, Perrault continues to work within, while specifying the focus of, the remarkable image of Louis holding sway over the rest of Europe.

Thus the spectacle of royal supremacy—"toute l'Europe armée contre vous, et toute l'Europe trop foible"—is unequivocally projected, in this final version of the epistle, beyond the portrait of the king's "Personne" into the larger political and historical dimension. Once that image of power is in place, its contextualization in the rest of the letter turns tellingly toward a narrative horizon. This move is intriguing because the narrative line is prophetic, running from present history toward the future, and because the prophecy takes as its groundwork the conversion of force on the battlefield into political power and correlates the exercise of power with the activity of language and culture. As Louis Marin's *Le Portrait du Roi* demonstrates with consummate insight, durable power—as opposed to expendable force—is a function of representation; the example of seventeenth-century France is particularly revealing because the perfection of the royal image becomes a veritable political program, a theorized strategy subjected to probing analysis in the work of Pascal.[27] The epistle points tellingly to the role of the French language and its dictionary as institutional vehicles in the complex process of representation—as expression and as delegation—whereby monarchic power is consolidated under Louis XIV. As in the draft, albeit more cogently, the academicians press their royal reader to imagine the process proleptically: since, from the standpoint of future generations, the power he achieves will continue to be exercised through the books and monuments representing him, in the last analysis it is the work of culture that will bring about his immortalization.

To what extent does Perrault's mini-tale about the future domi-

nance of French illuminate the letter's central turning point, the
poetic image of Louis's power transcending the difficulty of express-
ing his greatness in language? Projecting the impetus of narrative
backwards unsettles the domineering spectacle of a riveting image, a
scene that is firmly posited by the parallel and identical substantives
Europe/Europe (this paratactic phrase is a superb example of the
"figure de style" Fontanier names *l'enthymémisme*)[28] and supported
by the epithets "armée" and "foible" to the extent that they are
indicative of a fixed state. Insofar as the hypothetical story of con-
quest unfolds as an extended apposition to the spectacle radiating
out from the enthymemismic center, it discloses and densifies a
sense of temporal difference that is already at work in the truncated
texture of the image itself, a concatenation of two Europes, "armée
contre vous" and "trop foible." Indeed, the paratactic structure of
the hypotypotic climax enables it to shuttle across an incontrovert-
ible ambiguity, an irreducible duplicity, on which the whole of
the epistle turns and of which the central image appears to be a
metonymic condensation.

On the one hand, the evocation of Europe is one and unified; it
consummates decisively, once and for all, a process of meticulous
figuration, a preterition apt to turn the undescribable into descrip-
tion, to capture the royal sublime in a depictive sublimation. As
such, as a focal object captivating the attention of the universe, the
spectacle appears to be a singular, all-embracing picture, overpower-
ing and definitive in its integrative sweep and expressiveness; it
positions the monarch within representation, making him the abso-
lute subject who grounds his world as a structure of the attention he
gives and receives, as a hierarchical order of specularity. On the
other hand, owing at once to its bipolar composition and to the
evocation of a particular morsel of European history that it intro-
duces for the rest of the text to develop, the image constitutes, as it
comes into focus, a bridge leading from the descriptive to the narra-
tive, from the synchronic slice to the diachronic sequence, from
characterization to biography, from an instant of still-life portrayal as
immediate presence to the onrushing movement of a real-life story.
The paired—or opposed—epithets, "armée contre vous" and "trop
foible," may be read either as defining features belonging to the same
continuing present of triumphant superiority or as separate evoca-
tions of two distinct moments, the initial state of opposition being

followed by a later one of submission. Thus the representational power of the image lies in its dual troping capacity of fixation and transition; a static consummation in that it consumes the field of vision, transfixing the entire universe of viewers under the hold of panoramic wonder, it nonetheless traces a dynamic movement as it unfolds a scene in which the passage of time cannot not be reinscribed.

As an ensemble, the published epistle follows the trajectory that imposes historical narrative as the ultimate mode of monarchic representation, and thus gives precedence to our retrospective reading of the image, emphasizing the narrative movement germinating within it over the distillation of poetic stasis. On this account, the ultimate function of the hypotyposis is then to condense the statement articulated by the entire epistle by producing a dynamic image in and of history, by delineating a spectacle already penetrated by the narrative of events.[29] Of political events. Of national linguistic events. Of language subjected to political power and devoted to depicting it. This specification of narrative content is crucial. In the first place, it arrests Perrault's compliant response to the annotations, preparing the coda's forceful veer back toward the motif of omnipotent monarchic discourse that plagued paragraphs 1 and 2 of the draft. In the second place, it significantly qualifies the answer Perrault offers to the question about linguistic expression he had raised confusedly in his draft, but retained and reformulated more coherently in his revised text. The solution to the problem does indeed lie, as the text indicates, in deploying rhetoric to produce a graphic image, to conjure up an experience of presentification and shuttle it into the confines of visual representation.

That answer holds provided that the representational complexity and articulatory power of the image—its capacity to reach for the historical, to merge with a narrative of events that will come to constitute the horizon against which it is appreciated—are kept in view. Its essential argumentative consequence is that the potential tension between the linguistic weakness noted initially by the academicians and the strength of the language used to recount the reign of Louis XIV is resolved by the particular validation of narrative—as a vehicle of complex representations—that the image gives us to read. It filters what appeared to be a contradiction in the draft—expressive inadequacy versus perfected eloquence—into a complementary relation between description and narration in the final version. The passage into narration enacted by the central image in the published epistle infuses it with the sense of direction and cohesion that the draft lacked. It is, moreover, this essential compromise, effected by the power of narrative to capture and convey the pleasing qualities that resist expression through eulogistic description, that Perrault accredits when he applauds the character-portraying capacity of "le simple recit" in the preface to *Les Hommes illustres*. No doubt it is also to this compromise, expressive of his most productive instincts and formative of his most memorable achievements, that he adheres in *Les Contes du temps passé* and *Les Hommes illustres*. Yet as we shall see, he does not allow it to stand as the academicians' last word in the dedicatory epistle.

A Dictatorial Dictionary

Before Boileau and Racine were named to serve jointly as the *historiographes* of the king, the post had been held by Paul Pellison. The latter, a friend of Perrault's who had spent five years in the Bastille (1662–66) because of his association with the disgraced superintendent of finances, Nicolas Fouquet, had succeeded in obtaining the appointment in 1670. Louis Marin, in dissecting Pellison's remarkable "Projet de l'histoire de Louis XIV," shows how this proposal for a history of Louis XIV's reign works out an exceedingly subtle understanding of the process of representing absolute power.[30] Concomitantly, Marin analyzes in detail the strategy required for explaining persuasively to the king and to Colbert the mechanisms for constituting and manipulating the hypothetical reader of the still-to-be-written history. Through his contrivances, the historian serves to establish, between the power of the monarch as an actor on the stage of history and the power of the historical narrative of royal power, a relationship of reciprocity and mutual necessity. Pellison's "Projet" attends explicitly to the problematics of eulogistic discourse, focusing precisely on the pivotal connection between portrayal and narrative that Perrault's dedicatory epistle highlights. After evoking "ces manières de portraits, ou de caractères" in which the writer "sait en faire entendre toujours beaucoup plus qu'on n'en dit" (these sorts of portraits or character sketches in which the writer always manages to suggest much more than is said), Pellison writes: "Entre tous ces caractères, celui de Sa Majesté doit éclater. Il faut louer le Roy partout, mais pour ainsi dire sans louange, par un récit de tout ce qu'on lui a vu faire, dire et penser, qui paraisse désintéressé, mais qui soit vif, piquant, et soutenu, évitant dans les expressions tout ce qui tourne vers le panégyrique" (Among all these portraits, His Majesty's must stand out. The king must be praised everywhere, but so to speak without praise, through a narrative of all we have seen him do, say and think, a narrative that appears disinterested, yet is lively, stimulating, and sustained, in language that avoids anything that smacks of the panegyric).[31]

Pellison proposes an unsurprising itinerary for the historian—moving from the model portrait of the king's character to its display or manifestation in the action of history—that corresponds to the one in Perrault's epistle. In Pellison's vision of the narrative's effects, however, the paradoxical prescriptions of "praise without praise" and "disinterested interest," as it were, entail a passably striking nuance. They confer upon the well-wrought narrative of the king's actions the responsibility for producing an equivalent of praise that is, in effect, preferable to eulogistic discourse. It is precisely the effect of such a narrative on future readers that Louis XIV and Colbert can appropriately—with satisfaction and without embarrassment—be invited to contemplate; and in accord with this strategic discretion, Pellison structures his text so that the entire second half can be given over to the specification of what such a narrative can include and how it differs from memoirs or chronicles.

Quite as forcefully as Pellison, but without the restraint that would disallow a reversion from his narrative of linguistic imperialism to a new, lexicographic image of kingly dominance, Perrault, in closing his epistle, seeks to capitalize on the perspective of the future reader. In a letter addressed to King Louis, but to be published in a dictionary prepared by his institutional agents and intended to rule permanently over a lexicon established in response to his greatness, the academicians conclude by calling upon the king himself to weigh the reception of writing about himself by future generations—generations that will still be subservient to him, since they will have read about him in the timeless, definitive language of "le beau siècle de la France," the rule of which will be dictated, as it were, by the dictionary.

This tortuous formulation,[32] by underscoring the royal addressee's position in the face of the extravagant vision of present and posthumous monarchic hegemony that closes the revised epistle, seeks to mark a curious refractoriness in Perrault's approach to revision: it is as if, having reached an honorable compromise in the wake of Racine's annotations, he could not refrain from inflating his narrative disproportionately, so as to end by regenerating Racine's basic questions about what the academicians can appropriately write to the king. The coda fashions the dénouement to Perrault's tale about linguistico-military conquest out of a hyperclassic dream of the perfected tongue, definitively fixed by the dictionary "à ce glorieux point d'immutabilité" where it should no longer be dependent on "la tyrannie de l'Usage." Instead, according to the logic dutifully developed by Perrault throughout the second paragraph and laboriously reinforced by the coda, French is ultimately the language dependent on Louis XIV's position as the object to be represented in it.

Translation: the immutable language devolving from the king's greatness is freed from the tyranny of common usage at the price of its subjection to autocratic power and the tyrannical determination of what can or must be said or told. For read closely and as an ensemble that the coda attempts to integrate, the epistle inscribes in the image of Louis's triumph the story of monarchic ascendance spreading over the earth and through time in an inviolable language; it represents that tale of language-power as the master historical narrative that must be reread and recounted, not as the ongoing evolution of history, but in an endless order of repetition. Present-day French will be immortal, the coda claims, since it is the language of books and monuments that speak of His Majesty. By reverting to the portraiture of Louis's present power from which it devolved, the prophetic narrative ends, in short, by denying the immersion of language in history. The convolutions of the epistle's final period swell the spectacle of the king's power into an image of linguistic absolutism so consuming and so at odds with the common experience of language that one must ask if its eulogistic bombast does not cross what Louis Marin terms, in a brief chapter of *Le Portrait du roi* entitled "Le Discours du flatteur ou l'éloge du roi," the threshold of acceptability.

Thus the turgescent conclusion of the definitive epistle brings us back to the critical issue, barely adumbrated by Soriano in *La Brosse*

à reluire, of Perrault's curiously unstable position in relation to
French neoclassicism's explicit reflection on the practice—the rhet-
oric—of flattery: what can one say about the king, what can one say
to him, how—in what terms, tones, turns, modes—should one go
about it, what limits should one respect? The case made by Pellison,
Racine, La Fontaine, Boileau, et al.,[33] often while in direct contact
with Louis XIV, and long before 1694, invariably dwells on the art
of indirect statement and understatement, on the value of litotes
(nicely defined by Pellison's phrase "faire entendre toujours beau-
coup plus qu'on n'en dit") as opposed to hyperbole, of simplicity as
opposed to stylistic embellishment, of narrative as opposed to pan-
egyrics; and it undergirds this rhetorical caution with scruples about
plausibility or verisimilitude. Perrault's inclination to appropriate
this perspective is clear, and on the whole, the published epistle,
when compared with the draft, does seem to have moved toward the
discretion and sobriety of the classicist outlook, toward a typically
Perraldian compromise with the critical stance articulated in the
Racinian annotations.

Yet Perrault, having constructed such a compromise quite art-
fully, finally proceeded, if not flatly to deny it, at least to cripple it. In
all probability unwittingly (in any case without concern for the
incompatibility of the Moderns' position with the idea of an un-
changeable lexicon), he tacks onto the well-wrought praise implicit
in his narrative of monarchic exploits a fatuous but still disconcert-
ing totalitarian fantasy about an imperial France's rule by language.
At this precise point, where Perrault's prophetic narrative slides into
a fiction that is manifestly out of kilter with the geopolitical realities
it has invoked, the impulse to flattery seems to be marked for dismis-
sive reading. The marking has to be evident not only, as Soriano
rightly insists, for readers of our time, but—given the seventeenth-
century moralists' account of self-interest and the understanding of
flattery that emerges in the century's own discussions of eulogistic
rhetoric—for Louis XIV and his thoughtful subjects as well.

In order to appreciate from a Perraldian standpoint this tenden-
tious conclusion to the epistle, is it reasonable to invoke either
Soriano's stress on the author's tireless efforts to regain royal favor or
a certain recalcitrance toward Racine's annotations that the pub-
lished version would still reflect? Neither of these explanatory di-
mensions can have more than a hypothetical relevance. Perhaps,

however, Perrault's work—notable in passages such as the one we considered at the end of Chapter Two that disclose his thinking about history—does shed some helpful light on the matter. For at its core, the problem here is of a piece with the one that surfaced in his attempt to outline the cultural history of Louis XIV's century. In both the *Parallèle* and the *Hommes illustres*, his confidently advanced thesis, which we have also seen reflected in the draft and published epistles, treats the reigns of great monarchs (Alexander, Augustus, Louis XIV) as epochal. It is as if providence and nature conspired to surround these singularly dynamic, catalytic rulers with superabundant talent and propitious circumstances; as if the stellar prince were destined to provide the ambition and cohesion at the sociopolitical center that appears, in retrospect, to fecundate a historical concentration of great feats and great men (the absence of women from *Les Hommes illustres* is a telling sign). The monarch's ascendancy occasions a national, collective distinction that impels and warrants the extraordinary veneration and dominance he enjoys—an authority that the backing of so many great men only reinforces. Insofar as Perrault's defense of modernity needs to explain, justify, and exploit the programmed mythologization of Louis XIV in which he has enthusiastically participated, the recourse to the theory of epochmaking kingship opportunely furnishes him the advantages that accrue to historical perspective. History discovers and illumines the "proportion entre les Sujets et le Prince" that accounts for the pronounced superiority—"la derniere perfection" (ultimate perfection), as Perrault puts it in the third paragraph of the preface to *Les hommes illustres*—of Louis's century.

Already in the opening paragraph of this preface, however, Perrault takes note of an important corollary to his thesis: if nature is kind to the rare epochs it favors with great rulers and men, "ensuite elle s'arreste comme épuisée par la grandeur et par le nombre de ses profusions" (she then stops, as if she were exhausted by the greatness and abundance of her outpourings). The epoch of greatness correlates in time with the individual monarch's reign. At its end, which the *Parallèle's* metaphoric description of Louis's century terms the period of old age and leaves awkwardly empty, one must expect a vacuum. So according to his own theory, Perrault could not imagine the succession to Louis XIV in the manner of a consequent Modern, such as Fontenelle, who would envisage the future in the light of the ongoing progress of ideas and techniques that is ably described in the *Parallèle*. Instead, as the author of the dedicatory epistle, Perrault finds himself stuck with contradictory lines on the history of his century—the epochal account centered on the great king, and the comparative account centered on the idea of progress—that he cannot conciliate; and to make matters worse, he cannot present either of them in unqualified terms to the king. For in a letter to Louis from his servants in the academy, it is hardly possible for them to invite him or the public to contemplate his mortality and the inevitability of fatigue and decline that must follow in his wake, nor can they assure him that the march of progress is independent of his presence and will continue in his absence. Indeed, once engaged in foretelling the story of Louis's splendid century to him, they can hardly fail to represent its end in terms consistent with the reigning mythology and immediate circumstances (notably, the publication of the dictionary).

In groping for such terms, Perrault is again facing, albeit on a narrower horizon, the problem he left unresolved in his halting attempt, some five years earlier, to evoke the end of the century in volume 1 of the *Parallèle*. The choice he makes, privileging the epochal perspective and an absolutist vision of monarchic sovereignty, is clear. At the same time, he couches that view in a conventional sublimation of the type that would identify the king with his durable work or achievements, just as an author is identified with his writings. Via that standard metaphor, he would constitute for Louis XIV a figurative immortality. To a certain extent, then, the academy's dictionary—or a certain vision of the immortal power Louis will secure for himself in and through the dictionary that consecrates the French language for all time as the vehicle of his power—fills in the hole left empty in the schematic view of the century Perrault had sketched in 1688. The awkward ending it supplies does not point to an end-of-century generation of men and works; nor does it offer the terms and frames of a rhetoric that can reckon head-on with the coming end of Louis and his century. Rather, vis-à-vis Perrault's views on the role of great men in history and on technical, scientific progress, the ending constituted by the dictionarial enshrinement of the French language—by a prescriptive ordering of the lexicon that Perrault understands to be the most deeply rooted, domineering, and durable bearer of the king's presence in European culture—is an ironic legacy. Not only does Perrault support a conception of the dictionary that seems unfaithful to the stance of the Moderns (their outlook was, by and large, reflected in the stress that Antoine Furetière's dictionary placed on inclusiveness); he also ends up deflecting the emphasis of his historical vision away from the role of the great man (Louis XIV) onto the order of language. According to the logic submerged in the coda, princely power will be sustained only by its transfer from the individual to institutions, whether to language or to organs of state such as the academy. A patient reader of the proposition, upon perceiving this sobering outline of an inevitable historical drift, would doubtless ascribe less significance to the flattering rhetoric than to the deflation of flattery that lurks in the message.

PART II

Returns of Compromise: Perrault's Tales of Ogres

4

Food for Sight

The *Histoires ou contes du temps passé* (Stories or Tales from Times Past) appeared in 1697. Its last three stories—"Cendrillon" (Cinderella), "Riquet à la houppe" (Riquet with the Tuft), and "Le Petit Poucet" (Thumbkin)—were added to five retained from the 1695 manuscript of the *Contes de ma mère l'Oye* (Tales of Mother Goose): "La Belle au bois dormant" (Sleeping Beauty), "Le Petit Chaperon rouge" (Little Red Riding Hood), "La Barbe bleue" (Bluebeard), "Le Maître Chat ou le Chat botté" (The Master Cat or Puss in Boots), and "Les Fées" (The Fairies). Of the eight, only the relatively elaborate opening tale, "La Belle au bois dormant," seems to conform to the five-stage model of the traditional fairy tale or *conte merveilleux* set forth by Bengt Holbek in *The Interpretation of Fairy Tales*. It is, as Michèle Simonsen observes, the only tale in the small Perraldian corpus with a concluding drama that involves the acceptance of a young newlywed by in-laws, and the only one to end with the return of a hero(ine) finally able to stand up to parental figures and assume the master's role.[1] "La Belle" makes it clear from the start that Perrault's highly written texts, notwithstanding the popular sources of all except "Riquet à la houppe" (based on a story by Catherine Bernard), are intended for an adult audience. Versions of the tale expurgated for collections of children's stories commonly retain just the first half, the adventure of a "sleeping beauty" who awakens in the presence of a "prince charming."[2]

The closing segments of "La Belle au bois dormant" are crucial in setting the tone and establishing a context for the collection.

They shift the drama of royal succession to a new setting in which the beautiful princess is menaced, not by a maleficent fairy, but by her handsome husband's mother, an ogress whom his father had married strictly for her wealth. The son fears his wicked mother's appetite for human flesh and keeps his marriage secret until his father dies and he becomes king. But then, apparently believing his authority will protect his wife and two children, he ceremoniously installs them in his court, leaving them in the queen mother's custody when he goes off to war against the emperor Cantalabutte. The ogress decides to eat her daughter-in-law and grandchildren, planning to tell her son that they had been carried off by rabid wolves. Her project is foiled by her cook, who hides the princess and the children while tricking the queen mother with roasted lamb, goat, and venison served in Robert sauce. When the queen mother discovers the trickery, she has a great vat filled with various snakes and toads ("de crapauds, de vipères, de couleuvre, et de serpents"). Just as she is about to have her victims (daughter-in-law, grandchildren, the cook, and his wife) thrown into the vat, her son charges in on his horse, prompting his ogress-mother to throw herself into the vat, where "elle fut dévorée en un instant par les vilaines bêtes qu'elle y avait fait mettre" (she was instantly devoured by the foul creatures she had put there; 253).

It is no aberration that Perrault and his contemporaries made little if any discrimination among the terms *contes de fée* (fairy tales), *contes de ma mère l'Oye*" (Mother Goose tales), *contes d'ogre* (tales of ogres), and *contes de Peau-d'âne* (tales of Ass's Skin). "La Belle au bois dormant" clearly turns out to be no more an introduction to the world of fairies than it is to the world of ogredom (indeed, it suggests a linkage between the wicked fairy who ordains the death of the beautiful princess and the ogress, whose viperous vat conjures up a witch's cauldron). In a passage of the *Parallèle* that we examined in Chapter Two, in which the Chevalier points to examples of hyperbole in "contes de Peau-d'âne," he defines ogres as "certains hommes cruels qui sentent la chair fraîche et qui mangent les petits enfants" (cruel men who smell fresh flesh and eat little children; 3: 120; 227). In the same passage, Perrault mentions the seven-league boots owned by the ogre of "Le Petit Poucet," thus marking the association of a number of Perrault's ogres with supernatural power. Like the queen mother ogress, moreover, the ogres of the *Contes* generally have great wealth, and their fate is usually to be defeated by a hero(ine), whose victory appears to have a positive social sense: it purges a human family or community of a monstrous, alien force within it.

Yet in "La Belle," the fate of the ogress, whose death brings together elements of suicide and matricide without quite being either, has an all the more peculiar complexion because of the dietary twists and turns in the tale's dénouement. Instead of reverting to the ogre's natural, animalistic inclination to eat raw flesh, the cannibalistic queen mother holds onto the rituals of culture: she places an order for human meat disguised with a pungent sauce, and whether she is fed with meat from domestic animals or with game, she is well satisfied by the cook's fine cuisine. The picture becomes still more puzzling when the tables are turned and the ogress is herself devoured: the beasts who consume her are not carnivores, such as dogs or wolves; they are earth-crawling reptilian creatures— some of which are insect-eaters, some of which are poisonous— mingled in a *cuve*, that is, in a vessel usually associated with fermentation. Thus the prose tales open with a kind of interpretive enigma that centers on the ogress, her relation to food prepared for human consumption, and her transformation into food for lowly beasts. Through what lenses might we make sense of the tale's rather insistent entrenchment in a drama of overturned anthropophagy?

The Culinary System

In academic inquiry into the typology of foods, dietary systems, and eating practices, it has become almost obligatory to reckon with the analytical framework and general claims that Lévi-Strauss elaborates in his *Mythologiques*.[3] The insight most commonly appropriated from this work has to do with understanding the relation between nature and culture through the opposition of raw food, a product of nature, to cooked food, a product of culture. In the penultimate chapter of *The Origin of Table Manners*, a kind of theoretical summation aptly entitled "A Short Treatise on Culinary Ethnology," that duality is actually converted into a triangular schematic distinguishing three states of food, raw, cooked, and rotten, as well as three modes of food preparation, roasting, smoking, and boiling. The analysis of a given dish and its place within the nature/culture relation has to take into account not only the condition of the food after it has been prepared for eating, but also the process of cooking itself. Between the three major terms, moreover, there are grada- tions that depend on a number of variables: the type of cooking utensil or apparatus used, the distance of the food from the source of heat, the time of cooking and the level of heat required, the suc- culence or dryness of the food, the length of time food will keep before spoiling, and so forth.

The play of these variables makes for the apparent ambiguity or insecurity that emerges within the nature/culture opposition. For example, roasted meat may be well done or cooked on the outside, and thus on the side of culture, yet rare or raw on the inside, and thus still on the side of nature as well. Or, from the standpoint of the cooking method, a categorizer would place roasted meat on the side of nature, with smoked and boiled on the side of culture; whereas from the standpoint of the resulting foodstuffs, the smoked, since thoroughly transformed, would lie on the side of culture, while the roasted and boiled, when they retain their texture and succulence, end up on that of nature. These multiple ambiguities prompt Lévi- Strauss to draw the following conclusion: "The system demon- strates that the art of cooking is not entirely situated on the side of culture. Since it corresponds to the demands of the body, and is determined in each of its modes by the particular way in which, in various contexts, man fits into the world, cooking, being situated between nature and culture, has as its function to ensure their artic- ulation one with the other. It belongs to both domains and reflects this duality in each of its manifestations."[4] Insofar as this claim is valid for any society, ancient or modern, primitive or advanced, exotic or familiar, it can doubtless be qualified as "structuralist" and construed as an invitation to conduct synchronic analyses that re- gard a given culinary system as a variant on a general model of the vital if ambiguous nature/culture relation.

Moreover, as a practical matter (given the universality of the survival instinct and the need to combat starvation collectively), it is hardly surprising that the culinary system is vitally enmeshed in the processes of socialization and acculturation. For insofar as this sys- tem extends to prescriptions and prohibitions concerning the pro- duction, preparation, and consumption of food, it exercises a double function. On the one hand, Lévi-Strauss writes, dietary regimens, good manners, hygienic practices, and table utensils are muting or mediating objects that play the role of "insulators or mediators,"[5] suppressing or reducing the potentially dangerous tension between the social being and that person's (natural) body, or between the clothed and groomed body (of culture) and its physical drives. On the other hand, they also function as evaluative or prescriptive standards, as regulators that assign to physiological processes and social gestures an appropriate rhythm or duration, securing for individual and communal life a needed sense of periodicity. In short, to the extent that the culinary system serves simultaneously to hold individuals at a safe distance from one another or to mute the tensions within a single individual, yet still to keep them together, individually and collectively integrated through the bonding of society, its operation overlaps integrally with the moderating and mediating functions of culture itself. With this analytic superstructure in place, we can formulate a first hypothesis concerning the representation of food: to the extent—perhaps quite limited—that it embraces and discloses the operations of the culinary system, it is no less revelatory of a culture's vital ordering principles than representations of the other normative social systems—language, money, or kinship—with which it is presumably homologous.

No doubt the overarching framework of Lévi-Strauss's theoretical or philosophical reflections can indeed be reduced, in the end, to a set of oppositions: simple/complex, inside/outside, cause/effect, nature/culture, the raw/the cooked, and so forth. Once the systemic articulations or mediations between these terms, which prove to be subtle and multifaceted, have been grasped analytically, the ethnologist can construct his celebrated characterization of the dignity and complexity of primitive or mythic thought, and venture to compare "traditional" models of social behavior with the ideologies of modern western civilization. But in commenting on the order of the elaborated European culture that necessarily dominates the ethnologist's enterprise, Lévi-Strauss is not content with describing the practices of our civilization as if it were a monument or a continuum. Notwithstanding a commonplace criticism of the structuralist theses that Lévi-Strauss articulated in his *Mythologiques*, he repeatedly punctuates this monumental work with an explicitly historical point of view. In particular, he takes pains to evoke a constant evolution of the culinary system, comparable to the evolution of linguistic usage. In the final chapters of *The Origin of Table Manners*, in the process of building up a double-edged contrast between "so-called primitive peoples" and "the western world,"[6] he has occasion to refer to texts about table manners from the middle ages, the sixteenth century, the great *Encyclopedia* of the French Enlightenment, and the nineteenth century.

The first of the two major contrasts Lévi-Strauss evokes is a social one. For primitive peoples, table manners formed "a kind of adjustable code, the terms of which could be combined in such a way as to transmit different messages." For us, on the other hand, table manners have become so uniform that they are just good or bad; "eating habits for westerners no longer constitute a *free code*."[7] The evidence provided by texts of the last few centuries suggests that this shift has been subtle, gradual, and consummated only recently. The second and more celebrated contrast is a moral one. For the so-called primitive peoples, the commitment to good manners or to prescribed dietary and hygienic practices is grounded in the need to protect others, or society, or the human environment, from danger or corruption, whereas for us, says Lévi-Strauss, it is a matter of self-protection, of preserving the internal integrity of the subject against others or the outside world. Like the change in the signifying status of the code of table manners, this second shift is, he suggests, a relatively modern one. It appeared to start taking hold only in the Renaissance or early modern period of European history.

The Civilization Curve

From the attention to these overlapping historical processes, we can derive a second hypothesis about the representation of food: as this quiet sociomoral transformation slowly develops, the representation of food and of cooking and eating practices can hardly fail to manifest its effects. No doubt this broadly stroked historical hypothesis about our own culture that we can tease out of the speculative passages in *The Origin of Table Manners* is at one with its claims that the frames of cultural understanding have to be temporal as well as spatial. But unlike the first hypothesis, which the ethnographer tested massively in his analyses of South American cultures, it can hardly be qualified as more than a sketchy footnote to Lévi-Strauss's work. Thus it is necessary to look elsewhere for the pursuit and refinement of the historical inquiry that this second hypothesis subtends. In seventeenth-century studies, one highly instructive instance in which important scholarly investigations into cultural representation and its structure and processes have focused upon food is provided by the works of two formidably original scholars, Norbert Elias and Louis Marin. Their probing into the significance of alimentary production and consumption might be regarded as constituting a kind of fountainhead or watershed on which studies of specific cases in the culture of modern Europe can hardly fail to draw. Elias's sociohistorical account of the culinary system is a key element in the two fascinating volumes, *The History of Manners* and *Power and Civility*, of his study *The Civilizing Process*.[8] After recalling very briefly and partially the thrust of Elias's general thesis, I shall dwell at some length on Marin's remarkable study *La Parole mangée*, distilling from it a third hypothesis about the culinary system that focuses much more squarely on the problematics of representation itself.

Elias tracks the civilizing process in western societies over the past eight centuries in two distinct orbits: (1) the social and psychological existence of individuals and groups in their everyday life, their habits, customs, fears, and anxieties, and (2) the political and economic existence of feudal estates and modern nation-states understood as monopolizers of power. The historical process he evokes is a long-term, slow-moving evolution, largely imperceptible to those caught up in it. It has three main stages: a medieval period of *courtoisie*, characterized by the dispersion of political power and by diversity in the forms of social control; an intermediate, early modern period of *civilité*, running from the fifteenth through the eighteenth centuries, in which the rise of the absolutist state—epitomized by the France of Louis XIV—is accompanied by the development of codes of social behavior; and our own modern period of pervasive normalization and conformity, marked by the consolidation of state power and a very high degree of individual self-regulation in society.

Predictably enough, Elias's general claim is that developments in the two dimensions, civilized behavior and state power, go hand in hand, enabling and conditioning each other. This functional interdependence comes into view as one studies the spread of civility and the attitudes, emotions, and practices associated with it from the aristocratic court, where it originated, through the nobility at large, and then outward and downward through the bourgeoisie and eventually through all social classes: conformity to the centrally constituted model of behavior and personality structure at one and the same time enables the subjects of the monarch to partake of the power, military and monetary, concentrated in his hands and enables the monarch to extend his power ever more decisively over his subjects.

In describing what he sometimes terms "the civilization curve," Elias devotes considerable attention to two phenomena that may concern us here, the development of a ritual of eating habits and a change in the attitude toward eating meat. After a medieval phase marked by eating with the hands and by a relaxed standard of manners that imposed relatively minimal restraint on the play of emotions, the sixteenth century ushered in a phase of rapid development. During this phase, which was complete by the end of the eighteenth century, a new standard of table manners and the psychological condition corresponding to this behavior model extended across the whole of French society. The transformation that, for example, saw the common pot give way to plates for each individual, introduced the fork and spoon, and built up a bevy of taboos around the knife, had little to do with hygiene. Rather, developments such as the "fork ritual" had to do with a trend toward the formation of good taste and a sense of decency that depended fundamentally on the mechanisms by which individuals came to experience feelings of shame and revulsion. "The fork," Elias writes, "is nothing other than the embodiment of a specific standard of emotions and a specific level of revulsion. Behind the change in eating techniques between the Middle Ages and modern times appears the same process that emerged in the analysis of other incarnations of this kind: a change in the structure of drives and emotions."[9]

Unsurprisingly, the key factor among the phenomena that incarnated this advance in the threshold of embarrassment happens to be speech. In language, the all-encompassing medium of human contact, we encounter a spreading and tightening control of usage that closely paralleled the regulating of eating; and just as the rules for serving and eating food were not driven by a practical concern with hygiene, the code governing language use can hardly be understood as the effect of a rational concern with accurate expression.

Rather, the control of usage served the same sense of delicacy and politeness that the refinement of eating habits promoted, and it also demonstrated in the same way the power of the court and aristocratic circles to determine the standards and sensitivities to be adopted by the bourgeoisie and imposed by it on society at large. No doubt we should point out here that economic exchange was also a crucial parallel factor in this process. The development of money and taxation at the base of the economic system first enabled the king and his court to monopolize the definition of standards, then subsequently provided the framework for the monarchy's co-optative exercise of power in society with an ascendant bourgeoisie. As the monetary and marketing systems of mercantilism developed, this largely urban class gradually took over socioeconomic dominance from a waning aristocracy and helped recast the social order as an extension of the arm of state.

The argument of *Power and Civility* makes it clear that, in the value-forming process disclosed by the regulation of eating and speaking, one can discern still other pressures to conform, parallel to those that promoted polite manners, by tracing the development of the monetary system or the regulation of property. In any case, the economic hegemony of the bourgeois class was what gradually enabled it to coerce all facets of society into the civilizing process. Bourgeoisified civilization ultimately entailed making the acquisition and nationalization of the bourgeois class's values, feelings, and standards of conduct a matter of course, an unconscious and seemingly natural experience for children growing up in a society.

In elaborating on his claim that this sociohistorical process transformed personality structures and the psychological dynamics of human relationships, Elias suggests that the example of meat-eating is particularly instructive. In the seventeenth century, the practice of serving whole animals or large parts of large animals at the table disappeared; the century's rapidly articulated standard of taste suppressed reminders that meat-eating was connected with the killing of an animal and the eating of the dead animal by live human animals. Elias writes that "people, in the course of the civilizing process, seek to suppress in themselves every characteristic that they feel to be 'animal.' They likewise suppress such characteristics in their food. . . . The curve running from the carving of a large part of the animal or even the whole animal at table, through the advance in the threshold of repugnance at the sight of dead animals, to the removal of carving to specialized enclaves behind the scenes is a typical civilization curve."[10] We can readily see, in this case, how the requirements of the culinary system affect the presentation of meat to its consumer, that is, the people who buy it from a butcher, as well as those who gather at the table and participate in the ritual of eating it as food: the food we see and eat, that we represent in our culinary discourse, is a product of this acculturation or civilization; it contributes not simply to meeting our natural need for nourishment, but just as vitally, on the side of culture, to our practice of self-conception, of human identification.

Representation and Transignification

Elias's studies provide a concrete sense of the ways in which the slow historical process of sociomoral transformation, posited in the second general thesis about food and eating that we drew above from the writings of Lévi-Strauss, took shape in the late Renaissance and early modern periods. In the work of Louis Marin on the thought and culture of seventeenth-century France, there are numerous intersections with the investigatory horizons we have encountered in Lévi-Strauss and Elias. On the one hand, Marin appropriates the structuralist's view that the culinary system is a language, isomorphic with other cultural formations. On the other hand, he takes up, in *La Parole mangée*, a historical correlation that Elias sketches in broad strokes, the consolidation of political power under the absolute monarch in conjunction with the elaboration of neoclassical values and thought. In relation to this overarching background, Marin's insights on food in western culture inevitably have a special flavor simply because his analytical focus is relatively precise and propels him into a detailed reckoning with seminally important texts and artifacts of mid- to late-seventeenth-century France. But if he manages from the start to put a particularly original and challenging spin on his work in this domain, it is surely because the very ground of his reflections is the problematics of representation. Compared with the ethnologist's assimilation of cuisine to language, the import of this term and the framing it effects is considerable. For in its range and grasp, representation—subsuming not only language but the dimension of images and graphic forms as well—extends across the full spectrum of cultural formations, all of which become subject to conscious elaboration by virtue of being representable. It is, so to speak, the system of systems, the embracing fulcrum on which the recognition of cultural spheres and patterns, as well as the very possibility of articulating particular systems with one another, depends. To study representation is, we might say, to study the general order of culture, the very material and relations and activity of which culture is made.

It is not, moreover, a merely structural or historical account of representation that comes into play in *La Parole mangée*; it is, supplementally, an analysis of language, of images, of what Marin terms, rather than the culinary system, "the culinary sign," that pushes beyond the apprehension of functional relations and systemic developments toward the disclosure of what is absent, insecure, or dissembled within the processes of representation. From Marin's perspective on the cultural representation of food, it is necessary to add to our two hypotheses—one structural and one historical—a third one, according to which the role of food within the representational order is that of a *transignifier*, which is to say, of an operator or articulator uniquely well suited to playing in a double or multiple and transitive register so as, on the one hand, to dissimulate and to compensate for a potentially discomfiting inadequacy or missing link, an excess or lack in the general order of culture, which is that of representation, and on the other hand to provide for links or transfers or modulations, or indeed for jumps or slides, between orders or levels or terms that appear to be disconnected. To restate this hypothesis more simply, and in Marin's own terms, it suffices to refer to a passage in which he describes the culinary sign as the mechanism of the marvelous in the fairy tales of Perrault: in this fictional world, the culinary sign is a place or process, Marin writes, in and through which "the dialectic of *logos*, *eros*, and *sitos* is formed," where the figurative processes of *transsignifiance*—metonymy, synecdoche, and metaphor—convey and indeed carry out the articulation of society's major systems of exchange: words in a discursive system, wives in a matrimonial system, worldly goods in an economic system.[11] The third hypothesis thus posits the representation of food as a privileged sign, uniquely positioned for revealing the tensions and articulations between the various orders or spheres of culture.

Perhaps the optimal example of the culinary sign in Perrault's fiction is the Robert sauce that disguises the meats eaten by the ogress in the dénouement of "La Belle au bois dormant."[12] In the scenes of consumption we noted at the start of this chapter, which open onto the mystery of the ogress's alimentary behavior, the multiple dimensions of the act of eating are transparent. The narrative strongly underscores the "horrible envie" the ogress feels in the presence of little children. It is evident, then, that in combining the satisfaction of her appetite with the ritual prolongation of a fine dinner, she is managing a perverse expression of eroticism. At the same time, believing her acts of consumption effect a reordering of familial relations, she is conceiving the deceitful story she plans to tell her son. While the narrative of the ogress's failed regression into cannibalism thus relates the horizons of desire, kinship, and communication, its account of cooking and eating also shows how the process of transignification works. One should say that the Robert sauce, in transcending the opposition between human and animal flesh, is a sign that simply "transignifies" (rather than transubstantiates) because the substance of the flesh it accompanies does not change: the significance the sauce puts on the meat for the ogress causes her mistakenly to assume a relation of literal identity between the socially acceptable dish prepared by the cook and the serving of forbidden flesh she had ordered. In the more complex eucharistic model, the sign hides within itself the *transubstantiated* body of Christ: the bread's incorporation of the real body of Christ, which differs from it in substance, depends on a relation of *representation*— the sign stands for the thing—that the priest's sacramental discourse supplies. By contrast, the ogress's dish does not need to be infused with its body since the animal flesh persists throughout the process of cooking and eating.

Thus, in function and structure, transignification closely resembles the model provided by transubstantiation, yet it differs from transubstantiation to the extent that the culinary sign relies for its effect on a relation of immediacy or appurtenancy between sign and object: "the culinary sign, as a thing and as a sign, conceals the object, and it does so without their being any analytic relation, iconic or mimetic, between the sign and the object. The sign renders opaque the object to which it is joined, and it is more like an *ornament* than a symptom, more like a *mask* than an expressive look."[13] From the standpoint of the representational process, says

Marin, cooking is a ruseful art that belongs to the sphere of deceit or trickery; it functions as a *trompe l'oeil* that allows the sign to be confused with the thing. As for the act of consuming food, which, as Lévi-Strauss observes in *La Pensée sauvage*, so commonly figures the satisfaction of sexual desires, it takes on, for the eating subject, a seemingly transcendental articulatory power.[14] Since ingestion is a complex process in which the consuming subject simultaneously destroys, takes in, expends, and incorporates into itself the consumed object, it readily serves to figure the integrative transformations—absorption, assimilation, union, appropriation, reinvigoration, and so forth—that it literally carries out.

In order to appreciate the explicative power of Louis Marin's intriguing line on Perrault's tales, it is necessary to have in mind the larger historical scheme in which his reading of the tales takes root. Marin's understanding of the culinary sign stems from the study of representation and representationality that he elaborates in *La Critique du discours*, a study that takes the *Logique* of Port Royal to be the pivotal text in seventeenth-century French intellectual history. The *Logique* endeavors to construct for Cartesian rationalism a theory of representation and signification that Descartes left in a conspicuously underdeveloped state in his work. To put it crudely, that theory perceives the sign to be an adequate representation of or stand-in for an idea, which is an adequate representation or mental image of an object. Objectivity depends on a correspondence between object and idea and between idea and sign so perfect that representation as such—the activity of image- or thought-formation and the representing material (words, pictures)—passes unnoticed: the sign is transparent, the image is translucent, access to the represent*ed* is immediate. But for many reasons, the authors of the *Logique* could not make do with such a simple construct.

In the first place, like their colleague Pascal, Antoine Arnauld and Pierre Nicole of course realized that signs and images are produced by a subject whose awareness of the activity and medium of representing cannot be suppressed and whose use of signs inflects them with the effects and motives of desire. Hence the moral imperative to understand representation in order to restrict it to the service of truth. In the second place, and perhaps more significantly, the logicians of Port Royal, working in the Augustinian tradition of semiotics, were obliged to reckon with the mystery and the implica-

tions of the eucharistic sign. The singular utterance within the eu-
charistic ritual, *Hoc est corpus meum* ("this is my body"), is, Marin
writes, "at once the productive source of the representational model
of the sign and what throws the model into question."[15] Whereas
Arnauld and Nicole were constrained to conceal this origin, to treat
the sacramental speech act not as the enabling condition of their
general model for explaining the transformative capacity of the
word but merely as an illustration of the model, Marin asks if the
magical phrase should not be accorded a seminal theoretical and
critical position. He proposes to set forth explicitly the problem of
language brought to a head by the eucharistic mystery, and to study
its ramifications throughout the order of representation.

The thesis advanced here is a bold one. As we have seen, Marin
derives from the eucharistic sign the original model of *transsigni-
fiance*, of a metamorphosis he also designates, on occasion, with the
theological term *transubstantiation* (defining the process of conver-
sion whereby the bread becomes the spoken word, and the word
becomes the body eaten; whereby, under the proper conditions, the
authoritative speech act produces the divine body as the food of the
sacramental meal). Now as such, as the agent of an ontological
transformation effected by the force of signs, by effects of transig-
nification, the eucharistic formula is not only the model of the
culinary sign; it also constitutes, Marin suggests, the general model
of the communal process by which the force of signs is transformed
into power. Thus the utterance "this is my body" prefigures various
representations—historical narratives, panegyrics, paintings, medals,
portraits—that will serve to consecrate the power of the state, the
solemn discourse of the king being precisely an instance of speech
capable of transforming words into consumable goods.

To grasp the kind of understanding this insight affords, it suffices
to consider the correlation between the structure of the eucharistic
celebration and the imposing presence of the king that we encoun-
tered in analyzing Perrault's dedicatory epistle in Chapter Three. It
is as if the king's presence were embodied in his language or image so
that they could be taken in—"swallowed"—and absorbed by his
subjects. This parallel between the theological or ecclesiastical oper-
ation carried out by the words of Christ and the political operation
carried out by the words of the king underlies Marin's reading of
Perrault's tales. "Perhaps one might say," he writes, ". . . that every

culinary sign is in some sense and to some extent eucharistic; like-wise, that all cooking is a theological, ideological, political, and economic operation by means of which a nonsignified edible food-stuff is transformed into a sign-body that is eaten. It is this story, this dialectic of the edible and the consumed, of the thing and the body, of what is shown and its sign, of need and desire, that the tales never stop telling in their manner."[16]

So for Louis Marin, to read the culinary signs in Perrault's tales turns out to entail a further exploration of the eucharistic sign and thereby to be a(n un)cannily double-edged operation. On the theo-retical side, ferreting out the effects of transignification will expose the order of representation as an exercise of power; it will reveal the complicities of the rationalist theory of representation and signifi-cation with theological, ideological, and psychological operations that, in structuring human relations by, as well as in, representation, repeat essentially the same power play. Describing these operations analytically serves to shore up the general thesis on power and civil-ity set forth by Norbert Elias. From this theoretical standpoint, one could perceive in the queen mother's recourse to the ritual and refinements of artful cuisine in "La Belle au bois dormant" a sign of acculturation, a repression of animal instincts that serves the interests of power by enshrouding the violence at its origin in socially accept-able appearances. On the critical side, disclosing the forces—the forcing—at work in the processes of transignification will expose the strains and fissures that plague the order of representation; it will reveal the transactions and slippages that make representational practice an opportunity for strategic manipulation, for cooking up an enticing dish that hungry consumers will take from the *chef*—the chief—on faith. Describing the process that makes the enigmatic utterance efficacious opens onto the spectacle of fiction and illusion, onto the forces of dissension within representation. From this crit-ical perspective, one could detect in the cook's capacity to deceive the queen mother a breach in the fabric of royal power.

Transfiguration

Insofar as Louis Marin's thesis and his critical gambit in *La Parole mangée* consist in resurrecting the movement of the eucharistic sign in every culinary sign, they tie the operations structuring French

culture and society under Louis XIV to a quite particular ground—
one that is not simply theological in general and thus readily assimi-
lable to a certain theocentric version of Cartesian rationalism, but
that has to do with a specific religious event, the biblical meal under-
stood to be constitutive of the body of the Christian Church. In the
introduction to *Food for Thought*, the admirable English translation of
La Parole mangée, Marin refers explicitly to the withdrawal of the
divine body from the institution of the Church in the very sacra-
mental meal that founds it. He suggests that in Perrault's *Contes* we
can read traces of this scenario, situating the real presence of the
mystical body of Christ as the object of the Church's communal de-
sire: "The displacements and transformation of the culinary sign in
Perrault's *Tales* may be viewed as the figurative traces of this desire for
the divine body."[17] What is at stake here is perhaps less the value of a
Christological interpretation of Perrault's writings, the plausibility
of which can be reinforced by various details from the author's life
and works, than a very pointed account of the way in which Carte-
sian rationalism was appropriated by seventeenth-century French
culture.[18] On Marin's account, to put the point indelicately, the
midcentury elaboration of the Cartesian scheme in the Port Royal-
ists' theory and practice of representation provides for its politically
useful Christianization. For the early modern institutions of Church
and State, its reshaping of rationalism answers to an imperative: the
mechanisms of representation must enable their communities of
followers to fulfill their wish for mystical communion with the
holder of sacred authority. In other words, embedding the ecclesias-
tical model of allegiance to Christ in the general structure of repre-
sentation makes it appropriable as the model of allegiance to the
monarch. The ramifications of that historical development, while
given to be read in many places, receive their "most precise and
suggestive narrative expression" in Perrault's *Tales*.[19]

Since Louis Marin has demonstrated the fertility of his reading
hypothesis in a host of essays on Perrault, as well as in diverse analy-
ses of texts and icons that disclose the figural status of the king and
explain its effects, his perspective on the cultural representation of
food is hardly subject to refutation or correction. The question is
rather whether his description of the dynamics by which the ra-
tionalism of Descartes is complicated and recuperated by subsequent
cultural formations is the only workable account, or the most satis-

factory one. Concomitantly, in the case of Perrault's tales, the question is not whether the persistent invoking of the culinary sign in the narratives yields reinscriptions of the eucharistic sign and deploys its capacity to bridge across the other systems of exchange that are caught up in the mechanisms of the marvelous tale; rather, the question is whether those moments of transignification are indeed the most telling or dominant forces in the play of representation, and secondarily, whether other, essentially aesthetic signs—such as terms that evoke vision and intellection—are not just as capacious and pivotal as the culinary sign in exercising the transignifying function.

The answers to these queries, historical and technical, on the possibility of an alternative approach to the tales are of course interlocking. By now it should be evident that the questions themselves are implied and framed by the hypothesis elaborated in Part I. To formulate them explicitly here is to call for a testing of that hypothesis in readings of the tales. Accordingly, after briefly reviewing the account of Perrault's reaction to Descartes in Chapter One and the ensuing hypothesis on compromise formation elaborated in the rest of Part I, I shall take up the analysis of some especially significant tales in the light of that hypothesis. The first case to be studied is one of Perrault's three verse tales, "Peau d'âne." Marin treats "Peau d'âne" as a crucial watershed in *La Parole mangée*, owing to its inaugural and in many respects exemplary status. I propose to reexamine it in tandem with a second, quite celebrated tale, "Cendrillon," that Marin does not treat extensively, although he notes in passing that the fairy godmother's transformation of the pumpkin into a carriage offers a fine illustration of *transsignifiance*.

In Chapter One, I situated Perrault's recuperation of Descartes and his resistances to Cartesian rationalism in relation to the epistemic core of Descartes's foundational texts, the tightly controlled conversion of knowledge inherent in the speech of the subject into knowledge in the form of an image. The *cogito* emerges in representation via the Cartesian turn, that is, via the initial and, as it were, immediate envisualization of the proposition "I think," via the folding or displacement of thought onto sight or of sight into thought in a manner that marks their continuity and near-coincidence. Thus the representational movement or signifying event that a Cartesian theory of language or signification has to deal with is indeed a metamorphosis effected by a pivotal proposition, but one far more confined and discreet than the process of transubstantiation in the Eucharist or transignification in the realm of the marvelous; it is the subtle, metaphorical shift or shuttle or *tropos* whereby the sayable is shunted—or raised—into the visible, speech into image, assertion into figuration, knowledge into representation, the mind into the sphere of natural light; in short, a movement generative of the most elemental representation, a primary imaging that underlies the fundamental value of the visual—the clear and distinct idea—in Descartes's epistemology.

It is above all through this accreditation of the compelling visual image, faithfully reproducing its object for a thinking subject, that a certain Cartesian influence makes itself felt in Perrault's *Parallèle des anciens et des modernes*. Perrault's position is generally one of solidarity with the rationalist construction of a conventional mimeticism; this stance, a kind of mainstream, domesticated Cartesianism, supports the privileging of the visual in the work's aesthetics. However, when the work of Descartes is encountered directly, a counterposition appears that stresses not the continuity in the Cartesian turn, but the difference between the enabling ground of representation, visibility, and that of knowledge, mind. Mind engages the reason and intelligence and communicative powers that Cartesian rationalism reserves for man, whereas lower animals can perfectly well be endowed with the faculty of representation. Through this reversal that disconnects the image from cognition and leads Perrault's spokesman to posit a certain necessary inconceivability or irrepresentability within or beneath the conceptual knowledge he extols, the priority of visual representation is momentarily thrown into doubt.

Perrault's Cartesianism thus takes on an intriguingly critical edge or twist. The result is a compromise formation in which a simple, mainstream rationalism accrediting a stable, technological, continuist account of knowledge as well-formed representation—as delineation—is the dominant perspective. But rather than forcing the triumph of a thoroughly transcendental model that would finally assimilate all cognitive experience of the subject to conception modeled on the forming of an image, the compromise leaves open a lesser, subordinate space for knowledge or intuition that may prove to be irreducible to visualization. A certain tact or restraint with respect to alterity makes the Cartesian turn the exemplary model of such a compromise. If the turn's foundational movement displaces and covers the amorphous or contourless experience of self-sensation, it stops short of eradicating it; the movement shapes a relation guaranteeing for thought and knowledge their irrepressible capacity to wrap the conceivable order around the inconceivable, without crushing the resistances that emanate from the inconceivable, without relegating them to the sphere of the radically inaccessible or the necessarily unthought.

As we saw in studying the sublime and preteritional turns, Perrault's writing ranges across diverse subjects and contexts, and the terms in which he recasts the overarching opposition between the conceivable order (that of sublime style and expressible qualities) and its unequal counterpart, the inconceivable (that of the sublime and the inexpressible), vary accordingly: the animal versus the human, the visual versus the verbal (Chapter One); metaphor versus hyperbole, technique and calculation versus passion and genius (Chapter Two); representation/mediation versus presentification/ immediacy, description versus narration (Chapter Three). Since tales such as "Riquet à la houppe" and "Le Petit Poucet" cling to an openness or indecision that makes for articulations of the conceivable with the inconceivable analogous to those of the *Parallèle*, one must ask if Perrault's experiments with the writing of *contes merveilleux* do not reproduce such compromises systematically, primarily through the manipulation of narrative techniques and themes and secondarily through the *moralités*. If such formations prove to recur from tale to tale, their cumulative effect will constitute a pervasive background against which the work of the culinary sign—along with that of the culinary system—can be placed in perspective. Hence, a working hypothesis, according to which the signifying operations conveyed by the culinary sign belong to the apparatus of compromise formation. Thus, while they may serve to expose and on occasion to disturb or contest the mechanisms of power, their essential place would be one of complicity in a general movement that, whether textual or historical, enables the dominant order of visual conception to sustain itself, to incorporate and use productively the very resistances to or within representation that contest it.

Concretely, the focus of this hypothesis is the process of articulation within the general sphere of representation. Via this process, the opposed poles—the visible and the invisible, the conceivable and the inconceivable—come into a stable hierarchic relation. Already in the *Parallèle* one can distinguish between articulations that depend on the semantic breadth of terms such as knowledge and *esprit* and those that depend on analogy and simile, or on ambivalent images or figures such as the Abbé's mirror. The latter dimension, where the culinary sign and the process of transignification manifestly constitute an important resource, is, more generally, that of figuration or tropology; and drawing on the analogy with transignification, one might, without undue hesitation, name the general process that includes transignification *transfiguration*.[20] In the light of the hypothesis built around the Cartesian turn, one would expect the metaphorics of visuality and appearance, which Louis Marin evokes when he compares the culinary sign to a mask or an ornament, not merely to complement the metaphorics of cuisine, but to play a presiding role in the figurative domain. To illustrate this relation between vision and consumption, which will be the principal object of scrutiny in my analysis of "Peau d'âne," it is once again useful to recall the encounter between the princess's beauty and the ogress's destructive appetite in "La Belle au bois dormant."

The most prominent feature of the story's narrative structure is a function of repetition. In the marvelous drama marked by the interventions of fairies, the adorable princess who is condemned to death by the wicked old fairy can be saved only by waiting in slumber for 100 years; she is then rescued at the moment of her awakening by her courageous and loving prince. In the subsequent sequence with the ogress, the princess undergoes an analogous trial. Here, as the beautiful young queen, she is again threatened (along with her children) with death; this time her hiding (parallel to her slumber) is foiled by her enemy and a renewal of the death threat, but her husband, now the king, again turns up in time to save her. The global and embedded narrative sequences thus fit cohesively together in a drama of royal succession, inaugurated by the strenuous efforts of the princess's parents to have a child and successfully consummated by the preservation of the young queen against the sinister forces that assail her.

As the story's title and its descriptions of the princess/queen suggest, her survival is a triumph of beauty, played out, moreover, in scenes that mark the captivating power of visual spectacle and ocular communication. The first of the princess's gifts from the good fairies makes her "la plus belle personne du monde" (the most beautiful person in the world; 244). The portrait of the sleeping beauty places her "dans le plus bel appartement du Palais, sur un lit en broderie d'or et d'argent. On eût dit un Ange, tant elle était belle; car son évanouissement n'avait pas ôté les couleurs vives de son teint: ses joues étaient incarnates, et ses lèvres comme du corail; elle avait seulement les yeux fermés, mais on l'entendait respirer doucement, ce qui faisait voir qu'elle n'était pas morte" (in the finest apartment of the palace, on a bed embroidered with gold and silver. She was so beautiful one would have said she was an angel; for her swoon had not taken away the warmth of her complexion; her cheeks were crimson and her lips were like coral; though her eyes were closed, one could hear her gentle breathing, which showed that she was not dead; 245).

After the prince enters the castle and determines that "l'image de la mort" is only an appearance, he finds in the bedroom "le plus beau spectacle qu'il eût jamais vu: une Princesse . . . dont l'éclat resplendissant avait quelque chose de lumineux et de divin" (the finest spectacle he had ever seen: a princess whose radiant beauty made her seem luminous and divine; 247). Her awakening begins with the opening of the eyes that were marked as closed in the portrait, and they are immediately expressive: "la Princesse s'éveilla; et le regardant avec des yeux plus tendres qu'une première vue ne semblait le permettre" (the princess awoke, and looking at him with eyes more tender than a first look would seem to allow; 248). In describing the ensuing feast and marriage ceremony, the narrator notes that the princess's magnificent clothing was a century out of date; "elle n'en était pas moins belle" (it made her no less lovely). The motifs of beauty and luminosity are carried into the couple's procreation of lovely children, "dont le premier, qui fut une fille, fut nommée l'Aurore, et le second un fils, qu'on nomma le Jour, parce qu'il paraissait encore plus beau que sa soeur" (of whom the first, a daughter, was named Aurora, and the second, a son, was named Day, since he appeared even more beautiful than his sister; 249).

This gradual arraying of beauty across the first three-quarters of the story evanesces in the dénouement, precisely in the segments that place heavy emphasis on the culinary process as they narrate the foiling of the ogress/queen mother. It is noteworthy, however, that the very end of this closing drama—the moment of rescue, which

corresponds to the bedroom scene followed by the feast and marriage in the sleeping-beauty portion of the tale—resurrects the
framework of the spectacle and marks its decisive visual effect on the
ogress. The king "demanda tout étonné ce que voulait dire cet
horrible spectacle; personne n'osait l'en instruire, quand l'Ogresse,
enragée de voir ce qu'elle voyait, se jeta elle-même la tête la première dans la cuve" (asked in astonishment what this horrible spectacle meant; when no one dared inform him, the ogress, enraged to
see what she saw, threw herself head first into the vat; 253). To the
king's question, concerning the meaning ("ce que voulait dire") of
the spectacle, the text's answer is clear: it is grounded in what the
ogress sees ("ce qu'elle voyait") and the result of seeing it ("enragée
de voir"). The outcome—her head-first dive into the vat—carries
the public spectacle into a scene of eating, witnessed by the king, his
family, and his subjects. The narrative brushes lightly over the naturalistic contents of the intolerable sight. For the witnesses see, unmitigated, the very consumption of raw human flesh that the queen
mother had desired but failed to achieve: "Je le veux, dit la Reine (et
elle le dit d'un ton d'Ogresse qui a envie de manger de la chair
fraîche), et je la veux manger à la sauce-Robert" (I want it, said the
queen (and she said it in the manner of an ogress wanting to eat fresh
flesh), and I want to eat her with Robert sauce; 250). In opting to
have her victim's flesh prepared as a dish with Robert sauce and
thereby to give her reversion to cannibalism a less savage, more
savory appearance, the ogress succumbs sufficiently to the civilization curve to expose herself to culinary fraud. This acculturative
movement is reversed by her paroxysmal impulse to feed herself live
to the lowly creatures whose feasting will assimilate her to the ugliness and primitive instincts they symbolize.

Thus the suicidal end of the ogress's attempts to sustain a contradictory mix of anthropophagy with human culture emerges as a
self-decapitative ("la tête la première") plunge into bestialization,
marked by the activity of eating without cooking. The spectacle in
the vat—the swarm of seething beasts engulfing her body in a kind
of communal inosculation—converts the culinary vessel into the
arena of a natural slaughter. Rather than anthropophagy, the vat
houses and exposes the kind of stark animal violence—wolves consuming their human prey in the wilds of nature—that the mother
had planned to evoke to explain the disappearance of her daughter-

in-law and grandchildren to her son. The scene of ingestion effectively suspends the cultural sense of the culinary insofar as it sets cooking aside and exposes the carnage attendant to the devouring of raw meat. So "La Belle au bois dormant" ends with a graphic exposure of the eating process that puts representational frames—those of the spectacle of horror—around it. Significantly, it is precisely this exhibitionary turn, reinserting the metaphorics of consumption into play on or within the field of vision, that accompanies the arrival of the prince/king and identifies him as an agent of the spectacular: his heroic and royal destiny is that of beauty's servant who saves it from consumption; his arrivals in the castle and in the courtyard allow beauty to come out of confinement and into the sphere—designated by his children's names—of light. The last sentence of "La Belle," which follows immediately the one cited above reporting the devouring of the ogress, seems to confirm him in this role. "Le Roi ne laissa pas d'en être fâché: elle était sa mère; mais il s'en consola bientôt avec sa belle femme et ses enfants" (The king was nonetheless saddened by what had occurred: she was his mother; but he soon consoled himself with his wife and children). The spectacle of carnage has reestablished the conditions for the victorious reappearance of beauty, situating the latter, moreover, as it is incarnated by "sa belle femme et ses enfants," as the consoling value that enables culture to put behind it the specter of violence from which it has emerged.

Versions of a Master Tale

In *La Parole mangée*, Louis Marin offers a reading of "Peau d'âne" that stresses Perrault's artful writing down of a story so emblematic of the oral tradition of folktales that one could refer to them generically as *contes de Peau d'âne*. By writing down a paradigmatic or master tale that is also a story of a king and a father, Perrault the author positions himself as a surrogate father and surrogate king, inasmuch as the king is the ultimate origin—and thus, as it were, the presiding author—of all written cultural production. From this position, he—Perrault—dramatizes "what was at stake at a given time and place in a writing of orality and in the orality of writing,"[21] and enables the reader—Marin—to grasp all the ambivalences that are captured and figured by the mouth. The articulatory power of this flexible organ of speaking and eating is all the greater since it is also an erogenous zone: via the movements of the tongue, teeth, and lips, the mouth becomes the locus of an anaclitic relation mingling libidinal impulses with the instinct for self-preservation. The activation of this intra-oral relationship, says Marin, amounts to the inscription of a bodily desire, a bodily writing that takes place in the mouth. Hence the proposal to read the tale as a kind of dismantling of the opposition between the oral and the written.

Now, taking this account of the context-setting status of "Peau d'âne" to be valid, I propose to pursue a quite different tack, reading the story as the densified elaboration of the narrative structure of a sister-tale, "Cendrillon," or "Cinderella." The term sister-tale is appropriate since, according to the Aarne-Thompson classification of popular tales, the two stories belong to the same cycle.[22] The resemblance between "Cendrillon" and "Peau d'âne" begins with their titles (each is the nickname of its heroine), degrading names that foreshadow the sordid, bedraggled state into which a virtuous maiden has fallen. "Cendrillon" is the story of a lovely young girl whose mother dies and whose father remarries with a thoroughly disagreeable woman who has two self-centered daughters. Once Cinderella and her father have moved in with these three women, we hear no more of the father: the haughty stepmother and her daughters persecute Cinderella, relegating her to the role of household servant. Both of her nicknames, "Cendrillon" and the still more pejorative "Cucendron" (Cinderseat, Cinderfanny), are derived from the lowly spot she habitually occupies, sitting in cinders by the chimney; both suggest a kind of seating of her identity in the material her body contacts, just as Peau d'âne's name (Donkeyskin) suggests a kind of displacement of her identity onto that of the animal whose skin she wears.

When the king's son gave a ball for notables in the kingdom, of course the two daughters of Cinderella's stepmother were able to attend, decked out in splendid costumes, whereas poor Cinderella, clothed in her tattered rags, was expected to stay at home. But fortunately the good fairy godmother struck, using her magic wand to make a coach and coachmen from pumpkins, mice, and rats, then outfitting Cinderella in a beautiful jewel-studded gold and silver dress and dainty glass slippers. Thus she could attend the ball, provided she made it home before midnight. All went well: the prince was so taken with her that during the banquet he ate nothing, "tant il était occupé à la considérer" (he was so busy contemplating her; 277), and invited her back the next night. On this second evening all went so delightfully that Cinderella forgot to leave on time. Thus her costume and coach disintegrated as she ran from the ball at midnight, losing one of her glass slippers during her exit.[23] We learn that the prince picked up the glass slipper and until the ball was over, did nothing but gaze at it. A few days later, the prince announced that he would marry the woman whose foot fit the delicate shoe. In the ensuing shoefitting contest, after watching her stepsisters fail to squeeze the slipper on, Cinderella of course succeeds. After she pulls out the other glass slipper as clinching evidence of her identity, the fairy godmother turns up to dress her splendidly one last time. The tale ends with her marriage to the prince and her reconciliation with the two stepsisters.

In what sense does "Peau d'âne," the master tale, enact essentially the same plot we encounter here? In the opening sequence of "Peau d'âne," the heroine becomes, like Cinderella, a kind of disinherited victim of her parents. The sequence that reduces her to a plight comparable to Cinderella's is, to be sure, much longer and weightier in connotations. Peau d'âne is a princess who loses her beautiful and virtuous mother, just as Cinderella had lost her mother, whom the narrator simply described as "la meilleure personne du monde" ("the finest person in the world"; 274). But the dying queen had a vengeful streak: she made her husband, the greatest king on earth (219), swear not to remarry unless he found a woman superior to her in beauty and goodness. Entrapped, the king eventually discovers that only his lovely daughter can fill the bill and hatches a violent incestuous passion for her. On the advice of her fairy godmother, she tries to fend him off by erecting impossible obstacles: before marrying him she requires a dress the color of time; when the king's tailors produce the most beautiful blue dress imaginable, she adds a second demand, a dress the color of the moon, and a comparably gorgeous silver dress is produced; she then calls for a third dress, the color of the sun, which yields another marvel made of gold and diamond-laced cloth. At her wit's end, she follows her fairy godmother's suggestion to request of her father the skin of his prize donkey, an animal formed by Nature, we are told (222), so that, instead of feces, it excretes only silver and gold. Since the ass is the source of the great king's wealth and power ("comme il est toute sa ressource"), says the fairy, reason dictates that he will not grant this exorbitant request. But of course passion defeats reason, and the poor young girl, clothing herself in the donkeyskin and covering her extremities with dirt, takes flight. Peau d'âne is aided by the fairy, who enables her to take along the three beautiful dresses and other personal effects in a magic trunk that follows her underground.

All this elaboration of an Oedipal calamity compounded by an economic fiasco reduces Peau d'âne, as a family outcast, to the position that Cinderella occupied when she was at the bottom of the domestic ladder, unable to go to the ball. Our heroine ends up in another kingdom, working as a lowly kitchen servant on a royal farm and living in a miserable hovel. In her privacy she is sustained by the pleasurable experience she enacts on Sundays and holidays, when, staging for herself a secret commemoration of her beauty and culture, she puts on one of the three magnificent dresses and contemplates herself in a mirror. One holiday, the king's son happens into the barnyard, wanders about, and eventually looks through the keyhole in Peau d'âne's door; contemplating her, he is ravished with passion. After learning what people call her and that they consider her an ugly beast, the prince falls into a drastic lovesickness. Refusing to eat, he wastes away, saying his only desire is to have a cake made by Peau d'âne. While making him a fine cake, she drops a ring of gold and emerald into the batter. The famished prince eats this dessert so ravenously that he nearly swallows the ring; spotting it, however, he saves it under his pillow. Thereafter, his illness worsens. The doctors diagnose lovesickness and recommend treating it with marriage. The prince agrees and proposes a contest: he will marry the woman whose finger will fit into the ring extracted from Peau d'âne's cake. Like Cinderella fitting her foot into her glass slipper, the victorious Peau d'âne is the last contestant allowed to try the ring. With the ring on her finger, she then puts on one of her dresses and is accepted by the royal family, to whom the fairy recounts her story. Her marriage, like Cinderella's, is marked by a familial reconciliation as her father, wisened and chastened, turns up for the wedding.

To recapitulate the parallels between the stories of Cinderella and Peau d'âne, it is helpful to distinguish schematically a principal narrative structure, the locus of a drama within the heroine's family,

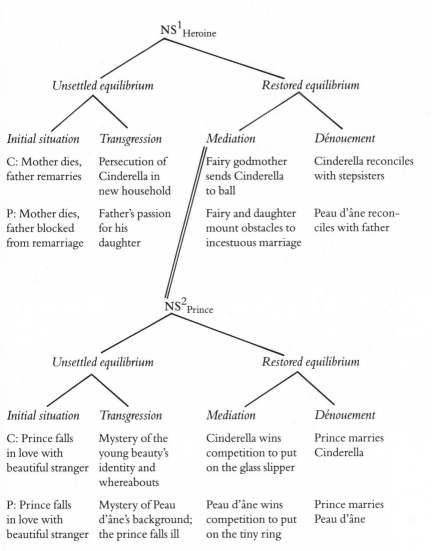

Fig. 1. The global (NS¹) and embedded (NS²) narrative structures of "Cendrillon" (C) and "Peau d'âne" (P). In each case, NS² is the elaboration of the mediation function of NS¹.

and an embedded structure, which consists of the recovery from her downtrodden state through an amorous adventure outside the family (see the tree diagrams in Fig. 1).[24] On the global level (NS[1]), the initial situation results from the death of the mother; the transgression that fuels the drama is the parental aggression against the heroine; the heroic response is the joint resistance undertaken by the heroine allied with the fairy godmother; and the dénouement is the family reconciliation. On the embedded level (NS[2]), which in each case is simply an extension or specification of the heroine's quest in the global sequence, the parallelism is still more striking. In each tale, the prince is quickly enraptured by the unknown beauty he discovers; the transgression stems from her mysterious identity and lowly status; the problem is solved in a vestmental ceremony that enables the heroine to don a key part of a costume that she alone can wear; and the dénouement is her marriage with the prince. The comparative framework provided by this schematic overview will enable us to see how "Peau d'âne," by filling in the blanks or gaps left in the sparer story of Cinderella, evokes the representation of food and its role in the shaping relations in and among the orders of the family, society, economy, and politics with a comprehensiveness that does indeed make it exemplary in the Perraldian corpus. Following the classical procedure of structural narratology, I propose to begin by noting some further parallels in the two tales, then veer toward the suggestive differences that emerge when we confront details such as the slipper and the ring.

Comparing Heroines

In both "Cendrillon" and "Peau d'âne," the trajectory of the heroine may be taken as an illustration of what Norbert Elias terms the civilizing process. Each heroine, in servitude, is characterized by insistent associations with dirt and animality. In "Cendrillon," the first case of a magical transformation of the type that Cinderella undergoes both instantly, before the ball, and gradually, as her story unfolds, is the fairy's nifty reincarnation of the pumpkin, mice, and rats as her coach and coachmen. That conversion illustrates a crossing over from nature to culture that "Peau d'âne" redoubles: the donkey first appears in the tale having already crossed the nature/culture divide to occupy a position of splendid luxury, as the idol at the center of the immaculate, manureless royal stable. When Peau d'âne takes on the donkey's skin and its name, she is treated as a "pauvre bête," so that her itinerary—like that of another Perraldian hero marked by a natural ugliness, Riquet à la houppe—involves shedding her visible animal features for human ones. But for both Cinderella and Peau d'âne, the mark of civilization that is stressed most decisively is the passage from a milieu of filth and dirt—Cinderella's cinders and the *crasse* or grime that Peau d'âne puts on as make-up—into their brilliant costumes, dresses that become progressively more scintillating and more compelling in impact as each story develops. The principal emblems of court society, the magnificent dresses and the heroine's glittering appearance, are indeed the exclusive locus of supernatural effects, for the fairies' artful deeds— as distinct from their words—bear upon nothing else: the supernatural here lies in the costuming and appointments of high society—in the embellishment of visible bodies and objects and in the control of appearances, which are the hallmark of neoclassical culture.

While the visual effects of dress seem paramount in the society of these tales, manifestations of the consonant culinary system are assuredly in evidence. At the ball, in a gesture connoting her charm and cleverness, as well as the flavor of the event, Cinderella gives her stepsisters the oranges and lemons (expensive fruits that were signs of luxury) the prince had presented to her as a mark of his favor. After Peau d'âne's disappearance from her father's castle, the pall that has been cast is evoked in these verses:

> Partout se répandit un triste et noir chagrin;
> Plus de Noces, plus de Festin,
> Plus de Tartes, plus de Dragées;
> Les Dames de la cour, toutes découragées,
> N'en dînerent point la plupart. (224)

> A dismal, dark dejection spread everywhere;
> No more matrimony, no more celebration,
> No more tarts or sugared almonds;
> Most of the women of the court, quite downtrodden,
> Had no dinner at all.

But what seems to bear out our initial hypothesis about the representation of food particularly well is the eating behavior of the

two princes. In "Cendrillon," as we have noted, the prince's infatua-
tion with the unknown young woman's beauty is signaled by his less
than impeccable table manners: instead of eating, he stared at her.
The prince in "Peau d'âne" likewise gets away with not eating when
he should eat during his seemingly self-styled lovesickness, and
when he does punctuate his abstinence with food, rather than
proper nourishment, he gorges himself with Peau d'âne's delectable
dessert. In each case, the suppression of appetite correlates with
visual behavior that seems excessive as the prince gives himself over
to the contemplation of a beautifully clothed stranger. The pre-
dominance of the scopic over the oral as a channel of desire seems no
less decisive than the capacity of apparel to signify beauty, wealth,
and above all social station.

In "Peau d'âne" one scene seems to record the dominance and
significance of visual experience with an insistence that has no par-
allel in "Cendrillon." While the prince gazes at Peau d'âne through
the keyhole, looking long enough, moreover, to pass through three
rounds of temptation to break through the door before he can tear
himself away, Peau d'âne is inside the room, decked out magnifi-
cently, going through her ritual of gazing at herself in a full-length
mirror. Upon evoking these conjoined spectacles of voyeuristic and
narcissistic pleasure (not exactly a commonplace concatenation in
neoclassical French literature), the Perraldian narrator glosses lightly
over the effects of eroticism, quickly shifting the focus from the
scopic dynamics to the objects seen and what they reveal, that is, to
the conventional opposition exploited with critical verve by the
French *moralistes*, that of appearances to being. The prince's moral
interpretation of the scene he observes is reassuring as he discerns
the perceptible marks of the young woman's beautiful soul and
noble birth. The spectacle of seeing a scene of self-admiration thus
coordinates the sphere of pleasure and desire, animated by Peau
d'âne's natural beauty, with both the sphere of economic resources,
evoked by the magnificence of her dress, jewelry, and full-length
mirror, and the sphere of social and psychological relations, which
are accessible to the prince's penetrating gaze. This process of coor-
dination and communication through the play of the visual dy-
namics is further marked, moreover, by a narratorial intervention.
The narrator suggests that Peau d'âne had noticed she was being
observed by the prince, owing to a kind of magnetic interaction of

the two gazes at work in this scene, and thus that her dispatch of the ring in the cake was not accidental, but contrived.

The extended development of a visual dynamics and meta-phorics in "Peau d'âne" differentiates the tale in degree, but not in kind, from "Cendrillon." Two features, however, do distinguish the two tales decisively. The first is the extended elaboration, in "Peau d'âne," of the mediation function in the global narrative, where the young woman and the fairy godmother pursue their unsuccessful attempts to fend off the father. The second is the scene of cake-baking and eating, which brings into play an intriguing operation of the culinary sign. It is the linkage of these segments—and specifically of their key signifiers, the gold-defecating donkey and the ring-bearing cake, that the narrative constructs and invites us to ponder.

In the strategy pursued by the fairy godmother and the fearful daughter, there is a curious echo of the dying mother's prohibition on remarriage by her husband: they attempt, as she had done, to set impossible conditions, and their failures tend to reinforce the asper-sions that the narrative casts on the mother figure. A comparably disparaging view of the domineering mother figure is developed in "Cendrillon," moreover; it is as if the mothers were somehow to blame for the fathers' irresponsibility toward their daughters; and yet, in each tale's dénouement, it turns out that the scene of familial recognition incorporates the satisfaction of the mother's wishes. In any case, Peau d'âne's imitation of the problem-causing maternal gesture appears to occasion her downfall, although for her, too, the strategy will eventually appear to have been a successful one. But the telling difference between "Peau d'âne" and "Cendrillon" lies in the transformational itinerary through which Peau d'âne passes: a deeper, steeper fall from a royal station to which she already belongs, into an apparent abjection that is nonetheless shrouded in an ambiva-lence missing from Cinderella's experience—followed by a drama of return toward her elevated social origin, crowned by a classic scene of recognition, whereas Cinderella's itinerary is more straightfor-wardly one of social ascension toward a new identity in a higher class.

Costuming and Cooking

The ambivalence of Peau d'âne's position stems, of course, from her costume: superficially, it is the ass's skin around her neck that causes the attendants of the prince's mother to describe her as "la bête en un mot la plus laide / Qu'on puisse voir après le Loup" (the ugliest beast one can see except for the wolf) and again as "une noire Taupe / Plus vilaine encore et plus gaupe / Que le plus sale Marmiton" (a dark mole more base and foul than the filthiest riffraff; 227). But for the reader who reckons with the power of clothing in the tale to invest the wearer with identifying marks, and who recalls that Peau d'âne's garment comes from the marvelous, idolized animal that had been worshiped as the source of her royal father's wealth, the significance of her evolving identity is rather more complex. For the same skin that transforms her identity for unknowing onlookers into that of Peau d'âne also clothes her in a salient reminder of the family drama she is fleeing—a drama in which her role became decisive when she requested the ass's skin and then appropriated it as the most telling of her garments. In other words, the skin that aids her by disguising her also accompanies her as the salient trace of a past that stubbornly clings to her in the present. Depicting her as both the recipient and the destroyer of all her father could offer her ("toute sa ressource"), the skin transfers onto her body—rather than the donkey's essential, money-minting core— only the exterior coating that surrounded it. Now, that displaced surface of animal remains adheres to her as a sign of what has been lost, the donkey's productive interiority that the victims of the debacle lack and that Peau d'âne, as the heroic wearer of the donkey's coat, is obliged to supply. So far from just escaping her father's grasp by wearing the donkeyskin, the outcast princess carries into her escape a heavy burden of symbolic material. As her private ritual of removing the costume that is bound up with her fall into debasement and putting on one of her beautiful dresses suggests, her appropriation of the donkeyskin makes it an impetus in her efforts to construct for herself a productive role, akin to the one played by the donkey in her father's kingdom.

To grasp the multiple ramifications of the father/king's gift of the donkey's skin to his consummately beautiful daughter, we must consider it from his standpoint as well as hers. For him, the gift entails sacrificing entirely the advantage he derives from having a uniquely independent and constant source of wealth. The economic implications of such an irrevocable and *unreserved* gift make it all the more excessive: the act by which the king accords higher

value to possessing his daughter's beauty than to preserving his lu-
crative ass cuts off the supply of gold that provides him with financial
self-sufficiency. Thus his monstrous sacrifice of a profitable resource
for his kingdom to his own incestuous pleasure presumably initiates,
or at least increases, the monarch's dependency on his taxable sub-
jects. In the absence of the donkey, he will have to extract his wealth
and power from them. So as a signifier, the ass's skin that his daugh-
ter takes and wears is the residue of that socially irresponsible deed;
it points back toward a ruler's crisis, the breakdown of an idyllic
(doubtless feudal) royalty, heretofore sustained by the surplus or
superabundance of its private resources, but now left to fend in a
more brutal worldly economy that is driven by competition for
wealth. Against this background, Peau d'âne's recourse to wearing
the donkeyskin is at once the act that saves her from further ensnare-
ment in her father's degradation and that marks her implication in it.
From both of these angles, it is an act by which she is assuming
responsibility for herself and her actions. Until she can definitively
shed the skin and rid herself of the connection to intrafamilial vio-
lence that it emblematizes, she and the beauty she incarnates will be
sullied, associable with the flowering of evil. By the same token,
what is at stake in her efforts to recover her rightful place in society
is the possibility of reasserting the moral dignity or purity of beauty.

For Peau d'âne, the ass's skin is the fourth and ultimate garment
she receives (after the three dresses) in the series of failed mediations.
As we have suggested, the various uses and meanings that wearing
the compromising gift from her father has for her (a protective
disguise, a sign of her victimhood, a metonymic link to the priceless
donkey, an impetus to pursue survival and rebirth, an assumption of
responsibility) make the donkeyskin a thoroughly ambiguous sign.
Notwithstanding its deceiving, animalizing effect on her appear-
ance, the brutish garment grounds and sustains an association with
the precious talent of the living, gold-making donkey, a producer of
cultural capital. It no more situates its wearer strictly on the side of
nature than it did when it still coated the donkey. Instead it gives
Peau d'âne a position comparable to that of the donkey, straddling
the nature/culture dichotomy. The symbol effecting her fall from
culture into nature—her descent from beauty into ugliness—no less
evidently links her to the inverse possibility, signaled by the lowly
donkey's prestigious stature and sanctification as a source of riches.

This symbolic reversibility invests the donkeyskin with a power of transignification that Perrault's text represents as a dynamics of disguise or travesty.

The skin's capacity to work as one of the heroine's possible costumes or guises is immediately signaled by the fairy, who refers to it as a "masque admirable" (223), an admirable mask or disguise; and the employment she acquires as a dishwasher in a distant corner of the royal kitchen is granted to her because of the steadfastness with which she maintains her practice of what the narrative pointedly describes, when she puts on the skin, as *travesty*: "la Princesse ainsi travestie" (223). The verb *travestir*—literally cross-dressing, costume switching—suggests that Peau d'âne is caught up in the practice of changing identities by changing clothes, a seesaw movement between public and private faces that she maintains by shifting back and forth between the donkeyskin and her three gorgeous dresses. Her problem in the visual order—in the sphere of being and appearances—will be solved precisely when she is able to eliminate the screen that shields the private side of her existence from view. In this respect, her position resembles not only that of Cinderella, trapped in her stepmother's house and visible only in tatters, but also that of the princess/queen in "La Belle au bois dormant," first isolated for 100 years in her inaccessible castle, later hidden with her children in the cook's house. In all three cases, the reader's interest tends to focus on the mechanism that will enable the heroine's resplendent beauty to be restored to full visibility.

Peau d'âne's method for recovering her lost visibility entails a remarkable deployment of the culinary sign, which functions unmistakably in the manner Louis Marin describes. Miraculously, she brings to her confection the quality of a master baker who, significantly, retires to her room, grooms herself, and puts on a silver vest in order to concoct her dessert in a worthy manner ("pour faire dignement son ouvrage"; 227). The tack she takes, that is to say, is to adjust the situation so that the scene's setting and costumes are in harmony with the reality of her production itself, so that being and appearance will be at one with each other. The crucial feature of her performance, however, has to do with the product, a cake so fine that, according to the narrator, "on ne pétrit jamais un si friand morceau" (never did anyone taste such a luscious piece; 228). But the quality that makes this culinary work of art so remarkable is what connects it with the production of the donkey. The unnatural, inedible object that emerges from the baking process and falls thereby into the hands of the prince ("il désire / que Peau d'âne lui fasse un gâteau de sa main"; he wants Peau d'âne to make him a cake with her own hands; 227) from the hand of the heroine ("De son doigt par hasard il tomba dans la pâte / Un de ses anneaux de grand prix"; One of her prized rings chanced to drop from her finger into the dough; 228) is of a piece with the gold coins from the donkey, *écus* and *Louis*, that turn up on the litter where one would expect to find not valuable, manufactured objects of culture but a natural waste product. Moreover, it is as if, by dint of the metonymic effects conveyed by the ring as an identifying part of the princess's hand and as an ingredient of the cake destined to be seen and held, but not eaten, the cake has linked product and producer and become a dessert not only made with her hands but *of her hand*, so that the cake provides, for the prince, a symbolic meal through which he is almost literally taking her hand. The narrative pointedly notes that the cake, quickly consumed, supplies more than one form of nourishment to the prince, both satisfying and whetting another appetite that eating does not assuage:

> Quand il en vit l'émeraude admirable,
> Et du jonc d'or le cercle étroit,
> Qui marquait la forme du doigt,
> Son coeur en fut touché d'une joie incroyable. (228)

> When he saw the admirable emerald,
> and the narrow circle of the golden band,
> that marked the form of her finger,
> his heart was filled with an incredible joy.

What Peau d'âne has cooked up for the prince supplies not only edible food to be consumed in the natural processes of ingestion and digestion, but a food supplement, we might say, in the form of an inedible object to be seen with the eyes—"il en vit l'émeraude admirable"—and prized for its form. The value of the ring here is doubtless very close to that of the glass slipper, a readily fetishizable object that Cendrillon's prince contemplated from the moment he picked it up until the end of the ball. For Peau d'âne's prince, the pleasure derived from imagining that erotic moment when the impeccably shaped bodily part slips delicately into the receiving hole is made rather more explicit. The key point, in any case, is that what Peau d'âne brings with her, in her ambivalence, via the metamorphosis that invests her first with the traits of the donkey and then, in the kitchen, with the donkey's alchemical skills of production, turns crucially on her success in drawing the food she cooks into her practice of travesty and in making that food the carrier of an enduring, visible object, the ring, that functions as a conventional symbol of a matrimonial exchange in the works, but also, more generally, as an artifact embodying the overriding articulatory power of the visual image in the civilizing process represented in Perrault's tales. The prince's consumption of the cake, because it offers up the beautiful bodily adornment for enduring contemplation, is perhaps the exemplary figuration in Perrault's work not only of the signifying power of the visual mark, but also of the dynamics through which it comes, in the tales, to embrace and be privileged over all others, including the culinary sign. So if the narrator of "Peau d'âne," as Louis Marin suggests, invites us to grasp a certain writing in or with the mouth or the voice, the tale itself invites us to apprehend a scopic culture, given over to eating with the eyes.

5

The Ogre's Genesis

The shortest of Perrault's fairy tales, "Le Petit Chaperon rouge" (Little Red Riding Hood; 254–56), seems to stand curiously alone in the corpus. No doubt this impression of singularity has to be ascribed less to the bare simplicity of the plot—the wolf learns the little girl is going to her grandmother's house, then races ahead and ambushes her there—than to the story's abruptly nightmarish ending ("ce méchant Loup se jeta sur le petit chaperon rouge, et la mangea"; this evil wolf threw himself on Little Red Riding Hood and ate her up). One other tale, "Les Fées," ends with a darkly trenchant observation: the foul-tempered sister, evicted by her mother, "alla mourir au coin d'un bois" (went off to die in the woods). This dismal fate may appear to be an exceedingly severe punishment for the villain's misdeed. It does not, however, produce an effect as chilling as that of the final sentence of "Le Petit Chaperon rouge" because it is a subordinate element in the story's predominantly comic dénouement, which presents the good sister's marriage with a handsome prince.

On the 1695 manuscript of "Le Petit Chaperon rouge," the stark ending is reinforced by a disconcerting marginal notation, according to which "on prononce ces mots d'une voix forte pour faire peur à l'enfant comme si le loup l'allait manger" (these words are pronounced in a stern voice in order to provoke fright, as if the wolf were going to eat the child; 256). This stage direction is noteworthy on two counts. First, by evoking the child's listening experience, it seems to invite the censorial attention of interpreters like Bruno Bettelheim, who strenuously objects to Perrault's version of "Little

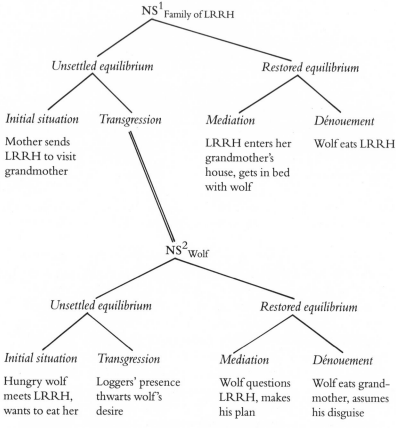

Fig. 2. The global (NS[1]) and embedded (NS[2]) narrative structures of "Le Petit Chaperon rouge."

Red Riding Hood" and declares it unfit for a collection of children's stories. Second, the comment marks a narratological feature of "Le Petit Chaperon rouge" that situates it vis-à-vis the rest of the tales as an inimitable limit case: ultimately its global narrative structure, represented in Fig. 2, is utterly monopolized by the villainous protagonist, the wolf, who takes over Little Red Riding Hood's story and her family's world.[1] Although Perrault's *moralités* often serve to soften or complicate a story's effect, here its bluntly terroristic thrust is reinforced. The *moralité* gradually turns its attention from young girls, in its first four lines, to wolves and their intrusions "jusque dans les ruelles" (all the way into private chambers) over the nine remaining lines; its message underscores the frequency with which the same brutal scenario of occupation leading to destruction occurs in polite society. The wolf manages to gain entry and devour so many women, the final lines warn, thanks to his wily and genteel behavior.

From the standpoint of character relations, the wolf's wicked exercise in wholesale destruction consists in usurping systematically the actantial functions initially held by Little Red Riding Hood (subject or heroine), her mother (dispatcher), and her grandmother (recipient). For in his first encounter with Little Red Riding Hood (mediation function of NS^2), the wolf engineers a superimposition of his universe onto that of Little Red Riding Hood's family (NS^1). He is able to send (from the mother's position) his prey to himself (in the grandmother's position) precisely because his victim, as he draws her out of her familial universe into his own, does not realize that he is deviously taking over her world. Indeed, as he rushes to the grandmother's house ahead of Little Red Riding Hood, he is carrying his co-optation even to the point of preceding her in her own function: he plays her role when he arrives at the door.

When we reconstruct the narrative syntax from the perspective of the dénouement, we apprehend the crushing finality of the alimentary ending in which the wolf incorporates his victim into his own body from two complementary angles: as the wolf finishes absorbing the role of his antagonist/victim, he simultaneously completes a thoroughgoing recasting of the actantial structure. Since the ending effaces the split of the subject-function in NS^1 between the two characters, it allows for a retrospective (or postdigestive) account according to which the surviving subject has sent himself to himself, just as he does in NS^2. Thus the overlapping and dovetailing of the global and embedded sequences make for a collapsing of the parallel structures into one another. By schematizing this elegant convergence, the tree diagram distills a narratological account of the story's tightly unified simplicity and devastating impact; it also records a degree of autotelic dominance on the part of the wolf that none of Perrault's other tales will match.

Marvelous Tale or Fable?

The hungry wolf's resolute violence recalls the end of La Fontaine's fable "Le Loup et l'agneau" to the extent that the peremptory destruction of the victim figures an act of rejection: of culture (set aside when Little Red Riding Hood obediently puts the cake and butter on the shelf) by nature, of mind (manifest in the characters' speech) by matter, of the spiritual order (dominant in the wolf's deceitful talk while he is hiding under the covers, but evanescent once the little girl sees his body) by brute physical force. The two tales of appetitive violence are different, however, in that the acculturated lamb of the fable is a far more accomplished victim than Little Red Riding Hood. The lamb, a well-domesticated animal who represents the values of humanity, mounts a strategy of reasoned dialogue by which the weak seek a means of resisting the strong. It is the lesson of its failure, "la raison du plus fort" (the rightness of the strong), that the fable invites us to ponder. In Perrault's tale, by contrast, the exercise of reason belongs to the agent of brute appetite; and within the general opposition of strength to weakness, the conflict presented in the narrative and Perrault's *moralité* highlights the difference between the sexes. For alongside the *moralité*'s picture of "jeunes Demoiselles" endangered by the overtures of "Loups doucereux," the tale sets off the wolf supercharged with traits of masculine power against three women marked by their apparent vulnerability.

Various commentators, treating red as the color of passion and strong emotion, have suggested, indeed, that the red headdress bestowed upon the extremely attractive girl ("la plus jolie qu'on eût su voir"; the prettiest ever seen) by her grandmother symbolizes sexuality, transferred to her by her less alluring elders.[2] Given this symbolism, the fact that the red hood "lui seyait si bien, que partout l'on l'appelait le Petit Chaperon rouge" (fit her so well that everyone called her Little Red Riding Hood) is at least doubly suggestive. On the one hand, from the perspective of a more or less Jungian symbolics that takes what covers the head as a sign of what goes on inside it, it is as if her head, rather than a locus of thought, has become a beacon of desire. On the other hand, the cranium's place at the top of the torso and its central functional significance for the individual—in hearing, seeing, thinking, speaking, and being recognized by others—makes for the classic Platonic association of the head with dignity, personal identity, and directive power. To form an image of the head fully endowed with its traits and capacities is to envisage that crowning corporal sphere as a world: it is the integral

figure of the world of the personality.[3] So in the perfect fit that
makes the headpiece such an indelible, defining coif that it surfaces
in Little Red Riding Hood's name (like the ass's skin that identifies
Peau d'âne), the integration achieved is that of identity with desire:
the red headpiece incorporates the hood of sex as the mark of the
controlling identity she has acquired from the gaze of others and as
an informing component in the image of her personal world that
the tale constructs.

Among Bettelheim's complaints about "Le Petit Chaperon
rouge," the most insistent casts Perrault's tale as much too trans-
parently a staging of seduction, in which a young woman, presum-
ably entering puberty, is mindlessly consensual in the face of temp-
tation because she is discovering her sexuality. As a result, no room is
left for imaginative and reassuring interpretations by children.[4] Most
of the fuel for Bettelheim's criticism doubtless comes from the much
interpreted final scene of the story, in which Little Red Riding
Hood follows the wolf-as-grandmother's direction to undress and
crawl into bed with "her." The dénouement thus seems almost
literally to carry out a sexual power play, to display emphatically the
conventional symbolic equivalence between eating and copulation
that we noted in "La Belle au bois dormant," and thus to cast the
satisfaction of the male's carnal drives as ultimately carnivorous, as a
destructive, potentially deadly physical menace. The intensity of the
stress on the carnal and physical is heightened by the celebrated
dialogue in which Little Red Riding Hood remarks upon the wolf's
bodily parts, his big arms, legs, ears, eyes, and teeth. Each time the
wolf answers by noting their instrumental functions—grasping, run-
ning, listening, looking, eating—that is, precisely the kind of physi-
cal activities of a beast of prey bent on satisfying its appetite that
characterize the wolf's behavior. No doubt one can defend Per-
rault's version of the story by situating it, as Marc Soriano does, in a
particular historical context. In Perrault's time, he suggests, "Le
Petit Chaperon rouge" had to be read as a *conte d'avertissement*, de-
signed to impress children with real dangers posed by wild animals.[5]
No doubt the interpretive context in the seventeenth century was
also inflected by authentic human fears of being devoured that
stemmed from actual cases of cannibalism, provoked by famine,
during the Middle Ages and the sixteenth century. But does this not
amount to agreeing with Bettelheim's suggestion that the story is

fundamentally not a *conte de fée* or *conte merveilleux*, and that it does not belong among Perrault's Mother Goose tales?

Just as it is important to acknowledge the extremes that make "Le Petit Chaperon rouge" a limit case in the *Contes*, it is vital to make plain the implications of our comparison to La Fontaine's fable and of the story's placement in Perrault's collection. Perrault's interest in folklore goes hand in hand with a long-term attachment to the beast fable tradition. That interest is well demonstrated by two of his works, "Le Labyrinthe de Versailles" (1679), a transposition of thirty-nine of Aesop's fables, and "Les Fables de Faërne" (1699), a free translation of *Fabulae centum* by Gabrielis Faërni.[6] In the fictional world evoked by fables, the attribution of human features and social relations to animals that nonetheless continue to act as animals in their natural environment makes for a reading on two registers, literal and allegorical. In fables that depict humanized animals confronting men in society, such as La Fontaine's "Le Loup et les Bergers," this ambivalence continues to function by the same conventions: on one level, the tale makes sense if the animal is treated as such; yet the invitation to interpret the thoughts and actions of the animal as those of a rational actor in a human drama is the key source of interest and pleasure. In the case of "Le Petit Chaperon rouge," the *moralité* clearly points to the possibility of such a double reading.

Another of Perrault's tales, "Le Maître Chat ou Le Chat botté" (Puss in Boots; 263–68), falls squarely in the beast fable tradition. As we shall see, some of its components make for an illuminating comparison with "Le Petit Chaperon rouge." The case of its feline hero offers a fine illustration of the humanized animal turning up as an authoritative player on the stage of contemporary society. Since "Le Chat botté" draws on Aesop and Phaedrus in a manner parallel to that of La Fontaine in "Le Chat et un vieux Rat" (*Fables* III, 18), Collinet perceives in the tale not only the process by which the storyteller blends fable material into his own intricate elaboration, but also a subtle imitative touch through which Perrault acknowledges his debt to La Fontaine. Now if "Le Petit Chaperon rouge" functions as a kind of extended prose fable, the key factor is the degree of humanization we encounter in the wolf. For the wolf of the in-bed dialogue, who has abandoned imposture in favor of direct sensual contact with the little girl, the gap he closes at the end of their exchange is not a split between a falsely human identity and a real animal one; rather it is the dissolving distance between his intention and its realization. The contrast between his knowing lust and Little Red Riding Hood's wondrous naiveté puts him rather more fully on the side of the human than she. He holds the position of the mature—if impatient and cruel—adult, talking down to the ignorant child.

Of Wolves and Ogres

With what sort of character, then, is it appropriate to associate the wolf in the folkloric milieu of Perrault's tales? The tradition that seems to originate largely with Perrault takes wolves and monsters to be surrogates of the ogre. The wolfishness of ogres is made explicit in "La Belle au bois dormant," where the ogress goes out stalking for prey in the evenings and plans to disguise her misdeeds by telling her son that his wife and children were dragged off by wolves. Ogres have central roles in "Le Petit Poucet" and "Le Chat botté," and although the appetites of the bluebearded villain of "La Barbe bleue" do not include the craving for raw flesh attributed to ogres in the *Parallèle* (3: 120), he has often been perceived as a variant on the ogre figure because his capacity to persist in unacceptable behavior seems to depend on resources that the ogres of the "Le Petit Poucet" and "Le Chat botté" also enjoy: he has great wealth and, through his magic key, a strange relation to supernatural power. In "Le Petit Poucet," the supernatural is emblematized by the ogre's seven-league boots, which are in fact fairy boots that shrink to fit Thumbkin when he steals them. In "Le Chat botté," the ogre's distinctive supernatural trait, "le don de [se] changer en toute sorte d'Animaux" (the ability to change into all sorts of animals; 266) happens to involve the very capacity for metamorphosis that the beast fables take in the reverse direction—by giving human faculties to animals such as the cat. Such a self-transformative capacity, moreover, underlies the ogre-like behavior of the wolf, whose masterful exploit is the impersonation of Little Red Riding Hood's grandmother. Indeed, "Le Petit Chaperon rouge" records what has been, by all odds, the most influential of the imaginary scenarios through which the wolf acquired the status of an ogre surrogate.

On the horizon of the ogredom evoked by the tales, it is "Le Petit Poucet" that contains the most evident parallels to "Le Petit

Chaperon rouge." The connection begins with the title, "Le Petit
Poucet" being another tale named for a smallish character, Thumb-
kin (cf. "Riquet à la houppe" as well), whose identity depends on
his appearance. When the ogre who intends to feast on Thumbkin
and his six brothers decides to butcher them during the night, he
mistakenly beheads his seven daughters. His error stems from a
cunning substitution made by Thumbkin, who swapped the sleep-
ing daughters' crowns and the seven brothers' caps. The victims are
thus identified by their headcoverings, just as is Little Red Rid-
ing Hood (whose name based on clothing marks her resemblance
to other titular Perraldian characters—Cendrillon, Peau d'âne, Le
Chat botté, La Barbe bleue, Riquet à la houppe—who are saddled
with identities that reflect their visible appearance or dress). It is
perhaps less obvious that, since the ogre's daughters undergo de-
capitation in a state of unconsciousness, their experience uncannily
resembles the demise of Little Red Riding Hood. For as it is experi-
enced by the helplessly naive girl, the wolf's move to devour her is so
sudden and unanticipated that for her the scene runs its course
without any possibility of recognition or resistance. Reduced, in her
fatal innocence and passivity, to what is corporal or animal in her
nature, she is consumed as raw flesh.

Hence, in the dénouement of 'Le Petit Chaperon rouge," a
skeletal drama of female victimage flowing from a male monopoly
of reason and force:

> "Ma mère-grand, que vous avez de grandes dents!"
> "C'est pour te manger."
> Et *en disant ces mots*, ce méchant Loup *se jeta sur* le petit chaperon rouge,
> *et la mangea*. (256; my italics)

> "Grandmother, what large teeth you have!" "They're for eating you."
> And upon saying these words, this wicked wolf threw himself on Little
> Red Riding Hood and ate her up.

The wolf's action here bears a curious resemblance to the pounce of
the cat who tricks the ogre into turning himself into a mouse in "Le
Chat botté":

> Impossible? reprit l'Ogre, vous allez voir, et *en même temps* il se changea en
> une souris, qui se mit à courir sur le plancher. Le Chat ne l'eut pas plus tôt
> aperçue qu'il *se jeta dessus, et la mangea*. (266–67; my italics)

"Impossible?" replied the ogre, "You shall see," and simultaneously he changed into a mouse that started running across the floor. No sooner did the cat perceive the mouse than he threw himself on it and ate it up.

If, in both cases, the narrator emphasizes the relation of continuity between speech and action, in the case of the cat that relation extends backward to the start of the tale. For the utility of the cat's speech—deceitful and forceful—has been his essential resource until this turning point, when the physical action he carries out, still with the mouth, is decisive. Yet the parallel between the wolf and the cat is all the more curious since the heroic cat ensures a welcome triumph by consuming the evil ogre/mouse, whereas the inverse occurs when the big bad ogre/wolf devours Little Red Riding Hood. Does this momentous difference—the divide between the comic and tragic dénouements—not simply disable the comparison?

The Ogre-eating Cat

As Louis Marin has shown in a brilliant reading of "Le Chat botté" in *Le Récit est un piège*, Perrault's modest tale actually recounts a fabulously complex and artful exercise in power brokerage. In that operation, the transformative functions of providing, discussing, and eating food are crucial to the cat's mastery. For our comparative purposes, however, the import of the cat's meal can be queried from a simple, pragmatic standpoint. What does the cat accomplish by devouring the ogre? Prior to the execution scene, the rational, ruseful feline servant has been warding off the fate that his master has in mind for him: to eat him and make a handwarmer from his skin. In turning the tables, the cat dismisses the deadly scenario that would convert him into food and clothing for his master in favor of his own clothing requirement—the boots mentioned in the title, "Le Chat *botté*," or "Puss *in* Boots"—and his own phenomenal exercise in food production for the king, his master, and himself. After much coming and going, the cat finally arrives at the last of the story's settings, the ogre's castle, where he will shortly receive the king, the king's daughter, and his master. His first move is to manipulate the dialogue with his monstrous host so as to dispatch the ogre, a victim of flattering temptation, definitively out of the human and into the beastly sphere; then, in his guise as the feline servant/hero, he rushes his victim through consumption as an edible object. "Maître Chat" himself does what comes naturally to cats (though this is the last time he does it by necessity), and thereby enables his own definitive occupation of a comfortable place in the aristocratic order. There, says the tale's last sentence, he becomes a great lord ("grand Seigneur"). In short, the cat's feast enacts an adroitly prepared role reversal through which he and his master dispossess and displace the ogre.

The master cat's performance provides a singularly suggestive illustration of one of Louis Marin's central theses in *La Parole mangée*. He argues that the underlying significance of acts of eating in Perrault's work is inflected by the deeply transformative symbolism of the eucharistic meal. According to the Christian doctrine Perrault invokes in the *Pensées chrétiennes* (see paras. 29 and 54), the communicant who ingests the body and blood of the resurrected Christ partakes of a spiritual union with the singular human who has known not merely the fear but the experience of death; the words of Christ addressed to followers celebrating the Eucharist grant them vicariously a foretaste of the immortality that awaits them. What trickles down from the sublime symbolism of the religious ritual is a sense that, under special conditions, certain acts of eating can be transformative, and that the nature of the transformation derives from the food consumed. That the cat of "Le Chat botté" has engineered the conditions for completing a far-reaching transformation of his lot is clear. For the scenario of cunning domination whereby the terrifying ogre is transformed and incorporated into the humanized cat's body records a particular, opportunistic version of society's victory over the monstrous forces, at once alien and internal, that menace it. Converting the ogre into an edible object and instantly eating him is no mere slaying of the barbarous monster whose elusive independence confronts the king with a troubling resistance to authority; rather, it serves to channel the act of eradicating him into a satisfying process of possession via nourishment.

Insofar as the ogre/mouse is food composed of natural, human, and supernatural elements, it enables the consumer-cat to partake symbolically of all three nutritive resources. At the same time, the cat's own "natural" metamorphic capacity overcomes that of the ogre, subjecting it to the thorough control and transformation achieved by digestion. In other words, in a process well designated as commodification and consumption, the cat is acting as society's agent. Through incorporation or appropriation, he is able to capitalize, as it were, on the ogre's value as raw material. Yet he does so in the proactive movement of self-protective aggression that wholly obliterates the threat of unassimilable difference that the ogre represents in the dominant cultural order. The cat's meal thus prefigures an exercise of absolute mastery: his immediate absorption or assimilation of the ogre's power is as absolute—as destructive of opposition—as the power the king will proceed to consolidate by bringing the ogre's domain into the royal fold. This integrative scenario of social consolidation is exemplary of the artful compromises that typically overlay the comic endings of Perrault's tales.

At this pivotal moment in the dénouement of "Le Chat botté," the narrative achieves a remarkable onrushing velocity. This effect results from a sequencing of verbs in the simple past and their knitting together by expressions of simultaneity. Those expressions are supplied, in the passage cited in the previous section, by "en même temps" and "ne l'eut pas plus tôt aperçue que," and in the very next sentence by "cependant" and "en passant": "Cependant le Roi, qui vit en passant le beau Château de l'Ogre, voulut entrer dedans" (meanwhile the approaching king saw the fine castle of the ogre and wanted to go inside; 267). Coupled with this energetic forward drive on the diegetic level, the quick-as-a-flash representation of the ogre/mouse's consumption by the cat glosses nimbly over the fact that the feline hero was not merely killing but also eating the momentary incarnation of a character whose primary state is that of a cruel, abnormal but still human being. A slight but telling textual modification makes the dissembling of the ogre's predominantly human nature more pronounced in the definitive edition of the tales (1697) than in the first edition (1695). In 1695, after the ogre first demonstrates his metamorphic prowess by becoming a lion, the cat sees that "l'Ogre avait repris sa forme d'homme" (the ogre had reassumed his form as a man); in 1697, "sa forme d'homme" gave way to "sa première forme" (his initial form). The deletion of direct reference to the ogre's humanity lessens the likelihood of censorial attention to the cat's action.

If the critical reader subsequently looks back at the consumption scene with the double identities of the cat (animal/human) and ogre (human/animal) in mind, four permutations are possible: (1) animal eats animal, (2) human eats animal, (3) animal eats human, (4) human eats human. The narrative makes the literal reading of (1) dominant while readily accommodating figurative interpretations based on (2) and (3). Although the disconcerting possibility of (4)—the cat-as-human eating human flesh—is not excluded, such a reading is improbable because figurative explications faithful to the story's elaborate characterization of the cat will tend to reappropriate the same playful, fablelike ambivalence that Perrault's tale builds up and maintains around its hero. Hence, rather than accounts that choose between two identities for the cat, as either animal or human, the predominance of those that persist in treating him as both animal and human.

By dispelling the dismissive view of animals expressed by his master at the beginning of the tale, the cat's accomplishment, like the feats of many animals in fables, doubtless fits implicitly into the critical questioning of the human/animal distinction that, as we saw in Chapter One, Perrault was eager to pursue. But in the end, the story at once closely links the hero's achievement of seigneurial status to the moment when his animal nature was vital to catching the mouse and reminds the reader that the ennobled cat could still chase mice for pleasure. Thus the cat's itinerary is not one of further humanization—he is no more human than he has been all along—but one of the animal's recuperation or integration by the human. After his helpful descent into the carnivorous and his return to entrepreneurial activity, the dénouement does take the process of feline domestication—elevation into the stable economy of the royal court—to unprecedented heights; it does not, however, withdraw the felinity that enables the master cat to inhabit that world as a representative of nature and the resources nature brings to the society controlling it. The cat's fate, then, fits congenially into the larger scenario of compromise we noted above: he incarnates the meld of nature and culture that also characterized the ogre's existence, but puts to rest the aggressive, menacing side of natural instinct emblematized by the ogre's metamorphosis into a lion.

"Le Chat botté" deftly controls and attenuates its reader's perspective on what happens when the cat eats the ogre by folding the image of an animal devouring a human—precisely the spectacle we encountered in the ogress's demise at the end of "La Belle au bois dormant"—into a near inverse: a humanized animal's eating of a bestialized human. In comparing this relative delicacy to the ending of "Le Petit Chaperon rouge," with its brutal "il la mangea," can we see anything but stark contrast? Still more significantly, is there a sound basis for comparing the cat's consumption of the ogre and the wolf's consumption of Little Red Riding Hood? Although the frightful ending of "Le Petit Chaperon rouge" is one of the features that make for its unique status among Perrault's tales, a scrupulous conclusion will be possible only after we look closely at the relations between the two main characters, Little Red Riding Hood and the wolf, and then, with the resulting context in mind, examine the wolf's two meals (he also devours the grandmother) more closely.

Maternal Authority

Before Little Red Riding Hood meets the wolf, she appears to exist solely through her relation to the maternal order: "sa mère en était folle, et sa mère-grand plus folle encor" (her mother was mad about her, and her grandmother even more so; 255). Given the broad semantic range of *la folie* (already covering, in seventeenth-century French, *trouble mental, déraison, manque de jugement, passion violente, extravagance*), should we understand the two occurrences of "folle" here as connoting anything beyond preoccupation and intense affection (the sense we see at the end of "Le Chat botté," where the king's daughter is described as mad—"folle"—about the Marquis de Carabas)? To a limited extent, the text does shed further light on this reference to "mères folles." Its first hint comes from the next sentence, where we learn that the grandmother made the red hood. The effect of the apposition is to suggest that a certain (grand) maternal folly was manifested precisely in the bestowal of that emblem—an extension of folly—on the little girl. It is as if the exorbitant emblem were a sign of the extent to which her identity has been determined by the motherly bond—between mother and grandmother—within the space of which her action in the tale—carrying her mother's gift to her grandmother—takes place.

Marc Soriano has called attention to the proliferation of unworthy parents in the *Contes en vers* and *Contes du temps passé*; he cites the folly of the mother and grandmother as a reason for including them in the group. It seems fair to add to his general comment that the incidence of absent fathers results in something of an imbalance:

there are far more self-centered, deficient, or maleficent mothers (in nine of eleven tales) than deplorable fathers (in five of eleven). In addition, while villainous ogre figures are crucial in five of the eight prose tales, mothers are the dominant villains in the other three ("Cendrillon," "Riquet à la houppe," "Les Fées"). Little Red Riding Hood's mother's single action before she disappears from the story reinforces the impression of parental delinquency. We learn by implication that she sent her obedient daughter off to see her grandmother without warning her about the dangers lurking in the outside world: "la pauvre enfant . . . *ne savait pas* qu'il est dangereux de s'arrêter à écouter un Loup" (the poor child did not know that it was dangerous to stop to listen to a wolf; 254). A factor in the feminine folly that takes shape around the disastrous visit to the grandmother, then, is this *non-savoir*, a foolish ignorance concordant with the construal of folly as opposed to reason and common sense. The young girl's lack of knowledge appears no less pronounced, moreover, within the domestic sphere occupied by the three feminine characters. In the dénouement, her surprised exclamations upon "comment sa Mère-grand était faite en son déshabillé" (how her grandmother looked in her nightgown) betray her unfamiliarity with the adult female body.

As for the grandmother, her position in the somewhat unmoored maternal order seems rather more delicate. The most salient index, a poetic one, seems to be the term *mère-grand* itself, which occurs no fewer than fourteen times in a tale of about 650 words. In a fine essay on Perrault's restricted, still thoroughly phallocratic "feminism," Béatrice Didier offers a remarkable commentary on this term. Taking the *mère-grand* as the epitome of women who bore the burden of transmitting tales to children, she links the author's "fascination pour la voix de mère-grand" (fascination for the grandmother's voice) to his attraction to contralto voices in opera and, more generally, to "une certaine ambiguïté des voix féminines graves" (a certain ambiguity of low feminine voices). The grandmother, she suggests, has reached an age at which she is no longer a woman in the conventional sense; it is "par delà la sexualité" (beyond sexuality) that she assumes the essential social identity and familial role of the storyteller. Perrault, the author who did not sign the tales, published them with a frontispiece illustration of three children listening to an elderly woman in that storytelling role. If he takes that role for himself, writes Didier, he does so "en s'identifiant à 'mère-grand'" (while identifying with "*mère-grand*").[7] Didier is content to link this conclusion fleetingly with Soriano's intriguing but elusive hypothesis attributing to Perrault a lifelong anguish about his sexual identity. Her insight is perhaps more relevant to the task of deciphering "Le Petit Chaperon rouge." On the one hand, offering a plausible rationale for understanding Little Red Riding Hood's walk to her grandmother's house as the action of a child happily setting out to visit her favorite storyteller, it opens the possibility of discerning in the tale a message—doubtless unique in the collection—about the didactic function of children's stories. On the other hand, if a certain ambiguity of narrative voice—or of its representation—in the Mother Goose tales is indeed encoded in sexual terms, it is appropriate to ask how this story's *mère-grand* embodies that ambiguity.

In "Le Petit Chaperon rouge," the indices confirming the suggestion of the frontispiece that the tales are meant to be read aloud are particularly abundant. They include, for example, the dramatizing effects with a cleverly onomatopoetic touch that are conveyed, at the door of grandmother's house, by "Toc. Toc. 'Qui est là?'" and by "Tire la chevillette, la bobinette cherra" (Knock, knock. "Who's there?"; Pull the pin, the latch will catch; 255). Moreover, the plot itself highlights connections between the disguised wolf and his two victims that are invisible, but audible. While noting twice that the wolf had to disguise his voice, first to imitate the little girl, then again to imitate the grandmother, the narrative also observes that Little Red Riding Hood was first frightened by the "grosse voix" (deep voice), but then assumed her grandmother had a cold. Indeed, until she climbs into bed with the wolf, her relation with him lies on a purely vocal register. We might say, following Didier's characterization of the grandmother, that it is imposed by a suspect, ambiguous, yet familiar voice, characterized by a low pitch that takes it partway toward the masculine horizon on which, wide-eyed, the child will finally see, but not know, the body of the wolf. In responding to the pretender's softened voice ("Le Loup lui cria en adoucissant sa voix") with her unfailing gullibility, she is doubtless giving herself over to the ambiguous voice she associates with a storyteller worthy of her confidence. The irony is that Little Red Riding Hood has formed this presumably pleasurable relation via voice and speech with the same grandmother whose gift of the red hood determined her own ensconcement in the visual order.

But the wolf's vocal tricks are episodic. Does the tale actually allow us to treat the lovely red-hooded girl, so clearly identified by her appearance, as a creature of speech, as a character entrenched by her gift of—or penchant for—gab in what she hears and says? The text does at least raise this question as soon as Little Red Riding Hood first meets the wolf and hears his two questions. With apparent enthusiasm, she adds to her direct answers—"Je vais voir ma Mère-grand" and "Oui"—significant details: "Je vais voir ma Mère-grand, et lui porter une galette avec un petit pot de beurre que ma Mère lui envoie" (I'm going to see my grandmother and take her a pastry and some butter that my mother is sending her). "Oh! oui, dit le petit chaperon rouge, c'est par-delà le moulin que vous voyez tout là-bas, là-bas, à la première maison du Village" (Oh yes, said Little Red Riding Hood, it's just beyond the mill you see way over there, the first house in the village). These are the effusive responses of a speaker unrestrained and essentially unreflecting in the face of her interlocutor's intentions. Caught up in the immediacy of her own orientation toward her grandmother and her house (indicated by the main verbs of her answers, *voir, porter, voir*), Little Red Riding Hood gives her undivided attention over to the objects (*mère-grand, galette/pot de beurre, maison*) of her discourse. In situating herself as the agent of a transmission from mother to grandmother, in representing herself in her grandmother's house in the act of seeing her and giving presents to her, Little Red Riding Hood is unwittingly revealing to the wolf the extent to which she exists *for* the grandmother, fixes upon her as the privileged other, the mirror or interlocutor from whom she derives her image or sense of self. As a result of her expressiveness, the wolf has the directions he needs and the line he will use at the grandmother's door. No doubt he also takes from the exchange a certain irritation because he would wish for more than the minimal notice she affords him. For she offers him so little in the way of recognition that, while playing readily into his hands, she effectively denies him a place in the structure of mutual identification she occupies with her mothers. So over and beyond strengthening the wolf's aggressive feelings toward her, a direct effect of her unwitting, yet fatal loquacity is to set up a triangular relationship in which the wolf has to perceive her grandmother as his rival, and the maternal order as an obstacle to be overcome.

The Talking Wolf

We can, then, consider Little Red Riding Hood's cheerful prat-
tling as a trait that comes down to her from her storytelling grand-
mother, one that is internal to their bonds of kinship and intimacy.
So what relation obtains between the girl's verbal facility and her
physical appearance, which is also linked to the grandmother? Has
she already overcome the antithesis, posited in the *Parallèle* and dra-
matized in "Riquet à la houppe," that opposes the visual order, of
which feminine beauty is the exemplary marker, and the spiritual
order, associated with male reason and speech? Here it is necessary
to consider the approach to Little Red Riding Hood by "compère
le Loup, qui eut bien envie de la manger; mais il n'osa, à cause de
quelques Bûcherons qui étaient dans la Forêt" (Comrade Wolf,
whose real urge was to eat her, but he didn't dare because of some
loggers who were in the forest). In La Fontaine's fables, the term
compère (comrade; but as the root *père* suggests, the noun can also
designate a godfather) typically signals the humanization of the ani-
mal in question and at times may imply a touch of connivance
between narrator and character as well. As the scene in the woods
develops, it turns above all on the wolf's response to the frustration
caused by the nearby woodsmen, whose presence forces him to hold
his instincts at bay. His potential victim belongs to their protective
society, to an oppressive human culture that invades the natural
world and doubtless fosters resentment on the part of sensitive ani-
mals. The feeling evoked by *envie* has to be understood as a compul-
sive craving, not merely appetite but an aggressive drive tinged with
hostility, jealousy, desire for possession. Yet "compère" wolf deals
with the woodsmen's presence through a solid reality principle. He
instantly appears in his affable, rational, calculating guise, repressing
his aggressive impulse in favor of wily questions followed by this
single, savvy rejoinder: "Hé bien, dit le Loup, je veux l'aller voir
aussi; je m'y en vais par ce chemin ici, et toi par ce chemin-là, et
nous verrons qui plus tôt y sera" (Well, said the wolf, I want to go
see her, too; I'll take this path, and you take that one, and we'll see
who gets there first).

This formulation is remarkable on several counts:

1. The wolf announces his intention to Little Red Riding
Hood with utmost clarity.

2. From the start, he establishes the parity of his desire and hers (he wants to do what she wants to do), and by imagining them taking parallel paths on the same plane, he installs them in an order of comparability and competition.

3. By the same token, placing her in parallel with him in a movement toward the separate grandmother, he marks out a triangular space in which the two of them (younger and ambulatory) can represent their difference from her (elderly and infirm).

4. His middle proposition subtly draws her into his discourse and makes her the subject of an observation that functions as a command, an assertion of authority.

5. The plural subject of his final proposition joins her to him in a presumptive bond that will entail, if she goes along with his game, their companionship.

6. Thanks to her acquiescence, his entire sentence functions with the performative force of a decision being rendered by a voice of authority.

7. Simultaneously, it constitutes a proleptic summation of most of the action to come, tells the story in advance.

Thus the wolf, in usurping the mother's role and conveying to Little Red Riding Hood knowledge that she lacks, also assumes the grandmother's storytelling role and becomes the consummate speaker in the tale, the skilled user of a discourse of power in the service of desire. For him, the encounter in the woods has two important, interlocking functions. In the first place, it establishes the position of discursive authority he will occupy in the grandmother's house, where Little Red Riding Hood's obedience to his orders simply continues the already established pattern. At that juncture, her experience in and of speech remains one of unthinking subordination to the interlocutors she confronts and to the object-world she constructs with her words. Language is a vehicle with which she mindlessly—pleasurably—registers what she sees and feels. Given the contrast between her naively expressive and referential use of language and the wolf's discourse of reason deployed as an instrument of manipulation, it seems necessary to interpret her speech as a sign of deficiency, of her lack of *esprit*. As long as the absence of a viable spiritual relation in speech persists, the dominant impression she makes on the wolf will continue to derive from the attractive red-topped image she projects to the world through her visible appearance.

Yet the second function of the wolf's response to Little Red Riding Hood in the woods has to do precisely with the possibility of overcoming this deficiency of *esprit*. Like the grandmother he will displace, the wolf addresses the young girl from the standpoint of an adult speaking to a child, of a responsible major speaking to an inexperienced minor. The potential educative value of the framework within which they communicate depends on the receptivity of the junior party, on her readiness for maturation, for discovery and learning, for a flowering of selfhood and subjectivity. According to a classic—that is, common to philosophy (Hegel, Heidegger) and psychoanalysis (Freud, Lacan)—psychological framing of the human subject's conjoined experiences of consciousness and desire, the "spiritual deficiency" we have observed in Little Red Riding Hood's outlook needs to be understood structurally, as a function of interpersonal dynamics.[8] Amid the many contending schemes that flood this zone of inquiry, one constant seems never to be denied: the constitution of the subject as consciousness or desire depends on (the mediation of) the other. Heretofore, indeed, we have glimpsed the dynamics determining Little Red Riding Hood's low-level, nonspecular, almost hypnotic consciousness and her primitive, juvenile desire in the key relationship with her grandmother. In this initiatory encounter with the other through her mother or grandmother, the child can discover a pleasing, supportive difference from self that is intimate and reassuring. The question is what could happen if the other, through whose perceptions and desires her own are formed and reflected back to her, were another—in this case, the wolf, who entices her into a reckoning with the unfamiliar.

When we contemplate the innocent girl's escape or removal from an aberrant and confining (grand)maternal bond, her potential itinerary becomes that of a nascent heroine entering a new stage in her sentimental education. But is the emergence of such a development at all plausible? Two impediments that prevailed in the woods must be overcome if the wolf is to engage Little Red Riding Hood in a second, potentially inspiriting encounter: he must abate his physical need for food, and he must be alone with the object of his attentions. The scene that intervenes after the initial encounter in the woods meets both needs. The wolf eliminates his grandmotherly rival with understandable efficiency. The short account of his raid again depicts his meld of human and animal traits, underscoring first his cunning imposture, then his ravenous hunger. Although the context for appreciating this preparatory meal is minimal in the spare text of "Le Petit Chaperon rouge," helpful insights turn up elsewhere in the Perraldian corpus. In the *Pensées chrétiennes*, Perrault contrasts the "plaisirs positifs" of the spirit with the imperfect pleasures derived from the cessation of need or pain: "Le plaisir de manger ne consiste qu'à faire cesser la faim" (The pleasure of eating consists simply in ending hunger; para. 32), he writes. In "La Belle au bois dormant," when the ogress orders the princess served up in a Robert sauce, Perrault humorously evokes the cook's concern with the difficulty of substituting an animal for someone whose 100 years of slumber had made her aged skin tough. No doubt the limited satisfaction to be had from the uninviting old woman is not such as to prompt the wolf to tarry over her in search of higher pleasures. Yet the cessation of hunger is a significant benefit. His appetite assuaged by this first repast, he can anticipate drawing more gratifying pleasures from the staging of his second encounter with Little Red Riding Hood.

The young girl's arrival at her grandmother's house initiates the story's final episode. It follows exactly the same movement from calculated deception to unbridled slaughter that occurred in the preceding episode, when the wolf arrived and quickly downed the grandmother. The scene is launched, moreover, by repetitions that call attention to the wolf's move into the grandmother's position and the granddaughter's duplication of the wolf's words and actions at the door. What is new and different here is the substantial elongation of the first part of the scenario as the wolf extends his game of deception in order to draw Little Red Riding Hood into bed and then further delays his second meal while their decisive dialogue runs its course. Up to this final encounter, there is an uncanny resemblance between the wolf's tactical success and that of the cat in "Le Chat botté." Like the cat, the wolf aims fundamentally for survival and channels his efforts through well-wrought speech and pretense. Both the cat and the wolf eliminate obstacles—the ogre and the grandmother—to the realization of their designs by devouring them and taking over their domains. Both, moreover, are engaged in the appropriation of a metamorphic power that the tales associate with the ogre's practice of anthropophagy.

Over against this convergence of the feline and lupine trajectories, it becomes clear that the questions brought to the fore by the manifest disparity of outcomes have to do with what they reveal about these wily creatures' intentions: in what respects do their designs ultimately diverge, and what is the significance of that divergence? For each of these animal protagonists, the crucial concern is clearly their relation to an other—the cat's master and the wolf's potential mistress, we might say—whose position or identity they undertake to transform. The cat's triumph ultimately lies not only in his own ascension in tandem with his master, but also in his willingness to continue in a position of mutually acceptable servitude. As we have seen, the wolf is caught in the inverse situation as a result of the authority he holds over his unequal partner in dialogue. The issue is ultimately what kind of meeting of minds and bodies his exercise of that authority and her response to it make possible.

From Speech to Violence

The last word on the wolf's communication with Little Red Riding Hood is delivered by the terminal scene, in bed, where the relation developed in discourse is decisively supplemented by a moment of vision:

Elle fut bien étonnée de voir comment sa Mère-grand était faite en son déshabillé. Elle lui dit: Ma mère-grand, que vous avez de grands bras!— C'est pour mieux t'embrasser, ma fille.—Ma mère-grand, que vous avez de grandes jambes!—C'est pour mieux courir, mon enfant.—Ma mère-grand, que vous avez de grandes oreilles!—C'est pour mieux écouter, mon enfant.—Ma mère-grand, que vous avez de grands yeux!—C'est pour mieux voir, mon enfant.—Ma mère-grand, que vous avez de grandes dents!— C'est pour te manger.

She was quite astonished to see how her grandmother looked in her nightgown. She said to her: "Grandmother, what big arms you have!" "It's for embracing you better, my dear." "Grandmother, what big legs you have!" "It's for running faster, my child." "Grandmother, what big ears you have!" "It's for hearing better, my child." "Grandmother, what big eyes you have!" "It's for seeing better, my child." "Grandmother, what big teeth you have!" "It's for eating you."

In contrast to the childish folly voiced by Little Red Riding Hood's exclamations, the wolf's discourse, in each of his five answers in the dialogue, is an assertion of reason—"c'est pour"—that also, as an indication of purpose and use, connotes the immediate coalescence of reason with intention and desire. The syntactic form that carries the propositional focus forward onto the infinitive—"pour mieux t'embrasser"—points, moreover, to the eclipse of reason by the force it sanctions. This first response condenses the essentials of the wolf's attempt to establish a rapport of intimacy with the entrapped girl. It tells her that the object of her gaze exists for the purpose of embracing—touching/holding/kissing/encompassing—her. That is, the significance of the wolf's body lies in his willful capacity to surround her with the contact through which she can perceive her own body, can experience a sensual revelation of herself to herself.

Two other linguistic phenomena call for comment here, the discursive function of the "c'est pour" and the comparative function of the adverb *mieux*. The formal significance of "c'est pour" is governed by the context of a dialogue made up of five exclamations by Little Red Riding Hood and five responses by the wolf. The deictic *ce* instantiates a relatively loose but clear reference back to the whole of the preceding proposition; caught up in the turn of phrase "c'est pour," it effectively recasts her exclamations—strong assertions of fact—as questions or requests for explanation. Thus, in response, the wolf is effectively appending to her exclamations third-person statements that amount to elaborations on what she has observed. While short-circuiting dialogue's conventional reciprocation between "I" and "you," the wolf draws his interlocutor's speech into fusion with his, as if his thinking were a framing extension of hers. At the same time, however, the "c'est pour" construction places a curiously impersonal inflection on the wolf's utterances, sparing him the need either to respond directly with a second-person "tu" (corresponding to her "vous") or to refer to himself. This guarded self-effacement or detachment expresses subtly the circumstantial awkwardness of the dialogic position he has staked out for himself. Having occupied the grandmother's place and thus invited Little Red Riding Hood's incorrect address to "mère-grand," he can in turn address her only in terms that are unavoidably caught in the ambiguity Didier imputes to the grand-

mother's role. He can neither deny the validity of the false identi-
fication to which she clings nor assume a discursive posture that
affirms it; instead, his words follow an intermediary course that
keeps the indices of a subject of enunciation to a bare minimum and
allows his interlocutor to interpret them (via linkage to mère-grand
or the wolf) on her own. If the wolf's reserve is consistent with
tactical concerns (correcting her would presumably repel her), it is
also a cogent expression of the seducer's interest in deriving his
satisfaction from the desire of the other: rather than identifying
himself to her, he seeks to be recognized by her.

The interest of the adverb *mieux* here stems from the ellipsis
of the comparison: better than what? than arms smaller than the
wolf's, such as the grandmother's? A key reason for treating the
adverb as a marker beckoning toward what distinguishes the wolf's
features from the grandmother's is that his subsequent responses—
pour mieux courir/écouter/voir—bring out that differentiation more
insistently. There are two telling signs of this discreet inching toward
self-characterization on the part of the wolf. The first is the verb
courir, which hardly conjures up grandmotherly activity, and indeed
in one of its seventeenth-century acceptations could refer to chasing
after women (as in "courir les femmes"). The second is the absence
of the direct object *te* referring to Little Red Riding Hood. Even if
the dialogic situation in which the wolf is pursuing, listening to, and
staring at her holds her in place as an implicit object of all three
verbs, and thus of a dialectical operation in which the wolf persists in
confronting her with the mirroring effects of his perceptions and the
stimulatory impulses of his desires, the withdrawal of the *te* dispenses
with the familiarity of personal address proper to a grandmother-to-
granddaughter exchange. In its stead, the wolf imposes the haunt-
ingly impersonal turn of these three propositions that invite her to
contemplate the bodily parts she has singled out in their phenome-
nal singularity, in their difference from what she has known in her
familial experience.

The pressure on Little Red Riding Hood to recognize the legs,
ears, and eyes as those of the wolf occasions a complementary ad-
justment in the sense of the closing allocutions: "ma fille" after
t'embrasser becomes "mon enfant" after *courir*, *écouter*, and *voir*. In the
first case, "ma fille" correlates with *te* so as to confirm the bonding
of personal intimacy between addresser and addressee that is central

to the proposition's content. But in the other three cases, not only does the daughterly "ma fille" give way to the less specific, more generic "mon enfant"; the allocution itself is left dangling as an appendage. Its function is no longer to link the listener to the proposition, but to separate her from it, to position her as the recipient of the speaker's message whose task is to examine the information conveyed from a discreet distance and reckon with it. Thus isolated, moreover, "mon enfant" takes on for the wolf an authentically designatory significance: he can say *my* child because for him she becomes ever more evidently in this dialogue the subject he is intent upon engendering (cf. *enfanter*), whose existence depends on his perceptions and desires.

The last of the wolf's five answers—"C'est pour te manger"— registers a sudden break in continuity that releases the pressure to which the wolf's visual and verbal assault has subjected Little Red Riding Hood. Predictably enough, the proposition differs in form (bearing the object *te* but suppressing the address to "mon enfant") and content (announcing her destruction) from the four preceding ones. The earlier responses appeared to engage communication and explanation; they closed with affectionate possessives ("ma fille" or "mon enfant") apt to secure her confidence, and they somewhat abstractly stated purposes compatible with the victim's continued existence as a dependent who is subject to the formative dominance of the speaker's faculties. The penultimate terms in the series of bodily parts and infinitives ("grands yeux" and "voir") designate the scopic or specular order in which male domination, grounded in the image of manhood returned to the male subject by his female mirror, might have been consolidated. By contrast, the ultimate pairing ("les dents"/"manger") signals the collapse of that possibility. The wolf's aggressively referential "te manger" instantly squeezes Little Red Riding Hood into the space of the little pronoun object that is, as it were, swallowed up by the verb. The passage from *voir* to *manger* is an abdication. No longer merely designating the wolf's impersonal authority, the potential for action that gives him controlling power, "c'est pour te manger" triggers the passage of power into destructive force. Too stifling, moreover, to be heard (or read) as a message, the death sentence is devoid of concern with the prisoner's response. It is as if the wolf, having renounced communication, were talking to himself, animating his own response. "Mon enfant" can be elided since the addressee the wolf has been creating and sustaining is now swept up in the pronominal *te* and, rather than before him, can better be pictured as already on her way into him. For according to the narrator's last sentence, the speaking and eating are nearly simultaneous in the wolf's mouth, part of a continuous movement that merges his enunciation with the masticatory act so as to make the final expression of rational intention coincident with its enactment by force.

By representing a ruseful, talking wolf capable of relishing deferred pleasure, "Le Petit Chaperon rouge" precludes ascribing his action to simple hunger. The scene of entrapment forces us toward the kind of allegorical understanding that Bettelheim found so objectionable. As willful masculine force applied to feminine weakness, the process of ingestion—biting, chewing, swallowing, digesting—figures a degree of castratory male violence that exceeds in intensity the effects achieved by the representation of feminine decapitation in other tales ("Le Petit Poucet," "La Barbe bleue," "La Belle au bois dormant"). The wolf's voracious charge manifests a drive to possess the feminine object so absolutely as to require the woman's incorporation into the male body. Toward what insight into this ogreish paroxysm do the relations we have been ferreting out of Perrault's tale take us? Does their fatal dialogue ultimately reveal a vicious wolf indulging in a few moments of sadistic pleasure before moving on to his dessert? Or should his plunge into ogredom be ascribed at least in part to other factors, including, as the foregoing analysis suggests, the abortion of communication in the dialogue?

In Little Red Riding Hood's question, the wolf encounters a certain awakening to his physical presence. She expresses her astonishment at what she sees by confronting the wolf with her perceptions of his size. This makes for a pronounced difference from their first encounter, when their exchange of words seemed unreal for want of a parallel exchange of looks or even the slightest hint that she was aware of his wolfishness. Yet the wily wolf can hardly regard the image of himself she now reflects back to him as satisfactory, as a recognition comparable to the one the cat in "Le Chat botté" provides for his master. For the wide-eyed Little Red Riding Hood, saying what she sees with her tunnel vision and her infantile infatuation with the immediate object, continues to express her ignorance, now specified by her exclamations as ignorance of her grand-mother's body and ipso facto of the male body as well. Just as impor-tant, however, as the doggedly mindless, primitive consciousness she sustains is the insistency with which she repeats the ritual allocution "Ma mère-grand." Thereby referring back to her intimate, posses-sive tie to the being whose nudity she believes she is now appre-hending, she unrelentingly (mis)names her bedmate while mistak-ing his male body for a female one. From her incorrigibly unwitting point of view, it is apparently still her grandmother with whom she is consorting and by whom she will be devoured.

Thus the hapless young girl sustains the sad irony that attends her ignorance of what has been happening, which here takes its ultimate form in her seeing the wolf without knowing him, without linking his corporal traits to his individuality and masculinity. For him, the persistence of Little Red Riding Hood's mindless, unknowing vi-sion can only spell renewed frustration. To be sure, her exclamations do spring from a rudimentary consciousness of difference; they do express her servile awareness that he is not she, is other than she, indeed other than what she can immediately recognize. Thus, like the slave vis-à-vis the master in Hegel's celebrated account of self-consciousness, she does at least confront him with the elemental work of the negative. But her perceptions, far from identifying him as her clever interlocutor, systematically reduce him to a body. Far from realizing that his mask has dropped, far from meeting his need for the same mirror of self-discovery that his encompassing presence affords her, she continues to identify him as another, as *mère-grand* (with no understanding, of course, of what this suggests to the wolf now that he has literally assimilated *mère-grand*).

We noted early on the lack of reciprocity that informs this situa-tion and the tenacious paradox that it brings into focus. To the wolf, who has pursued the effort to form a self-satisfying relation of au-thority with the acuity of a masterful reflexive consciousness, of human reason placed in the service of desire, Little Red Riding Hood responds subhumanly, as it were; and in its substance, her response constitutes a double-edged dehumanizing message. On the one hand, in the exchange of gazes they fix upon each other's bodies, her perceptions thrust him back toward his natural, animal state. On the other hand, in the confrontation of their respective desires, he is addressed in human terms by the object of his desire, but merely as the feeble *mère-grand* whom he has absorbed and whose role he seeks to relinquish in favor of his own male identity. Having liquidated the maternal order headed by the grandmother, the wolf has succeeded only in paving the way for his attempt at seduction. He still has to draw Little Red Riding Hood into the phallocratic order in which masculine power, desire, and vision— the forces manifest in the parts of his body that she observes—hold sway. To the extent that he can perceive in Little Red Riding Hood a subject expressive of desire, that desire remains inchoate, innocent, and immutable, still bound up in her childlike attachment to the maternal. Her unselfconsciousness erodes for him the very possibility of "desiring the desire of the other " (to use Borch-Jacobsen's phrase).[9] Hers is not a desire he can covet, that can serve as a foil for his own.

It is therefore necessary to grasp in the dénouement of "Le Petit Chaperon rouge" not so much a continuation of the wolf's successful project of deception and entrapment as the failure of his project of seduction. His recourse to violence neither satisfies his desire for recognition nor induces his victim to give up her fixation on the maternal in favor of subjugation to the phallocratic order he represents; it is essentially an outburst by which he expresses and breaks away from his frustration. For if the act of killing and eating his victim entails an erotic intensity that compensates for libidinal pleasures denied him by Little Red Riding Hood, it also disables the particular search for authority and self-identification that he may have been seeking through a relationship with her. In the last analysis, one can perhaps ascribe the wolf's failure to get what he wanted from Little Red Riding Hood to an error of judgment. While pursuing a victim who was, like her grandmother, well suited to serve him as an object of prey, he somehow decided—or succumbed to the temptation—to seek more from her, to draw out his lustful chase into an interpersonal and sensual adventure. "Le Petit Chaperon rouge" remains an interpretive enigma since the text exposes little of the wolf's motivation for embarking on this potentially less beastly, more human enterprise, and since it leaves his future enshrouded in mystery.

The surprise lurking in the exceedingly bare text of Perrault's prose fable lies neither in the wolf's extended display of human qualities nor in the diverse details suggesting that his entrapment and devouring of the little girl delineate an allegorical representation of seduction that gives way to rape. Rather, it lies in the characterization of Little Red Riding Hood herself, notably in the resoluteness with which the narrative threads preserve her status as a child—not even an adolescent—whose unpreparedness eventually leaves her at a loss, unresponsive to the advances of a *coureur* or womanizer. In the end, nothing mutes or palliates the representation of sexual child abuse. Its irrecusable effect is to magnify the horror of the story. Concomitantly, since the act of devouring the victim results in the same total, remainderless assimilation we noted in the cat's consumption of the ogre, the extremity exposed here—indeed, set off in stark relief—demands to be called, unreservedly, *absolute violence*. For in one and the same breath, the wolf announces to his victim that he is cancelling the existence she has been fleetingly accorded through dialogue with him, that henceforth she is to be, in him, absolutely nothing, and he asserts for himself, reduced by her intolerable naiveté to the lonely necessity of self-possession or self-incorporation, that he is reconstituting himself with the nothingness he inflicts upon/takes from her.

To eat the other, to eat precisely the death of the other, to appropriate an experience that can only belong to the other for himself in a violation of life and of death that forces the venue of their coalescence into his own mouth, is, to be sure, not to eat nothing; it is rather, for the wolf, at once to quell and to internalize the voice of the negative—the essential "you are not me"—with which the poor girl, even if hardly more engaging or perceptive than the gorgeous younger sister unsparingly depicted in "Riquet à la houppe" as a "pauvre bête," ceaselessly confronted him. The tale's inattention to the aftermath of this killing assimilation of life and death makes it all the more disconcerting. Whether, within the wolf, the work of the negative is silenced or regenerated is a question it appears to leave in suspense.

In La Fontaine's "Le Loup et les Bergers" (*Fables X*, 5), a reflective wolf tempted by the attractions of culture undertakes his own humanization, only to discover the savagery of the men he would imitate. He thus wisely decides to reassert the laws of nature, killing and eating the lamb he had meant to spare. Reading "Le Petit Chaperon rouge" in the light of that fable, one could take the wolf's meal as an aggressive reassertion of his natural integrative power, as an act that signals his decisive retreat from human society into the wise animal's cultivation of private satisfaction and autonomous self-mastery. The difficulty that reinforces the uniqueness of "Le Petit Chaperon rouge" is that the story makes it just as easy to perceive exactly the contrary scenario, according to which a frustrated wolf, losing control, falls back into the throes of need and deprivation. His natural experience would then merely reproduce the collision with human culture that converts the struggle for survival into a pursuit of self-recognition and would therefore lead to more dramatic face-offs with human others. Neither the gruesome ending nor the narrator's closing characterization of the wolf as "méchant" suffice to impose one of these readings over the other, nor indeed to indicate whether they are mutually exclusive or complementary. Similarly, the tale's *moralité*, asserting that "tous les loups ne sont pas de la même sorte" (not all wolves are of the same kind) allows for the play of this narrative indecision. It evokes both the ravenous creature that precipitously eats young children as prey and the clever scheming of human wolves who chase after "jeunes Demoiselles . . . jusque dans les ruelles."

Hence the importance of placing the story in the *Contes du temps passé*, which furnish a context in which the wolf's experience can be both illuminating and further illuminated. As the comparisons we have made with "La Belle au bois dormant," "Le Petit Poucet," and especially "Le Chat botté" suggest, a key affinity underlying an important subset of stories is the role accorded to ogre figures. Among these tales, "Le Petit Chaperon rouge" is seminal insofar as its central allegory pertains to the ogre's experience and status, insofar as the itinerary leading to the wolf's consumption of the little girl manifestly offers an account of ogre formation.[10] In this process, the wolf's maneuvering can be situated on two horizons: (1) it activates the conceptual distinctions that are so often at issue in La Fontaine's universe—the animal versus the human, nature versus culture—and (2) it unleashes concurrently a drama of sexual difference that opposes the feminine to the masculine, the maternal to the paternal.

In both of these dimensions, "Le Chat botté" and "La Belle au bois dormant" appear in sharp contrast to "Le Petit Chaperon rouge." To the extent that in each the social framework of a kingdom presupposes the dominance of the established paternal order, the opposition of the sexes has already been resolved; and in each a satisfactory compromise between the pressures of nature and culture results precisely from the suppression of the ogre figures. However, for insight into the development of the wolf's itinerary once he has emerged in the ogre's role, it suffices to look no further than the story that succeeds "Le Petit Chaperon rouge" in the *Contes*, "La Barbe bleue." If that tale is almost as evidently a companion to "Le Petit Chaperon rouge" as "Cendrillon" is to "Peau d'âne," it is because, in the first place, its ogreish protagonist's career, which consists in acquiring and beheading one wife after another, can be regarded as a logical extension of the wolf's itinerary as an ogre, and because, in the second place, quite as poignantly as the wolf's encounter with Little Red Riding Hood, Bluebeard's encounter with his last wife reenacts the dramatic opposition of the sexes. It is as if the wolf's experience provides background for understanding Bluebeard's behavior, while Bluebeard's story is a sequel that provides a prognosis of the wolf's future. It is reasonable to ask, moreover, if the trajectory traversed in "La Barbe bleue" is not pivotal for the *Contes* as a whole. The story resurrects the enigma of violence that "Le Petit Chaperon rouge" presents in the uncompromising form of a limit case and proceeds to reckon with it in a reconstructive dénouement that seems to typify the remaining tales of the collection. If this hypothesis about the connection between "Le Petit Chaperon rouge" and "La Barbe bleue" and about their exemplary status in the corpus of tales proves to be sound, it will of course lay to rest the objection that the former is out of place in Perrault's collection.

6

Bluebeard's Secret

Since "Le Petit Chaperon rouge" and "Le Chat botté" set forth very decisive representations of the wolf's consumption of Little Red Riding Hood and the cat's consumption of the ogre, we have assumed, perhaps somewhat incautiously, that the process of ingesting and digesting victims results in their total assimilation, in a liquidation that leaves no traces of the consumers' violent acts. The victims in these tales disappear definitively, irreversibly, because the act of eating integrates the singular, spectacularly marked bodies of the red-hooded girl and the ogre into the composite bodies that engulf them. Particularly in the case of the animal who wolfs down his prey in the privacy of the grandmother's house, there may be no awareness of his identity, no evidence pointing to him as the murderous beast. Insofar as he alone knows what he has done, his violence becomes his secret. That is, his feminine victims, whom he must initially separate out and recognize as the contents of his secret (Latin *secernere*, to separate), are thereafter "secreted away" by his act of crushing their singular bodies into his own corporal mass, where they are reduced to undifferentiated, homogeneous components. Their dissimulation is thus an effect of their indistinguishability—which is to say that the secret is an effect of the sameness or oneness the incorporated bodies come to share with all parts of the wolf's body.

Henceforth, the wolf's preservation of his secret will depend on his ability to appear integrally natural or normal, unaffected by his absorption of Little Red Riding Hood and her grandmother. Behavior displaying a difference between himself and other wolves could—if it reflected the consumption of human flesh—result in the betrayal of his secret. This structuring of the secret enables a "logical" or strategic formulation of the enigma we have heretofore grasped on the level of consciousness (does the wolf experience self-recognition or alienation?) or desire (does he experience self-satisfaction or frustration?). From the standpoint of secrecy, the crucial factor is memory. Has the wolf, by total consumption, achieved a definitive dissimulation, has he completed a process that will sink into oblivion? Or will the process of dissimulation in fact problematize the keeping of the secret, will the work of instinct and desire occasion a remembering of the violent event that triggers the dramas of secrecy? The issue remains unresolved in "Le Petit Chaperon rouge" because the abrupt ending precludes establishing the minimal conditions under which the play of secrecy can take hold. In an essay in *Lectures traversières*, "Logiques du secret," Louis Marin describes those minimal conditions as a triangular configuration in which two characters collude in hiding something from a third character who has an interest in knowing it. Thus, the wolf's knowledge of himself and his past could come into play as a secret only at the point when he would confide to someone else the fact that he has a secret that needs to be kept.

Among the reasons that "La Barbe bleue" seems to pick up where "Le Petit Chaperon rouge" leaves off and to promise to shed light on the little tale that immediately precedes it in the collection, the structurally primary one concerns the ominously mysterious past of the disturbing protagonist, Bluebeard. As the story gradually brings to light his penchant for ensnaring wives and murdering them, it seems almost as if this terrifying womanizer were a human reincarnation of the wolf, compulsively repeating the attempt to draw his female victim into a satisfying relationship. To the extent that Bluebeard's drama forms a sequel to the wolf's adventure, it takes on a special twist precisely because he constructs his project of marital coercion around his secret, seeks to force his young wife to cooperate with him in preserving it.

Within the *Contes du temps passé*, "La Barbe bleue" is one of four medium-length tales; similar in complexity of elaboration to "Le Chat botté," it is more than twice as long as "Le Petit Chaperon rouge," and its narrative practice appears to entail a far more studied and intricate orchestration of details. Yet the story's plot can be reduced to five simple segments, each of which is marked either by the presence or the absence (noted in parentheses in the following list) of the husband:

1. Bluebeard marries the younger of two sisters from a neighboring family (=period in which the two main characters are brought together).

2. The young wife violates her husband's command and enters the forbidden chamber, where she discovers the corpses of his previous wives (=period of Bluebeard's absence on a presumably feigned business trip).

3. After a suspenseful drama during which the wife, aided by her sister, manages to delay her punishment, her two brothers arrive just in time to rescue her (=period in which the protagonists are reunited after Bluebeard's return).

4. The two brothers enact the reversal of the punishment the husband was about to administer to his wife by killing Bluebeard (=moment of the definitive separation of the two central characters).

5. The young widow organizes a comic dénouement that provides rewards for the two brothers, a new marriage for herself, and a marriage for her cooperative sister (=period in which the heroine is brought together with a husband who replaces the deceased one, i.e., a revised version of the action in segment 1).

Overall, then, the plot consists of a series of episodes that moves from unification, through separation, reunification, and reseparation, to a final unification. It conforms patently to the conventional folkloric structure, in which the ending restores the beginning equilibrium that has been upset in the body of the tale. Represented schematically (see Fig. 3), it bears a striking resemblance to the plot of "Le Petit Chaperon rouge."[1] For here again, the embedding of a single sequence (NS^2) under the transgression function of the global sequence (NS^1) constitutes a simple narrative syntax that puts into relief the confrontation of two protagonists—a male ogre figure and a female victim whom he entraps—and their respective dramas. However, the relation between the beginning and the ending makes for a significant difference in the global structure (NS^1): unlike Little Red Riding Hood, the young wife escapes, is able to claim the heroine's role; whereas unlike the wolf, the frightful villain under-

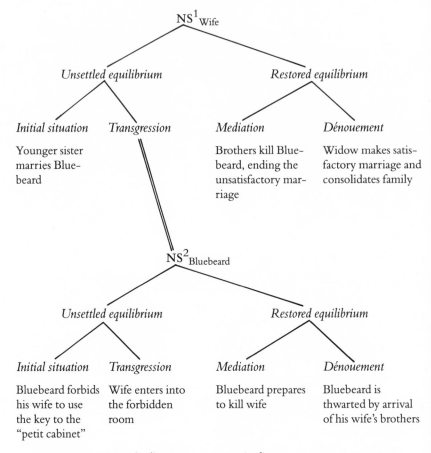

Fig. 3. The global (NS[1]) and embedded (NS[2]) narrative structures of "La Barbe bleue."

goes a punishment that enables the young woman and her family to triumph.

Within this global structure, the embedded sequence (NS[2]) or subplot—Bluebeard's plot against his wife—is the dominant locus of interest since it embraces all but the opening and closing lines of the narrative. Moreover, when we compare the tree diagrams of "Le Petit Chaperon rouge" and "La Barbe bleue," the striking difference in syntax turns out to lie in the placement of the failed dénouements: in the former, it concludes the global sequence (that of the female protagonist's family) and leaves each protagonist's story cut off, suspended in a terminal violence that merely repeats the violence already enacted at the end of NS^2, whereas in the latter, the protagonist's failure occupies precisely the crucial transition point at the end of the embedded sequence, and in that position it forms the bridge to a comic restoration of equilibrium in NS^1. So when the end of NS^2 in "La Barbe bleue" dissolves the correspondence between the two dramas, its crucial effect is to break off the pattern of repetitive violence that prevails in the two narrative sequences of "Le Petit Chaperon rouge," as well as in the several recurrences of Bluebeard's wife-killing ritual. Thus the structural comparison of these tales draws our attention to the shift from the ogre figure's dominance to an alternative scenario, introduced by the last two paragraphs of "La Barbe bleue" (which recount the mediation and dénouement of NS^1). What light does this tale's elaboration and transformation of "Le Petit Chaperon rouge" shed upon the *Contes du temps passé*?

A Narrative of Role Reversal

The subplot of "La Barbe bleue," which draws upon a quite conventional stock of tales about disobedient, overly curious wives, is very clearly framed by the narrator's presentation. In the first place, it is introduced by a single proposition in which the heroine's viewpoint suddenly displaces the narrator's: "Enfin tout alla si bien [narrator's viewpoint] que la Cadette commença à trouver [the young woman's viewpoint] que le Maître du logis n'avait plus la barbe si bleue, et que c'était un fort honnête homme" (Finally everything went so well that the younger sister began to find that the master of the household did not have such a blue beard, and that he was a quite honorable man; 257–58). From the new perspective, Bluebeard no longer seems so frightening and unnatural. His humanization is faster and goes farther than the wolf's, which is gradually achieved through clever speech. For the term "honnête homme" deftly assimilates him to a reassuring figure, a paragon of social grace and polite culture. Made all the more marriageable by his great wealth, he becomes forthwith the protagonist in the ensuing disobedient-wife sequence. In the second place, the embedded sequence is concluded by a rigorously analogous proposition that signals a switch back onto the level of the global narrative structure: "on heurta si fort à la porte [narrator's report, corresponding to "tout alla si bien que"], que la Barbe bleue s'arrêta tout court" [Bluebeard's standpoint, corresponding to "la Cadette commença à trouver"] (Someone banged so loudly against the door that Bluebeard stopped short; 261). So in each case a relation of strong impression to its effect on the character—marked conjunctively by the phrases "si bien que" and "si fort que"—occasions the change in viewpoint: the pleasureful effect on the young woman signals the switch into Bluebeard's sequence; the disruptive effect on Bluebeard signals the return to the level of the global structure dominated by the heroine.

The focus that this clear-cut framing of the two narrative sequences imposes on the reading of the tale has to do with a dual role reversal: Bluebeard's fall from the role of executioner into that of victim dovetails with his unnamed wife's ascent from that of disobedient wife to heroine. The historical background uncovered by Soriano's study of folkloric sources tends to support the notion that understanding the reversal of roles is a fundamental interpretive task.[2] According to Soriano, one of Perrault's principal contributions to the story was a modernizing, indeed a kind of Christianizing, of more primitive, barbaric versions of the disobedient wife's drama. In the version to which Soriano traces "La Barbe bleue," the wife prepares to die, not by praying to God as in Perrault's tale, but by changing into her wedding dress and then submitting to a pagan ritual of execution; here the ritual murder would then enact absolutely, in the stark reality of an embellished and, as it were, contractual death haunted by fateful overtones, the imposition of male authority that was only symbolic in marriage. But Perrault substitutes prayer for the profanation of the marriage rite; and, as we have noted, his narrative is structured so as to highlight the significance of the reversal that substitutes the salvation of the terrified wife for the vengeance of the tyrannical husband. Perrault's description of this latter substitution includes socioeconomic details that indicate the story's compliance with the demands of a late-seventeenth-century audience.

These signs of modernization lend support to the thesis suggested by parallels in plot and character development: among Perrault's tales "La Barbe bleue" is an illustration, still more telling than "Le Chat botté," of polite society's reaction to the ogre's menace—a reversion to primitive, natural violence—that is so baldly highlighted in "Le Petit Chaperon rouge." Still another factor external to the narrative also marks the significance of the change in victims that yields the happy ending: the play between the two *moralités* Perrault offers as a postscript. The first lesson, referring back primarily to the embedded sequence, turns on the theme of the over-curious wife, bemoaning the vice of the fair sex. The second one, however, refers to the entire story, to the global structure, and in moral terms, it sounds a modern note, recognizing the potentially equal or perhaps superior position of the wife in the marital relationship. Thus the move from the first to the second moral corresponds to the reversal of marital positions (from husband's dominance to wife's dominance) in the story.

As we noted above, the tree diagram of narrative syntax situates the crucial role reversal at the point where the embedded and global sequences are reunited (i.e., in the articulation between the dénouement of NS^2 and the mediation function of NS^1). The story's tension reaches its apex precisely in the insistently theatrical scene in which the heroine struggles to stay her execution until her brothers can arrive and impale the executioner. Until the suspense is ended, the narrative effectively produces a prorogation in the assignment of the transgression function in NS^1: will the transgressor in the global sequence be Bluebeard or his wife? Indeed, this amounts to asking whose sequence will turn out to be the global one, his (as was the case in the experiences of his previous wives) or hers. The taut drama played out in the tale's climax is a function of this narrative indecision; the deferral in the embedded sequence, by dragging out Bluebeard's implementing of his plot into the failure that terminates NS^2, is, as it were, the negative condition enabling the successful mediation of NS^1. What this narrative necessarily underscores, then, is the vital time-killing role played by those rather curious scenes—the frightened heroine's preparation for death and her dramatic dialogue with her sister, Anne—that intervene between Bluebeard's confrontation with his wife over her guilt and his failed attempt to behead her.

Mimetic Rivalry

Through the overlapping and coalescence of the plot and the subplot, a pronounced structural resemblance between them also emerges. Until the divergence in the respective dénouements ap-

pears, the heroine's plot—her marriage with Bluebeard, her viola-
tion of his prohibition, her resistance to the fate he has in store for
her, her success—corresponds point for point with Bluebeard's
subplot—his marriage, his wife's violation of his prohibition, his
attempt to repeat the punishment he had inflicted on his previous
wives, his failure. This similarity is strongly reinforced by the paral-
lelism of the actantial relations articulated in each of the narrative
structures. In NS^2, Bluebeard is not merely the dispatcher and provi-
sional hero; his aim, evidenced by his demonic trickery and dark
past, is apparently to consolidate a sadistic authority in his own
household, so that he is also the recipient of his own dispatch and
beneficiary of his action upon the woman he seeks to entomb in
his claustrophobic, prisonlike castle. In NS^1, owing to the marital
scenario, the dispatcher function at first appears to belong to the
mother or the family; the heroic function of mediation develops
around the heroine's delaying action and is also a collective enter-
prise of the family (the two brothers and the two sisters). As the
story develops, the heroine comes to stand more and more clearly as
the family's principal representative. In pursuing her acquisitive,
family-supporting desire to partake of Bluebeard's wealth, she as-
sumes the mother's authority both at the beginning, when she de-
cides to proceed with the dubious marriage, and in the ending.
There, having inherited her deceased husband's possessions, she acts
as the head of the family (the mother is not mentioned after the
story's third sentence) in treating her good fortune as their collective
bounty.[3]

The actantial framework thus provides a kind of teleological
overview of the parallels between the embedded and global narra-
tive structures. Each of them manifests a tendency to amalgamate
actants (hero, dispatcher, and receiver) in the activity of a single
agent or character, Bluebeard in NS^2, the young wife in NS^1; each
character is essentially autotelic, seeks the satisfaction to be derived
from addressing oneself (as hero or heroine) from oneself (as dis-
patcher) to oneself (as beneficiary), so as to integrate one's world
as an extension or image or dependency of oneself. Moreover,
the nature of the conflict between these characters also begins to
emerge out of this parallelism. Since, in each case, they display a
manifest interest in wealth and the power it affords, their relation-
ship offers a classic instance of mimetic rivalry. Given the dovetailing

of the motives that each projects toward the other, the evident difference between them that sets the stage for conflict lies elsewhere—in the opposition, given from the outset, of a dominant (actual) male possessor to a subordinate (potential) female possessor. As the dramas within the plot and subplot develop, the nature and implications of the difference indicated by these oppositions (actual/potential, dominant/subordinate, male/female) will be gradually exposed and articulated dramatically as a challenge to that difference.

The effects of the parallelism between NS^1 and NS^2 are magnified by the embedding of the latter in the former. In particular, this structure—whereby the background evoked by NS^1, although muted, continues to shape the understanding of NS^2 from a distance—has the effect of doubling the reader's perception of each main character. In the case of Bluebeard, it is fair to say that, from the start of NS^2, he is an ambivalent figure whose initially negative image ("cet homme avait la Barbe bleue: cela le rendait si laid et si terrible, qu'il n'était ni femme ni fille qui ne s'enfuît devant lui"; this man had a blue beard; it made him so ugly and frightening that there was not a woman, young or old, who did not flee from him; 257) has to some extent been neutralized by the young wife's more positive, self-interested view of him. Yet insofar as the two faces of Bluebeard are kept in view, the perspective established in NS^1, in which he is the villain, continuously shadows the embedded sequence even as it unfolds.

Subsequently, the ambivalence first encountered in the figure of Bluebeard resurfaces with renewed acuity when his wife begins to share in it. The implications of the young wife's intense curiosity ("Elle fut si pressée de sa curiosité. . . . Elle y descendit . . . avec tant de précipitation"; She was so driven by her curiosity. . . . She went down there . . . with such haste; 259) emerge mordantly in the dramatic episode at the door of the forbidden chamber. When she discovers the corpses hanging on the wall, she drops the key, whereupon it magically picks up an indelible mark of blood from the floor of the crypt. Because the mark will constitute evidence of her misdeed in Bluebeard's eyes, this discovery scene has a dual revelatory consequence: it shows the wife to be a transgressor of the marital edict even while it divulges Bluebeard's shocking transgressions against the laws of society. From this moment on, husband and wife occupy symmetrical positions; he is simultaneously the disobeyed husband, the victim of his wife's violation of authority, and a ruthless pervert whom society should punish; likewise, she is both her treacherous temptor's next victim and the violator, the breaker of her own promise, whom her husband should punish. As the drama of suspense develops, the duality of each character's position is rigorously maintained right up to the decisive moment of Bluebeard's execution, which therefore entails the substitution of one victim who is simultaneously wrong and wronged, guilty and aggrieved, for another. There can be no innocence here, no simple overcoming of vice by virtue. In its logic and dramatic force, the violent act of punishment that Bluebeard was about to commit against his wife is virtually identical to the one he undergoes; the latter ending is the double of the former, short-circuited one that it displaces.

The Place of the Secret

Within this framework of essential sameness, the opposition of the two protagonists comes to light around Bluebeard's secret.[4] His privileged knowledge, whether construed as what he knows or as the mere fact of knowing something his wife is not allowed to know, is the advantage that grounds his superiority and preserves his power, even when he is sharing his wealth. With the temptation scene that Bluebeard stages in order to provoke his wife's curiosity about this particular knowledge, he shrewdly complicates the doubling they experience as mimetic rivals by edging her into a split position that differs from his. On the one hand, she is his partner— the custodian of his keys and nearly all of his possessions—and a party to his practice of keeping a secret, constrained to help him keep it from everyone else. On the other hand, since she knows of the secret without knowing it, since he denies her access to the tabooed little room and whatever he may be hiding there, she is also placed among those who have an interest in acquiring the knowledge from which they are excluded. She is caught within this structure of simultaneous inclusion and exclusion, a double bind insofar as she feels compelled both to penetrate into the forbidden room and to respect its privacy.[5]

The contradictory impulses to which Bluebeard has thus subjected his wife correspond to the reversible connotations of the word *key*. These are brought into view by the conjunction of permission—Bluebeard first gives his wife the set of keys she is allowed to use—and prohibition—he then gives her the key she is forbidden to use. In the first case, the key's import is determined by the function of unlocking, opening, making available, so that by metonymic extension the usable instrument stands for the power of appropriation or possession: the keys thus serve as a symbol of their holder's authority, of control over the belongings they make accessible. But in the second case, Bluebeard's prohibition situates the key as an implement that locks up, closes, seals away, so that by metonymic extension it signifies what is hidden, the missing link or veiled truth: here the little key that naturally functions as the proverbial symbol of knowledge, representing the pathway to an explanation or solution, also serves as the agent of concealment, representing the secret to be kept.[6] This uncanny double edge or duplicity is the basic semantic load that the little key assumes in the temptation scene, where the young newlywed immediately faces the opportunity to use it, not for protecting the secret but for uncovering it—as if the little key would have for her the possessive function of the other keys, and thus enable her to appropriate the hidden knowledge as power.

For the woman whose interest in making wealth and luxurious living available to herself and her family and friends has proved strong enough to overcome her revulsion for Bluebeard, the opportunity to use the little key is a further temptation, fills her with a new upsurge of desire. Although she hesitated for a moment at the door of the forbidden room, "la tentation était si forte qu'elle ne put la surmonter" (the temptation was so strong she could not overcome it; 259). Her yearning to know what is behind the locked door thus proves to be a match for her husband's determination to hold the power of a secret over her. Were she simply to obey Bluebeard's orders, to keep the promise by which she accepted his exclusive control over the chamber, she would allow him to link their nominal parity—attachment to each other through the possessions they share—to a deeper disparity—to an agreement denying her any part in belongings whose nature and value she can gauge only negatively, through his portentous threat: "Pour ce petit cabinet, je vous défends d'y entrer, et je vous le défends de telle sorte, que s'il vous arrive de l'ouvrir, il n'y a rien que vous ne deviez attendre de ma colère" (As for this little room, I forbid you to enter it, and my prohibition is such that if you happen to open it, there is nothing you should not expect from my anger; 258). In violating this emphatic prohibition, the wife is refusing to recognize an ultimate authority that the husband seeks to anchor in her ignorance of the chamber's contents. Thus knowledge—the desire to secure knowledge, which for him is to secrete it away and for her is to obtain it—is the key mode of the difference between these similar characters and the primary object of the wife's drive toward sameness.

Now the contents of the villain's private knowledge—the wives' mutilated bodies he stores in his vault—raise in themselves some significant questions about Bluebeard's character and motives. For the hidden cadavers are unmistakably signs of misdeeds—of earlier episodes of sadonarcissistic conduct toward victims of ensnarement—that society would surely punish if they were disclosed. Were he intent on making the fate of his previous wives a really impenetrable secret, he would obviously not keep them, but would seek to destroy all traces of them, and might try to trump up an acceptable account of their disappearances. So why does he prefer to run the risk of keeping them secretively?

In order to appreciate their status as objects that belong, evidently enough, among his treasured possessions, let us revert hypothetically to Bluebeard's first marriage. At that point, a presumably empty room meant that Bluebeard merely wanted his wife to believe he was keeping a secret from her, that there was really nothing substantive beneath his pretense, that he had nothing significant to hide from a wife. Thus the paradoxical core at the origin of his secret had to be its falseness or emptiness: the truth of the secret is that there is no secret. In these circumstances, the victim's ordeal was essentially a test of her obedience, while the perpetrator's experience—including, along with the frustration caused by her disobedience, his discovery of the perverse pleasures accessible to killers and undertakers—entailed compensating for his lack of a genuine secret by constituting one after the fact. For if Bluebeard's first wife confronted him, in the manner of a poker player calling the adversary's bluff, with the hollow pretense of his secret, with the embarrassing fact that he had nothing hidden away that she should be constrained to lack or ignore, he could not fail to recognize the risk inherent to authority based on deception. If only to spare himself the pain of being exposed as a sham, but also in order to maintain the upper hand in his marital game, he needed to anchor his prohibition in an authentic ground, to provide a real, consequential reason for declaring the little chamber off limits.

Hence the supposition that Bluebeard's fashioning of a genuine secret consisted in substituting for the nothingness of his feigned initial secret the corpse of the violated woman who had refused to ignore that nullity. There are at least two passages in the text of Perrault's narrative in which Bluebeard hints at the eery associative logic linking the woman's corpse to the emptiness of the original secret. The first of these is the warning he appends to his restated prohibition against entering the forbidden chamber: "S'il vous arrive de l'ouvrir, il n'y a rien que vous ne deviez attendre de ma colère" (If it happens that you open it, there is nothing you should not expect from my anger; 258). The violence ("colère") and total negation ("il n'y a rien que") evoked by this formula record Bluebeard's position on his wives' usurpation of his exclusive authority: the extreme punishment they incur literally inflicts on them the strangely unthinkable nothingness of the originally nonexistent secret that they violate and are then forced to embody; it deposits each victim's dead body in the empty room as the visible image, the tangible sign of the inaccessible nothingness—the inert reality, so to speak, of deadness, as opposed to the lived experience of death—that remains the core of the secret. The formula "il n'y a rien" is thus a positive, absolutist assertion, excluding every exception, that overrides the opposition of "all" to "nothing" with a sweeping "all *and* nothing," "all" finally dissolving into "nothing"; since the vengeance it promises embraces every extreme of violence, the "all" can include the positive state "nothingness" designated by "rien," can incorporate as its logically ultimate manifestation the negation of life.

In the second of these passages, Bluebeard informs the heroine of the fate she has brought onto herself by looking into the forbidden room. He marks the poetic justice of his death sentence in these terms: "Vous avez voulu entrer dans le cabinet! Hé bien, Madame, vous y entrerez, et irez prendre votre place auprès des Dames que vous y avez vues" (You wanted to enter the chamber! Very well, Madam, you will enter it and take your place beside the women you saw there; 260). Here the darkly ironic sense of Bluebeard's "prendre

votre place" points to the woman's own role in the constitution of
the forbidden sanctum as a sepulcher in which, as in the rest of their
house, she has elected—albeit in this unique case against the owner's
will—to stake her claim. Bluebeard's accusation bears no more upon
his wife's misdeed as such than upon the unrealized desire—"vous
avez *voulu* entrer dans le cabinet"—that he now aims to satisfy in a
manner that will make its object unmistakably her death. Prior to
this moment, the extreme force of negation conveyed by "il n'y a
rien" has been, moreover, the only indication of what awaits her in
the forbidden room, the only hint about its contents that Blue-
beard's temptation dangles before his wife. Since, at the door to the
crypt, the young woman "si pressée de sa curiosité" pauses, "son-
geant à la défense que son mari lui avait faite, et songeant qu'il
pourrait lui arriver quelque malheur d'avoir été désobéissante" (re-
flecting on the prohibition her husband had issued to her, and imag-
ining that some misfortune might result from being disobedient;
259), one must ask if her curiosity is not somehow expressly focused
on the warning's ominous specter of all-embracing negation.

In other words, does the *vouloir* Bluebeard has triggered in his
wife and now perceives at work in her not reflect an uncanny fas-
cination with the threat of annihilation that can be heard in his
forbidding warning? For the young woman who, unlike her sister,
was susceptible to being charmed by the alarming man with the
sinister blue beard, is peril not a lure? Is the temptation to see the
forbidden room not intensified precisely by the incentive of high
stakes, by the prospect of flirting with danger? Is she not subject
from the start not only to her acquisitive and self-protective in-
stincts, but also to the obscure attraction of a death drive? The sense
that she is caught up in multiple and irresistible impulses is made all
the more plausible by her response to the death sentence. No sooner
does Bluebeard enunciate his implacable "il faut mourir" than his
wife, who has been pleading for forgiveness, integrates the proposi-
tion into her suddenly compliant response: "Puisqu'il faut mourir,
répondit-elle, en le regardant les yeux baignés de larmes, donnez-
moi un peu de temps pour prier Dieu" (Since it is necessary to die,
she answered, looking at him with tearful eyes, give me a little time
to pray to God; 260). Assuming the imperative of her persecutor's "il
faut mourir," Perrault's heroine thus invites us to appreciate the
coexistence of her resignation with her equally apparent struggle to

survive. Her life-preserving effort to delay the execution coincides with her preparation for an encounter with death.

From Bluebeard's perspective, each of the wives he proceeds to entomb in the little chamber has chosen her fateful place, is satisfying a death wish his temptation has induced her to discover. The bodies can be kept there safely precisely because it is a space that he dominates absolutely, a space he submerges autocratically in the nothingness incarnated by the dead women. Far more vividly than an ordinary grave, the eery chamber within the household evokes the deeply personal, self-orienting value that living mortals mythically invest in their memorial relationship to the dead. Insofar as the headless cadavers are products of a premeditated exercise designed to reassure Bluebeard of his authoritative otherness vis-à-vis his feminine companion, they can at least serve him—perversely, but no less surely than would wifely obedience—as visible signs of the difference he deems vital to his own identity. Yet insofar as, lifeless, they cannot furnish him the active recognition he sought to secure from wifely obedience, his relation to them leads to the disappointment that rekindles his search for satisfaction through marriage. In effect, his experience replicates the frustration of the wolf who finally broke off his dialogue with Little Red Riding Hood and ate her up. To perceive an essential parallelism between the ogre figures of "Le Petit Chaperon rouge" and "La Barbe bleue," it suffices to connect the wolf's recourse to the substitute eroticism afforded by the eating of his victim to Bluebeard's apparent discovery and cultivation of sadistic and necrophilic pleasures in the execution of his wives. If, as Bluebeard's manifest concern with his castle suggests, its design and contents can be read as an image of the architect's self-construction, as a metaphoric structure corresponding to his own organic constitution, the placement of the dead women at its core—in the very bowels of that organism—is equivalent to their consumption and absorption, to their incorporation into his domain as constituents of his identity.[7]

Here, moreover, the Christianization introduced by Perrault is highly suggestive. Bluebeard the judge and executioner allows his wife a few minutes to pray, and as he raises the executioner's knife above her neck, saying "recommande-toi bien à Dieu (commend yourself to God), his posture borders on the sacerdotal. In conducting this mortuary ritual, he displays a complicity with his wife's religious sense of life that sheds a curiously ambivalent light on his burial practice. On the one hand, by burying the women in a tomb within his own domain, he accords them a place of funerary honor and intimacy appropriate for wives whose loss is mourned and whose protected remains position the crypt as a kind of reliquary, sacralized by their ritual inhumation. From this memorial angle, Bluebeard's practice would simply invert the symbolic connection, at the center of "La Belle au bois dormant," that makes the secret nuptial chamber where the princess lies for 100 years a euphemized sepulcher.[8] On the other hand, the macabre display of the cadavers hanging from the walls hardly conjures up either the Christian's reverential notion of the sacred that links it to divinity, holiness, and veneration, or the symbolism of a Christian burial that ties the handling of the dead to the conception of death as a passage from flesh to spirit. Instead, it infests the tomb with the darker connotation of the double-edged Latin root *sacer*, the more primitive and pagan sense of the sacred evocative of an ineffaceable stain, of accursed beings who provoke horror.[9] Bluebeard's performance of the ceremonies of execution and burial thus entails a mixing of Christian and pagan motifs. It is almost as if his necrophilia were fueled by a demonic logic of sacrilege, enacted in a profane sacrificial rite. The death required of his guilt-stained victims—"il faut mourir"—removes them from the human order and allows for their enshrinement as cherished objects. Yet its effect is not to rid the victim (or the humanity the victim might represent) of contamination, not to enable a spiritual relation with the divine, but rather to consummate—to consecrate by sadistic force—an abject relation of subjugation that Bluebeard effectively celebrates by forming and filling his crypt.

Yet the story devotes little attention to Bluebeard's direct relation to the skeletons that are hidden away. There is no suggestion, for example, that they serve their keeper as objects of pleasurable contemplation. Rather, his perverse pleasure apparently derives from a retributive fantasy, from imagining the shock that strikes his wife when she encounters the lifeless bodies grotesquely displayed in the little chamber. It is here, however, in his clear anticipation of her disobedience, of her (unheroic) inability to emerge unscathed from the trial to which his tempting interdiction summons her, that the logic of his secret starts to look devious. For the sharply delineated paradox is that Bluebeard expects his wife to see the room he has declared off-limits, to use the key he has declared unusable. In short, he means for her to unveil his secret and to have to reckon with it. To grasp what is at stake, then, in this studied yet mysterious practice of secrecy, it is necessary to probe further into the relations between husband and wife that his baleful wife-controlling schemes generate.

A Mirror of Difference

As we have seen, the narrative frames of "La Barbe bleue" allow the wife's discovery of her husband's secret to bring into focus their essential likeness: each appears as both criminal and victim, and their respective marital itineraries make each the mimetic rival of the other. Hence a classic instance of identity-in-difference, where simple identity to or with oneself is undermined because the very project of self-determined identity is caught up in a representational structure that forces the characters to apprehend themselves through their resemblances to each other. Now in the horror scene at the door of the crypt, the uncanny dual dynamics of doubling—as imitation, repetition, copying on the one hand, as duality, ambivalence, two-sidedness on the other—is further magnified by a remarkable process of mirroring. The text presents the discovery as follows: "D'abord elle ne vit rien, parce que les fenêtres étaient fermées; après quelques moments elle commença à voir que le plancher était tout couvert de sang caillé, et que dans ce sang se miraient les corps de plusieurs femmes mortes et attachées le long des murs" (At first she saw nothing, because the windows were closed; after a few moments she began to see that the floor was covered with caked blood, and that the bodies of several dead women attached to the walls were reflected in the blood; 259). Perrault thus makes this scene of revelation a drama of perception, focused on what the young woman can see, by the light she lets in by the open door, in and through the blood on the floor. In this compound sentence, the main verb of each independent clause is *voir*, and the emphasis falls squarely on its direct object, the blood-covered floor, first pointed out as such, then re-marked as a container of reflection ("*dans* ce sang se miraient") in which the livid images of the bodies on the walls appear to their stunned ("elle pensa mourir de peur"; she nearly died of fright) beholder.

Thus that body-reflecting blood is positioned as an intermediary between the frightened heroine and the corpses on the walls. In the mirror that it gradually forms as her eyes adapt to the shadowy light, she can hardly fail to grasp the link between herself and them: she, the present wife, belongs to this group made up of Bluebeard's mysteriously missing previous wives. Thus, beyond her apprehension of Bluebeard's maleficent identity, she has to see herself mixed in among the images reflected by the blood. Her discovery is a self-discovery, a self-identification, mediated by the shady mirror that reflects self and other—self with other—in a figural condensation of the process of identification that reveals the self in and as the other. The bruising effect of this self-recognition, in which the live victim is forced to identify with her dead predecessors, is to immerse her experience of identity and desire in anxiety, to relate them to the coming of her own death. This advent of anxiety and awareness of mortality sharply distinguishes Bluebeard's adult heroine from the wolf's innocent victim in "Le Petit Chaperon rouge." Whereas the innocent child, trapped by her maternal fixation in an excessive alterity, could not afford her suitor the recognition that he sought, the adult woman's shattering experience enables her to match Bluebeard's acute awareness of self and other, to confront him with an all too effective mirror of identification.

Even on first reading, then, the eery mirror behind the locked door is no ordinary speculum: it is literally a mirror stage, positioning the mirror as the floor, the very ground of identity, and merging it with the blood, the symbolic essence of familial relations. At the core of this specter of genealogical violence, the accumulated blood composes, in its darkish substance, a kind of monstrous collective identity in death for the women whose headless bodies remain separate, but whose life-draining hemorrhages have flowed together so as to mix and congeal their bloodlines into a gory mass, a kind of literal consanguinity. The medium of caked or clotted blood brings into play a substance, a sense of depth, density, precisely a coagulation, a driving-together (*co* + *agere*) or fusion of depth and surface; the transparent film on which the reflected images are seen also lets through the tincture of its strange, nonmetallic tain or backing. The reflecting clot is thus amorphous and tenebrous: it both reflects and absorbs light, reveals itself as well as the objects before it.

So the mirror on the floor cannot be imagined as a flat plate sending back an exact, limpid image of the bodily surfaces suspended above it. Although it is a murky and incongruous mixture, a viscid slab formed of dregs drained from beneath those suspended corporal surfaces, its images uncannily transmit the essence of the objects it reflects because it con*tains* them—because its lusterless tain is the inside of those feminine bodies now reflecting back the skeletal remains, coloring the mirrored surfaces with the shades of passion that the speculum of blood embodies, restoring to the perception of the image a spectral sense of the depth and viscosity that is invisible behind the glassy screen of a plate-glass mirror. The deposit of blood, then, functioning both as a reflector and as an opaque object heavily charged with symbolic meanings, is a double and transformative mirror: it reveals depth as well as surface, inside as well as outside, the covered(-up) as well as the covering, the lingering ruddiness symbolic of the life principle as well as the sickly pallor of death, so as to underlay the reflections it transmits with its own signifying effects as a substance. The blood, in short, is the double agent of the dual perception we have observed in the wife's experience of discovery. Indeed, it is the very epitome, the integrating medium, of the duality that repeatedly informs the process of revelation through reflection, a fluid process of doubling and redoubling in which surfaces and depths, selves and others, are unrelentingly recast as images or ramifications of one another.

Around this reflective process of revelation that discloses the work of duality—of doubling and difference—within the mechanisms of representation, "La Barbe bleue" constructs an elaborate spectacle. The revelatory effects of the discovery scene are quickly displaced into a still more complex configuration because a speck from the blood-mirror clings to the little key to the secret chamber. If this special, magical object functions as a kind of textual talisman, becomes the veritable key to the story, it is because much more than its commonplace value as a trope and symbol now comes into play. For while the little key plays its part as the object of the central exchange between Bluebeard and his wife, it becomes the bearer of the bloody reflection in the vault; it is then the mobile reflector that brings the stuff of the unveiled secret, the mirror of blood, out of the crypt into the visitable sphere of the castle. There the displaceable yet indelible bloodstain on the key, evidence of both the husband's and wife's transgressions, will lurk in stark contrast to the magnificent mirrors that are presented in the paragraph just before the scene of discovery as the very framework of luxury: "Des miroirs où l'on se voyait depuis les pieds jusqu'à la tête, et dont les bordures, les unes de glace, les autres d'argent et de vermeil doré, étaient les plus belles et les plus magnifiques qu'on eût jamais vues" (Mirrors in which one could see oneself from head to toe, and whose frames, some of glass and others of silver and gilded crimson, were the finest and most magnificent ever seen; 258–59). No doubt the captivating interest of these prized full-length mirrors, developed by Italian artisans and introduced into France during the seventeenth century, lies in their power to provide stable self-perception, to send back exact, luminous likenesses of the viewing subject that afford the individual a sense of autonomy, of self-control, of freedom from the riveting gaze of the other. The value of their mirror images is sealed, as it were, by the splendor of the singular, superlative frames.

Since the marital drama in Bluebeard's castle takes place against this majestic backdrop, its villainous owner appears to have reckoned with a choice equivalent to the one confronting the wolf at the end of "Le Petit Chaperon rouge." Whereas the ambiguous status of the reasoning beast in the prose fable makes for an alternative opposing autonomous self-satisfaction and disdain for the human other to a continual struggle for self-recognition mediated by the other, Bluebeard's human, intrasocial situation is already beyond that point, is one in which the ogre's choice has been made. Although he has the option—highlighted, as we have seen, in Perrault's early tale "Le Miroir, ou la métamorphose d'Orante"—of taking refuge in the narcissistic pleasures of self-contemplation, in a passive, purely scopic and wholly present relation to a faithfully reflected but otherwise unmediated corporal image, he is clearly not content with the form of private, anonymous recognition he can secure on his own in and from an image. Rather, as his pursuit of a new wife after each of his murders shows, within society he seeks, beyond imagination, durable and thus memorable identification— the recognition that only the active, fluid mirroring of the other, in visual and in lingual exchange, affords. His engagement with the symbolically charged mirror of blood bespeaks his immersion in the density of human relations and his irrevocable attachment to the work of memory.

A Spectacle of Troping: The Magic Key

The mysterious, ineradicable, reflective bloodspot greatly expands the little key's figurative capacity and sphere of action—of magical and magnetic action, "car la clef était Fée, et il n'y avait pas moyen de la nettoyer tout à fait" (for the key was a fairy, and there was no way to clean it completely; 259). After the blueness of Bluebeard's beard, this fairyness of the fairy-key is the only marvelous element in the tale, the only one that Perrault retained from the folklore version, in which there was a good fairy who aided the young wife by summoning the two brothers. Within the *Contes du temps passé*, ogres are consistently endowed with the properties of the *féerique* (*fée*, from L. *fatum*, evokes the magical, the marvelous, the fabulous, the enchanting, the demonic, the fateful). The fairy-key's role as the villain's agent links Bluebeard to the ogre figure who possesses fairy boots in " Le Petit Poucet" (no doubt the strange blue hue of his beard should also be construed as a sign of the fantastic, picking up on the connotation of the expression *conte bleu*[10]). If Bluebeard seems quite as eery and menacing as the ogre figures in "Le Petit Poucet," "Le Chat botté," and "La Belle au bois dormant," it is because their scariness derives not just from the supernatural powers of transformation they wield, but also from their almost entirely human appearance and their capacity to interact with others as "natural" human beings.

Similarly, Bluebeard's fairy-key initially has a perfectly ordinary, familiar appearance. As an instrument of the castle-owner's power, it seems to be distinguished from the other keys by its small size and unusability. Yet in the phrase that introduces the fairy motif—"car la clef était Fée, et il n'y avait pas moyen de la nettoyer tout à fait"—its special symbolic status suddenly receives a further and spectacular marking. The phrase slips into the tale a rare flare of poetic prose in which the assonant clusters (on ε / e) and the rhythm (pauses on clef/ Feé/fait) call attention to the assimilation of *clef* to *fée*, and within this linkage, to their common letter, *f*. It is as if the *f*, silent in the pronunciation of *clef*, yet positioned by the semantic equivalence as the pivot of the *clef-fée* articulation, were the inscription of a fairy effect that the word *clef* comes to bear as it attains, after ample preparation, the allure of a textual fetish.[11] Moreover, in the elaboration on the phrase asserting the key's magical essence, the assonance of *fée/fait* overlays the closing "nettoyer tout à *fait*" with a delicately double and perfectly complementary thrust. Insofar as *fait* denotes fact, "nettoyer tout à fait" is a literal pointing to fact that indicates the key's irreducibility to natural reality. Insofar as one also hears in *fait* an echo of *fée*, and thus an adverbial "à fée" (cf. "à fond"), "nettoyer tout à fait" points to the physical inaccessibility of the key's fairyness. The effect of this pairing by poetic association is to bring into collusion terms (*fée* and *fait*) that express the dissociation of the objective from the magical, of the natural fact from the supernatural effect. The thrust of that collusion—the key can be reduced neither to a natural nor to a supernatural object, but somehow retains both qualities, or gravitates between them, partaking of a duality comparable to that of the mirror on the floor of the crypt—is not merely to underscore the remarkable operational or articulatory power that the text manages to confer upon the key; it is also to make the key central to the understanding of Bluebeard's secret now that it has been, in a sense, unlocked.

When the blood comes forth on the little key, the dark mirror of violence steals into view as a dim, fleeting, but fatal reflection, taking the form of a taint or stain. Indeed, the marvelous property of the key is above all its tarnishability, its capacity to pick up and hold onto a spot from that sinister mirror stage which darkens and densifies and deadens the image it transmits. Attaching a speck of the reflective blood to itself as a mobile blot—the ineradicable blood, although surrounded by metal, thus remains unfixed, irreducible, resistant to framing and polishing—the magnetic key serves in turn to figure, on its own hard surface, the tarnishing of the lustrous luxury of Bluebeard's world. The lifeless blood extracted from the crypt is a sign that brings back into the open the suppressed yet ineradicable presence of violence and death—a constant that Bluebeard will soon underscore by enunciating, in response to his wife's guilt, the hauntingly impersonal and oracular universal, "il faut mourir." The tarnished key re-presents the evidence of the castle's deadly metaphysical underground to a civilized society devoted to the dissimulation of violence and insouciance toward death. Although belonging to the world of splendor that Bluebeard's castle represents, the little key thus interferes with that world's repression of its anchorage in destructive impulses, confronts it with its dependency on controlling them. In its form and its relation to the metallic surface, the recalcitrant stain incarnates—like the blue beard in relation to Bluebeard's appearance as an "honnête homme"—a kind of rift or dissension or heterogeneity; the dark blot stands out as an uncontrollable excess, a contaminant, an alien, amorphous graft that needs, as the frantic wife realizes, to be removed. In its intractability, the furtive, mysterious, yet tenacious taint at once discloses the lapsed status of Bluebeard's secret and prevents his wife from keeping her own transgression secret.

With calculated alacrity, Perrault's text focuses on the mode of revelation that the bloodspeck forces into play: "quand on ôtait le sang d'un côté, il revenait de l'autre" (when the blood was removed from one side, it returned on the other; 259). This return of the same ("le sang . . . revenait") on the other side poignantly inscribes on the magic key the perpetual immersion of "La Barbe bleue" in duality and its users' entrenchment in the inescapable play of otherness that was first figured in the blood on the floor. Indeed, it is as if the key itself has become the milieu of a perverse process of "dismirroring," whereby the stain is reproduced on one side, then the other, in a back-and-forth movement that substitutes for a one-to-one correspondence between like sides a zero-to-one correspondence between the image on one side and its negation on the other. Because this figuring of an ongoing disfiguring is carried out by the mobile speck, it confronts the viewer not only with a reflection of self with and as the other, but also with the inevitable and perpetual displacement of that reflection, with an alterity adrift in a milieu of alternation. It thus makes a shambles of the very possibility of personal identity, disabling not only the identification of self to self, but that of self to other as well. In its tireless reversibility, this figurative process that the fearful wife discovers at work on the surface of the key mimics the turning movement of a key in the hole of a lock, the shifting between opening and closing that turns the key into a trope—a kind of reciprocating metonym—of duality, of *ambiva*-lence, of unsettled meaning. Indeed, her repeated turning of the key from one side, wiped spotless, to the other, restained, figures the very movement of troping insofar as a trope results from the twist or turn of a word or image away from its basic or literal meaning—the *key* as an implement for opening or closing locks—into other, associated or figural meanings—the *key* as knowledge, cipher, pathway, secret, code, musical tonality, and so forth.[12]

An Economy of Dominance: Knowledge as Power

The fairy-key, then, has a representational capacity that enables it to do more than evidence the frightful link between the forbidden room and the rest of the castle. It unveils the substance of that link in its unmanageability, in its essential, untamable otherness, even as it functions in the familiar symbolic role of the key of knowledge—the key to the special privilege-preserving knowledge Bluebeard had reserved for himself while permitting his wife to explore and use everything else in his castle. Moreover, because Bluebeard exchanges his full set of keys with his wife in return for a promise upon his departure and retrieves them upon his return, the keys take on a central intermediary function and value in the husband-wife relationship. The economic overtones of the exchange are evident from the outset. For the wife, the keys are the instruments that make Bluebeard's wealth available for her own use; for the couple, they provide, essentially, for the control and safeguarding of their shared wealth. The terms on which the keys change hands—his orders, her promise—constitute a kind of primitive contract. It grants the wife the use of the keys to her husband's usable, negotiable riches in return for her nonuse of the special key, the one securing access to the forbidden vault where Bluebeard's private reserves are, as it were, held in maximum security. No doubt the circumstances—his departure on the alleged business trip and especially his account of the various keys' functions—prompt the young woman to suppose that the contents of the little room must be his most precious treasure.

The function of reserves in a monetary system is to constitute a standard measure of value that serves as the basis and guarantee for minted, expendable currency; the latter, in turn, provides a ready yardstick in an everyday context for determining the value of the marketable assets that cumulatively constitute visible wealth. The reserves are then the ultimate treasure to which the other assets are tied, and while their status requires that they be protected at all costs, it is also necessary that their existence and authenticity be reliably verified. Now if the proprietary economy of Bluebeard's household is similarly anchored in a primary treasure that must be held in reserve, it is nonetheless at odds with the logic that secures the operation of a system of exchange for multiple users. The immediate problem lies not with the ghastly nature of the treasured reserves—rather than gold, silver, and jewels, which Bluebeard explicitly places at his wife's disposal, they consist of human remains—but with their secret status. As long as the contents of the forbidden room are unknown, one can wonder what they are, what they are worth, or even whether the vault might be empty; thus the basis for confidence and cooperation on the part of other members of the household is subject to doubt, and the wife's wish to see the room seems all the more understandable.

For his marriage partner, the force of Bluebeard's edict that places the (key to the) forbidden room under taboo is to make her respect for his authority contingent upon her willingness to live with the unknown, to make her submission a practice of resisting her desire to know. Their relationship is therefore essentially identical, in its structure, to the one that Yahweh established with Adam (before the creation of Eve) in ordering him to refrain from eating the fruit produced by the tree of knowledge of good and evil in the Garden of Eden.[13] In the case of the biblical prototype, the holder of authority also reserves for himself a superiority that depends on knowledge from which others are expressly excluded. Although this knowledge lies readily accessible in the abode where God communes with man, failure on man's part to respect Yahweh's secretive stance would amount not simply to rebelling against divine rule but, according to Genesis 3:22, to making himself equal to God. The punishment with which Yahweh threatened Adam upon enunciating his prohibition was death (Gen. 2:16). After determining what had happened when Adam and Eve succumbed to the serpent's temptation, he actually applied a lesser penalty—banishment from Eden—that nonetheless ultimately entailed death. For the purpose of exiling man from paradise was to deny him absolutely the opportunity to eat of the tree of life and thereby to be like God not only through a knowledge of good and evil but through immortality. In the story of the temptation and fall of man, then, authority based on knowledge and the collapse of that authority are linked forcefully to the menace of death and the condition of mortality. In "La Barbe bleue," where using the key to forbidden knowledge is equivalent to eating the fruit of forbidden knowledge, it is likewise the linkage of knowledge with death that proves to be fundamentally at stake.

When the little key—used, tarnished, diminished in value—is returned to Bluebeard, the dialogue immediately foregrounds the operation of the knowledge factor in the husband-wife relation: "Pourquoi y a-t-il du sang sur cette clef?—Je n'en sais rien, répondit la pauvre femme, plus pâle que la mort.—Vous n'en savez rien, reprit la Barbe bleue, je la sais bien, moi; vous avez voulu entrer dans le cabinet!" (Why is there blood on this key? I know nothing about it, answered the poor woman, paler than death. You know nothing, responded Bluebeard, but I myself know perfectly well; you wanted to enter the little room!; 260; my italics). In its most evident sense, this exchange seems to entail Bluebeard's dismissal of a puerile denial and his assertion that the young woman really knows that the key is bloodspotted because she tried to enter the chamber. With the key back in hand, he has momentarily recovered his superiority over his wife, but its basis has shifted: the key, instead of standing for his knowledge of the secret, now enables Bluebeard to recognize her knowledge, allows him to correct her denial and express his anger. The bloodspot that divulges her transgression to him is a signifier no less inculpatory than the fig leaves that Adam and Eve put on to hide the nudity their fall into knowledge has revealed to them. Understanding that the knowledge his wife has acquired cannot be repossessed, he is obliged, as Yahweh was, to deal with the problem of the shared secret: how to reinstate his mastery now that he no longer monopolizes the knowledge on which it rested.

To appreciate Bluebeard's unstinting decisiveness in this confrontation, it suffices to consider whether the key that informs him of his wife's misdeed does not embody a continuing superiority that he can hold over her in the domain of knowledge. In the long run, has his authority not been just a matter of degree, of the relatively modest advantage he preserves by retaining only one special privilege while sharing the rest of his domain with his wife? Could the master not then hold or recover the upper hand over his vassal or pupil by demonstrating his greater knowledge and insight? This question is raised by a closer, less obvious, but equally plausible reading of this exchange that assumes the entrapped wife has nothing to gain by lying. In this case, her "je n'en sais rien" would mean simply that she does not know why the blood sticks to the key. In response, Bluebeard would be acknowledging her lack of understanding when he answers "vous n'en savez rien, je le sais bien"; he would be granting that, for want of having entered the tomb, of having fully embodied her mortality, she has not yet attained the knowledge that she was seeking and that he now intends to give her. Whether Bluebeard is agreeing or disagreeing with her, it would be possible for each of them to infer that his knowledge derives from an inalterably privileged relation to the bloodmarked key, that his understanding would thus remain superior since he benefits from the key's supernatural assistance.

Why, then, as he goes on to imply forthwith in his implacable declaration of her fate, must he reconstitute the contents of the little chamber as his authoritative knowledge? Is his exclusive possession of the power anchored in that particular body of knowledge absolutely urgent, a matter of life and death? The basis on which this latter judgment takes precedence has nothing to do with the dimension of the marvelous (to which, after the phrase "la clef était Fée," the tale makes no further explanatory appeal). Rather, it has to do with the economy of exchange or interchange that inhabits the couple's relationship once the wife acts on her desire to know and acquires knowledge of his secret. If one sets aside strategic considerations (such as the threat of denunciation), the supplemental knowledge afforded to Bluebeard by the tainted key cannot give him a lasting advantage because of what it reveals to him about the two of them. Owing to the mutual insight that enables each party to the exchange to decipher the bloodmark on the key as evidence incriminating both her/himself and the other, his knowledge of her knowledge will quickly be matched by her knowledge of his knowledge. For both, the blood endows the key with a mirror effect duplicating that of the little room's floor, but also extending it dramatically, since each character sees the double-mirror while the two of them, in flesh and blood, are facing one another.

In that face-off, the magic key thus becomes the agent of identification that retriggers the recognition of an alarming resemblance. The doubling of husband by wife and wife by husband reemerges as the structuring principle of a veritable identity exchange: the wife giving back the key to the husband returns to him his identity, which she has taken on, along/aligned with her own, of which his now bears the mark, symbolically attached to the little key in which his authority is invested. In the sphere of (self-)knowledge, this process of re-semblance—doubling and mirroring that draw separate identities back into a fateful likeness, a dominant similitude—is threatening to the individual precisely because it is a great equalizer. Allowing for no higher perspective, no secure "meta-knowledge," it compromises or submerges the very difference in identity—here the mark distinguishing husband from wife—that would justify a hierarchic relationship between them. Having observed the collapse of his attempt to anchor authority in secret knowledge, Bluebeard understands that any further attempt to gain respect for a secret would only provoke his wife to discover it and, by her knowledge, to undermine its significance. Here again the position of Yahweh vis-à-vis Adam and Eve offers an instructive analogy. By creating man in his own image (Gen. 1:26–27) and as his interlocutor, Yahweh instituted the possibility of rivalry between himself and humans seeking to assert, as did Adam and Eve, their godlikeness. Confronted with their violation of his trust, he was still able to impose a definitive differentiation between himself and them: expelling them from his garden, he condemned them to an arduous life of cultivating the earth into which they would, as mortals, return. Moreover, in the biblical scenario of the fall of man, it is doubtless significant that human mortality and woman's subjection seem to go hand in hand. For in suppressing the rivalry of the human with the divine, Yahweh set the stage for its resurgence between man and woman by decreeing as one of the wife's particular punishments that she would henceforth be subordinate to her husband (Gen. 3:16).

Bluebeard's problem, then, is analogous to Yahweh's, in the sense that he is threatened by his wife's ascent into likeness and equality. His solution has to be different, however, precisely because, as a mortal ensconced in human society, he lacks the resources of a god; he can neither retreat into a unique attribute that his wife lacks nor resort to banishing her from his domain. To restore the regimen of inequality, he has but one secure option, the retributive position enunciated by Yahweh with respect to the fruits of knowledge: "the day when you partake of them, you will surely die" (Gen. 2:17). So Bluebeard's instant move from verdict to death sentence is entirely consequential: to hold power based on privileged knowledge, he must deny that knowledge once and for all to his rival; to reestablish his authority when she overturns the denial, he has no recourse other than to reimpose not-knowing on her. That he can do only by killing her.

Instrumental Power: The Phallic Keys

In tying his authority to the edict he enunciates concerning the little key to the forbidden chamber, Bluebeard confers upon the instrument his wife uses in violating his law the capacity to symbolize both his secret knowledge and his marital power. In taking back the tainted key and articulating the mortal significance of the spot it bears, he is simply respecifying the object of the knowledge he has forced upon his wife by inducing her to use the little key: his fatal physical power over his wives. As an agent and image of that power, like the cutlass that replaces it as Bluebeard's instrument in the ensuing execution scene, the key is then, just as obviously as it is a conventional symbol of knowledge, a phallic symbol. It is important to understand, after Freud, that the little object's phallic function does not derive unproblematically from some crude universal symbolism. If Freud imputes a typical meaning to certain symbols in dreams,[14] that hardly forces us to take every example of a key that opens a door into a dark room as a fetishized emblem of male sexuality, representing a penis breaking its way into a taboo-protected vagina. Rather, the phallic position of the key in Bluebeard's universe depends on its role in structuring the relation between him and his wife, on its power to signify the one difference that persists between the two doubles when the key is returned: the same difference between the sexes, underscored by the two *moralités* of "La Barbe bleue," that is so blatantly brought to the fore in "Le Petit Chaperon rouge."[15] As in "Le Petit Chaperon rouge," moreover, the gruesome end that Bluebeard seeks to impose on the male-female confrontation evokes an explosion of phallocratic force precisely because the scenario of violent incorporation begins with decapitation, that is, with a symbolic equivalent of castration.

To appreciate the role of the bloodspot on the little key in triggering the drama of castration, the mobile stain on the phallic object must be seen not merely as a sign of wifely guilt, but also as a vital symbol of the feminine. Luce Irigaray, in *Speculum de l'autre femme*, offers an account of the value of woman's blood that both illuminates from an immediately apposite angle the phallic function of the key and clarifies what is at stake in its re-presentation of the bloody mirror. In order to account for the status of red blood as a positive and defining value for woman, Irigaray traces the suppression of its "prehistoric" priority, its productive, profitable status, to its displacement, under the patriarchal order, by other values, such as money, the child, and the penis, that are equivalences of excrement in an anal economy. But the dislodging of blood from its place as a primary value is, to be sure, far from an eradication; rather, it ushers in the conditions under which blood can function, as it does in "La Barbe bleue," as an ambiguous value, a polyvalent sign. Once the primitive value of blood has been repressed, blood has an augmented capacity to stand *symbolically* for maternal power, and it plays as well a crucial role "in the sadistic and masochistic fantasies and practices that underlie the erotic pleasure of almost every 'subject.' [The man] will (re)discover pleasure only by (re)opening—if only imaginarily—the vein of blood. Red blood. Only by (re)starting the bloodshed. Of the mother. Wife, virgin. Of this proscribed taste, sacred and impure, vicious, the expression will occur only in the secrets of bedchambers, only in phantasmatic productions that are painfully confessed."[16] Otherwise, bloodshed is the object of a taboo that works to suppress woman because she is, says Irigaray, the "reserve" or repository, the secret holder of the blood-value who recognizes its worth only in pain and humiliation, in defeat at the hands of the family head.[17]

In a later and crucial chapter of *Speculum* on Hegel, Irigaray is able to take her account of femininity as the "guardian of the link to blood" further, to relate the repression of the blood-value to the masculine regimen of optics—co-optics—and specularity. The chapter opens with an astounding epigraph from Hegel, in which the anatomic distinction of man, the active invaginator, from woman, the passive recipient, turns on the role of blood.[18] Whereas blood flows strongly, productively, in man, swelling and hardening up the mesh of spongy tissue around the urethra, it is wasted away in woman in the shameful outflows of menstruation. This difference is quickly modulated into the most traditional of dichotomies, positioning man—the "active principle"—as the unified subject and woman—the "passive principle"—as the material element. Instead of attacking this account head on, Irigaray proceeds to rework her way through the opening pages of section 6, "Spirit," in the *Phenomenology of the Spirit*, where Hegel puts less stress on the relation of husband to wife than on that of brother to sister. Far more insistently than Hegel, who invokes Sophocles's *Antigone* in passing, Irigaray makes much of the relation of Antigone to one of her brothers, Polyneices, whom she buried in spite of Creon's prohibition. In its ideal form, the brother-sister relation—devoid of rape, murder, bodily injury, bloodshed, disruption by desire—would also be pre-patriarchal, would balance the ethics of matriarchy and patriarchy in a peaceful coexistence. The maternal/material value of red blood would be aligned with the sublated or sublimated sense of blood as consanguinity, as the essence of family bonds—bloodlines—expressed in the process of naming, in the genealogical priority of the name-of-the-father.

But under the patriarchal vision informing Hegel's account of this relation, the equilibrium is already lost: the noble Antigone who recognizes herself in her brother and buries him in the wake of a bloody internecine battle has already "digested the masculine";[19] she has taken the place of the *"living mirror"* vis-à-vis her dead brother so as to provide for him, though not for herself, the "harmonious (con)fusion in each other of the red blood and of the *semblant.*" Antigone thus combines the real, material, red blood valued by woman and the figurative blood or semblance (homonymically *semblant* = *sang blanc*, white or clear blood, such as the male's white semen or the clear lymphic fluid of vision) that counts for the man of the family. Thus Antigone, despite all that is admirable in her at once virile and tender commitment to her brother's identity in death, can eventually be seen, from a Hegelian standpoint, in a position of feminine submission, and her role in Sophocles's play comes to resonate with the leitmotifs of the first section of *Speculum,* where Irigaray deconstructs the oppressive operation of a specular economy in Freud's account of femininity.

In the relation of woman to man, the dominant register is that of sameness, of the Same, which overrides whatever real sexual differences might distinguish them with, precisely, the engulfing sweep of semblance or resemblance, making woman man's likeness, less-than-fully man, but man enough, like enough to him, to serve him reassuringly as a mirror of himself, to support the narcissistic constructs he employs to fend off the death instinct:

For this [male] ego to have value, there has to be a "mirror" to assure, to reassure it of its validity. Woman will ground this specular doubling, sending back to man "his" image, repeating him as the "same." The intervention of an image that is "other," of a mirror that is "other," always entails the risk of a deadly crisis. Woman will then embody the same—except for an inversion—since, as mother, she will allow the repetition of the same, with disregard for her difference. Sexual difference. Moreover, with "penis envy" she will compensate for whatever, in this specula(riza)tion, might fall short. Conjuring up, again as always, that *remainder* which dissolves in mirrors, that sexual energy necessary for the elaboration of the work. Of death.[20]

This passage is but one of many in *Speculum* that expose Freud's use of castration to structure a certain differential relation—positioning woman as simply the contrary or inverse or specular opposite of man—within the same. For the restricted analytic purpose of piecing together an interpretative frame, it is doubtless legitimate to delineate the kind of supplementarity Irigaray unearths, after Derrida, as follows: woman is like man except for her lack of a penis; but lacking a penis, she both desires (to have) one and covers up her lack of one; thus, by desire and by semblance or sham, she compensates or supplies for her lack; and doing so, she is all the more like man, since, via the castration complex, she takes on his relation to the (phallocratic) origin, and since, via the penis envy set off by her "actual castration," she aligns herself with his (phallic) desire. "This 'realized castration,' that Freud ascribes to 'nature,' to 'anatomy,' could also, or rather, be interpreted as making it impossible, prohibited for woman . . . to imagine, to figure (for herself), to represent (for herself), to symbolize, etc. (none of these terms is adequate since all are borrowed from a discourse that complies with this impossibility, this prohibition), her relation to the beginning."[21] For the little girl, to assume the castration that makes her the "opposite" of the little boy is to accept the defining status of the child's relation to the father; it is to give up the daughter's initial relation of desire for the mother and to install herself, like the little boy, in an Oedipal complex; it is to situate the father, with his penis, at the origin (where the sublatable image/value of the penis as the inseminating initiator in the reproductive process will thus take precedence over its pleasure-producing function) and as the object of her desire (which in due course will become a desire to absorb from man the male organ woman misses, thus a desire she can satisfy only through seduction, only by making herself an attractive object for man the subject).

This selective glimpse of Irigaray's analysis of the Freudian line on womanhood suffices to bring out an essential if familiar point about the phallus, insofar as the phallic structure subtends and subsumes the penis and other figurations of masculine desire/power rather than simply deriving from it/them. For, as Irigaray says bluntly of the phallus, "it would not attain its status as the privileged signifier of the penis, or even of power or erotic pleasure, were it not interpreted as the *appropriation of the relation to the origin, of the desire (of) origin*."[22] What, then, forms this relation—a relation of desire— to the origin that the key signifier "appropriates"? On this score, at least, Irigaray has to agree with Lacan about the core of the Freudian account:[23] there is but one ruling desire, only one commanding relation to the origin, the one that first emerges in the man's relation of desire to the/his mother. During the phallic phase, both the girl and the boy, having discovered the "fact" of woman's castration, buy definitively into the univocal order of desire that is structured by his capacity to "give" her the missing phallus (whether literally, as the penis, or symbolically, as a child). In subsequent phases of development, that one-way transfer—man giving his masculine desire/ pleasure to the woman—will be the underlying model articulating all the forms that sexual relations may take. Preeminently, to be sure, these will be the simple relations formative of the Oedipal triangle: the father-subject giving the child to the mother-object, and so forth.

In all the possible variants of this family-romance structure, male superiority is assured, since the man gives the phallus without giving it up, grants use or a share, but not control or full possession. Because the object that supplies (makes up) for the woman's lack remains his, it is also for her, continually, what supplies (makes) the lack, by remaining what cannot be hers. In this self-sustaining operation, supply both meets and makes demand; giving the phallus takes it away; repairing castration restores it. Thus, by the now quite familiar logic of supplementarity, the "fact of castration" is converted into the economic principle—continuing castration, recastration— that governs the relation between the sexes: the gift of the phallus compensates for the lack, or satisfies the desire, only at the price of reinforcing it, of placing woman at the mercy of the supplier, of subjecting her to man's willingness to repeat or sustain his gift.

As a privileged signifier, an instrument of appropriation, the phallus settles that structure of castrational supplementarity into a generative position in discourse. In Lacan's account, it is the under- cover agent—"it can play its role only when veiled"—that makes masculine desire the law of language.[24] It is the lingual/figural back- ground behind all those signifiers—phallic "symbols"—that, while

taking shape through the metaphorical formations of penis-equiva-
lence, repeat metonymically the predominant relation to the origin
that inhabits all expressions of sexual desire. As such, the phallus
inscribes cryptographically, as it were, the clandestine hold of the
masculine order—of the patriarchal, the Oedipal, the paternal, the
patrilineal—on discourse itself. The appropriation it effects—that is,
the process of integrating, making proper, appropriate, normal—
corresponds, in terms of psychological development, to that mo-
ment when the little girl assumes once and for all the feminine
position of castrated object in the founding relation with the father-
subject; no doubt it harks back as well to that mytho-historical
scenario, evoked by Irigaray in regard to *Antigone*, wherein the shift
from matriarchy to patriarchy occasioned woman's loss of the pos-
sibility of being the desiring subject in the marital relation and
holding the dominant position in the genealogical order. The ap-
propriation carried out by the phallus would be, in short, the veiled
implantation of the father's determining position in language, and
the phallic back- or underground would thus secure the discursive
terrain for the overt operations of the name-of-the-father.

To interpret Bluebeard's magic key as a conventional phallic
symbol is initially to recognize that it supports his demonic exercise
of power over his wife and unleashes the acting-out of a scene of
perverse pleasure. But to grasp the full extent of the little key's role
in this phallocratic operation, it is necessary to describe its shifting
within the structure of castrational supplementarity. In the ex-
change of keys between the two rivals that culminates in their con-
frontational crisis, the entire set of keys handed over and back ap-
pears to have a phallic function. Bluebeard, in giving his keys to his
wife, puts her in touch with what she lacks (knowledge, power,
wealth, pleasure, subjectivity, relation to the origin, and so forth),
but hardly in order to overcome her deficiency once and for all with
wholeness and self-sufficiency. His aim in giving them is eventually
to take them back, so as to reposition her opposite him, endowed
with his desires, but on the side of the lack—a lack she must feel all
the more acutely as *dis*satisfaction since, having been the custodian
of the keys, having held and used the phallus, she has experienced
the possessive power and pleasure it affords her husband and grasped
what it means to be in his position. She has, in sum, realized her
likeness to him. Thus for her, his double, the gift at once satisfies and

dissatisfies: it meets and reinforces her need to be like him; it fulfills and rekindles her wish to have what he has, consolidating her adoption of his desire so as to shape and nourish their mimetic rivalry. From this position of difference (her deficiency) in sameness (their shared desire), the very lack that constitutes her difference from him also plays the pivotal role of reinforcing her resemblance to him. Its dual role is thus exactly what makes it possible for her to be his mirror-object. Insofar as holding the keys to his knowledge and power makes her like him, she mirrors him; he can see himself in her. Yet insofar as his repossession of the keys shows that she is still unlike—or only *like*, only a reflection of—him, she is still a lesser, castrated object; her role in returning the keys is to reveal his wholeness and autonomy to him, the viewing subject. Had she complied with Bluebeard's order, upon returning the keys she would simply have settled into the classic position of the dependent wife/subservient woman. For Bluebeard, by contrast, her obedience would have consolidated a process of (self-) representation within which the keys serve as indices of man's control over the visible or inspectible, of his right to determine what will be open to view. Phallic, the keys are signs of man's scopic and specular dominance.

The Protophallic Symbol

But the itinerary of the magic key complicates the smooth consolidation of the recastration scenario. Within the exchange structure, the little key has the same phallic position and function as the other keys to the extent that it, too, must be returned and will represent man's ascendancy in the marital relation. Yet at the same time, it stands out among them because it is the object of a prohibition on use—which is to say that it cannot be a supplement in the *us*ual sense since it is expressly not supposed to fill in or supply for a lack, but primarily, even as it is held by its recipient, to impose and represent an insuperable lack. Bluebeard emphasizes the aggressive, privative role he ascribes to this singular phallus when, in the portentous warning we have previously underscored, he invokes the consequences of using the little key to gain entry into the forbidden chamber: "Je vous le défends de telle sorte que, s'il vous arrive de l'ouvrir, il n'y a rien que vous ne deviez attendre de ma colère." Forced upon the woman but unusable for her, thus serving only to confront her with an irreparable difference, to instill a lack, to deny her definitively access to a secret reserved for man, compelling her then both to safeguard the phallus as what she must lack and to accept along with it the impossibility of achieving sameness or full equality with man by taking it—him—in or on, the mini-phallus would then have for its recipient a single, predominant sense: it would reenact and openly represent her inaugural castration, "factual," irreversible, and insurmountable, a given of the phallogocentric male-female relation. As such, it would put in place the need for substitute phalli—for the other keys that are like it but cannot be it, that can serve as surrogates enabling her to take on and satisfy many of man's desires, but not to have his desire fully as her own.

Within the structure of castrational supplementarity, this founding castration holds a logically primary position comparable to that of the child's model-forming discovery of woman's castration in the phallic phase. In other words, the bond between the originating constraint of castration and the form it prescribes for future male-female relations parallels the link between the magic key and the other keys in Perrault's tale. In the first place, the transfer of the unusable key fixes in place the castrated position that woman has to accept, forcing upon her a wish she cannot fulfill. It thus figures in its aggressive form—as a motivated exercise, and therefore not as a mere "fact" of nature—man's appropriative "gift" to woman of castration itself: the gift of the phallus in the form of a lack. In the second place, the gift of the usable, supplemental keys will furnish the recipient a certain compensation for the deficiency imposed on her by castration. So the other phallic gifts, which are offered as substitutes for the original one, not only repeat but also make up for the denial of the phallus; they provide their supplement along with the lack, articulating the phallic order as one of substitution in which women are allowed an always only partial and derivative experience of the possession and pleasure that, for men, are full and original.

The language of Bluebeard's interdiction provides a telling illustration of the process by which the man's phallic gift relegates the feminine subject to a lesser, "castrated"—that is, deprived, deficient, inadequate, envious—position in their relationship. The insinuatory veer of his temptational imperative is made especially poignant by the curious form of the subordinate clause, "s'il vous arrive de l'ouvrir." This phrase punctuates the act of illocution with a reference to the future circumstance in which he will temporarily be unable to prevent his wife from doing as she pleases. In introducing the expansive version of his prohibition with the vague modulatory turn "de telle sorte que," Bluebeard seems to be groping for a way to express his vacillation between two images of woman, obedient and disobedient: the former is qualified to share some, though not all, of the male subject's traits, whereas the latter is thoroughly disqualified. The conditional phrase "s'il vous arrive" brings the possibility of noncompliance into play, muddling what was initially a straightforward relation of authority, stated in the form of a simple imperative ("je vous défends d'y entrer").

Once the shift to third-person discourse intervenes, the wife is no longer treated simply as the interlocutor to whom the order is addressed by the speaker and of whom the speech situation demands her ensuing promise of obedience. The "vous" of "s'il vous arrive" confronts her with an alternative representation of herself: no longer a subject who can act to keep her promise, she is reduced by her husband's verbal aggression to the position of a passive object. Instead of imagining her carrying out the act of door-opening, Bluebeard envisages the transgression of his edict as an event just happening to her unwittingly, as it were, by dint of fateful forces beyond her control. Thus his order, pointedly recast so as to stress the immersion of his speech in willful action, institutes a demoralizing relation between husband and wife in which her position is already wavering and contradictory. If he starts by granting her rights ("ouvrez tout, allez partout") and responsibility ("mais pour ce petit cabinet je vous défends d'y entrer") in return for resisting just one vital impulse among the various desires she has taken from him, he must accord her a moral and psychological capacity for obedience. But in the same breath, he qualifies his proscriptive terms so that they project a scenario in which the interdiction supposes, perhaps even determines ("je vous le défends de telle sorte que"), her lack of competence for such a role, denies her the place and will of a decision-making subject. Moreover, his intent to monopolize that role in their relationship is reaffirmed by the warning itself, which depicts her in the passive state of waiting for his response.

Although the little key is associated with the secrecy that the lock is supposed to protect, its role and work are patent: insofar as its

owner's threat invests it with a positive and ongoing significance, it is
not assimilable to the (always veiled and latent) Lacanian phallus. An
inescapably visible symbol, it functions as an overt, continuing pres-
ence, an iterable origination that accompanies and recurs within the
substitutive relations it spawns; thus it might well be imagined as a
kind of protophallus, as the negative condition that predetermines
the function and meaning of its surrogates: in relation to its priority,
they have to be interpreted reductively, as the woman's less than
satisfactory alternatives to the self-possessive phallicity it reserves for
man. The protophallus is, as it were, the lever holding up the phal-
locratic operation: the absolute prohibition on the use of the little
key makes it possible—should make it safe, and also worth his
while—for Bluebeard to offer his wife the use of his other keys, to
allow her a relative grip on the phallic surrogates. No doubt this
security results in part from a logic of last resort that Bluebeard
himself apparently relishes: if, in the end, his law is transgressed, he
can always fall back on violent force, revert to brandishing the lethal
instrument of castration he uses in beheading his wives. But were
the little key to make her subservient in accord with his apparent
intent, the security would result from the normalized operation of
castrational supplementarity, from her consensual use of the other
keys. This obedience would repeatedly reestablish and make bear-
able the dominance of the castrating relationship. To stabilize the
marital relationship it would suffice, and be necessary, to make the
give-and-take emblematized by the exchange of keys a continuing
operation.

The decisively foregrounded symbolic role of the magic key in
"La Barbe bleue" thus beckons toward the possibility of elucidating
the project of the tale's sadistic hero by grasping what undermines
his attempt to set up a marital/sexual economy—a would-be phal-
lotocracy—with the exchange of keys. Now, as we have seen, the
operation designed to ensure male dominance in a marital relation is
short-circuited when the young wife uses the unusable key. Treating
the protophallic key as if it were one of the usable phallic keys
amounts to disregarding its commanding status and wagering that
she can erase the difference between it and the other keys. Using it,
however, occasions the discovery of her inability to hold onto it: the
phallus that escapes her usurpative grasp and falls to the floor is the
decisive sign of her loss of (self)-control, and her futile attempts to

clean its surface are a further sign of her inability to use it possessively, to make it her own. Still more significantly, the little key,
once tainted by its fall into the blood, will in turn, true to its role as
the agent of doubling, also come to be a sign for Bluebeard of his loss
of (self-)control, since it conveys the violability not only of (the
dead) women, but also of his instigatory instrument, of the phallic
order itself. Thus the bloodstain picked up by the key does not
merely re-mark the opposition the young woman chose not to
respect as an indelible difference—between the protophallus and its
surrogates, between husband and wife. It also magnifies the load of
meaning put on the little key, so as to make the protophallic signifier
something more and other than just a critical phallic symbol that
would assure man of his stable identity.

When Bluebeard, together with the wife who is returning the
little key to him, examines the surface of the symbolically supercharged phallus and sees there a trace of the reflecting surface it
brings back from the floor of the crypt into the living space of his
castle, what is figured for him? The mobile spot that attaches the
darkly figurative blood of woman to the reigning symbol of male
domination has turned the protophallus into a marvelous condensation of all the dualities and ambivalences that the narrative of "La
Barbe bleue" has been accumulating. If the spectral blood deposited
by male violence represents the mirror function that enables him to
subjugate his wife as his foil and double, if it can also be relished as a
sign of the fluid that the sadist extracts from his victims and exacts as
a source of erotic pleasure, it confronts him as well with the darkly
figurative and positive blood-value of womanhood, of matriarchy or
maternal power. In its eerily fleeting form, the bloodspeck animates
the phallic symbol with a movement of reversibility that is alien,
other, resistant and resilient rather than submissive. Instead of allowing the protophallic key to serve as the secure image of a "normal,"
essentially visual economy—ocularity, specularity—of phallogocentrism, it subjects that image to an unsettling reconfiguration,
converting the surface of the hard metallic object into a bizarre,
borderless frame for the mobile trace of the bloody mirror on the
floor of the crypt. Having failed to keep the blood locked out of
sight, the key now prevents it from being removed from sight. The
work of framing it performs is uncanny and paradoxical, since it
disallows the stabilization of the representation/reflection it con-

tains. Thus, far from signifying for Bluebeard his wholeness or oneness, far from confirming his unique phallocratic role, it pictures a phallic order that is no less marred by the uncontrollable excess grafted onto its signifying surface than the feminine order it seeks to ground in deprivation is marred by deficiency.

Identity in Crisis

Hence for the phallotocracy there is a crisis—in and of sexual difference. This crisis, precipitated by the breakdown of a relation with woman that would guarantee man a satisfactory self-representation, is reflected in Bluebeard's aggressive reaction upon seeing the blood-stained key. While his wife seeks to defer the beheading he has prepared, he loudly presses her to hurry, pursuing anxiously a physical violence and an autarkic pleasure that carries the reimposition of phallocratic force out of control and into a raging anticipation of vengeful pleasures: he would overcome the bloodspot's tarnishing of the masculine signifier and its menacing mirror effect precisely by reopening the outflow of the woman's blood, so as to replenish the reserves in the tomb with a fresh supply. He would thus, as it were, restore order by putting the intolerable feminine blood his wife has exposed back in its place.[25] Graphically, the butcher's knife raised above the young wife's head is the tale's ultimate phallic symbol. The bloodletting Bluebeard covets figures a total, definitive cut-off that would substitute for the less absolute castration, tempered by the gift of phallic supplements, that his wife had failed to accept. The fatal recastration would punish woman for abusing and contaminating man's protophallic image of his dominance—for profaning a phallus that offered her the gift of castration less violently, in the form of a lack instead of death, of a denial of knowledge/power/identity rather than the absolute denial that nullifies life itself.

When the temptor who seeks wifely compliance via castrational supplementarity turns into the executioner who revels in punishing the noncompliance he has fostered, what does he accomplish, and to what end? The pattern of reenactment, whereby Bluebeard persists in remarrying and rekilling, clearly implies that his acts of execution, if they prove his power and provide a certain pleasure, nonetheless fail to satisfy him fully. Each sequence of death and

burial results in a void to be filled by another woman.[26] While his
wife-killing makes retribution for the women's tarnishing resistance
to his phallic empire, it also deprives him of the living mirror that
reflects and sustains that empire's ground in sexual difference. His
violent restoration of the difference his wife has challenged thus
reconstitutes, for him, a lack—a renewed need for his double—that
he is driven to fill. Which is to say that Bluebeard's ogreish incor-
poration of his wives, if it succeeds in bringing off their symbolic
integration into his universe, is incomplete; it is not a thorough-
going, obliterative digestion, comparable to that of the master cat in
"Le Chat botté," but a constitution of the memory traces figura-
tively embodied by the corpses in his domestic tomb. The process of
symbolic incorporation with preservation makes him a victim of the
same supplemental logic that he manipulates against his wife. The
blood-based mirror of doubling and difference on the floor of
the crypt or on the phallic key never ceases to figure a dual and
contradictory necessity: incarnating a resistance—difference—he
needs to break, woman's blood also appears as the essence of a foil—
doubling—he needs to retain (re-tain); displaying an excess (of dif-
ference) he cannot tolerate, it also points to a lack (of sameness) he
has to overcome.

The cruel use to which Bluebeard devotes the blood and corpses
in the crypt suggests, then, that he cannot give up his manhandling
of feminine difference, that his construction of an identity depends
on his ability to continue putting woman's blood in its burial place
so as to reserve it for his masterful exploitation. The role of the
phallus is precisely to position sexuality as a function, not of real,
physical union of man and woman, but of representation—of an
order in which man's phallic aggression consists in denying to
woman his rights of vision and representation. The ordering of
domestic space in Bluebeard's castle makes for a kind of architectural
institution of that denial. For in storing the corpses and blood in the
little room at the end of the gallery in his quarters—even if he does
not view them as the locked treasure reserved for his private inspec-
tion—he is keeping them in a relation of contiguity with what is on
open display. The floor plan of Bluebeard's castle thus sets off in
relief the intimate bond between the visible (gallery) and the invis-
ible (tomb), between the exposed and the concealed, between self-
perception in the present and perception by the other in the past.

Here Bluebeard's knowledge of that past is the key: it is the place of
women as the hidden ground of representation that he cannot give
up; it is his privilege as the sole viewer of that ground that he forever
needs, with the aid of a wife/woman, to (re)establish. This is to say
that the objective his reign of terror seeks to consolidate—the regi-
men of oculocentricity itself—falls prey, like all forms of male domi-
nance, to the same dependency on the perception and manipulation
of the other—of woman—that infuses the contaminative logic of
castrational supplementarity: the phallus becomes precious for its
male owner only after the desire it represents has been taken in and
inflected (in-spected) by woman. Bluebeard could not escape from
the evidence of this logic. He did not have, nor could he fabricate, a
secret that would free him from bondage to his feminine double.

Crisis Arrested: Doubling in Death

Bluebeard's execution is, spectacularly, another substitute castra-
tion: thwarting his decapitation of their sister, his wife's brothers run
their swords through his body. In its wake, the close resemblance of
the wife's experience to that of her husband reemerges in this cu-
rious description: "La pauvre femme était presque aussi morte que
son mari, et n'avait pas la force de se lever pour embrasser ses Frères"
(The poor woman was almost as dead as her husband, and did not
have the strength to get up to greet her brothers; 261). Almost as
dead, but not quite. To what extent does Perrault's narrative ac-
count for the mix of sameness and difference in this odd com-
parison? The death scene resonates with Bluebeard's twice-repeated
phrase "il faut mourir," which, devoid of personal reference, desig-
nates a necessity that appears absolute and excludes no one. Even if
the context makes it appear to apply directly to his wife, the abstract
proposition asserts the same necessity of death *for Bluebeard*. Since
neither husband nor wife can escape from the necessity of dying, the
comparison of their deaths points to another instance of doubling:
both died, albeit differently. Within this ultimate identity in differ-
ence, Bluebeard dies physically, absolutely; his wife, "psychologi-
cally," as it were. So in what sense can her experience of dying—a
figurative death through fright from which she can in due course
rise up in a new guise—be understood as the same as his, and in what
respect are they different?

When the narrative of "La Barbe bleue" begins to move back from Bluebeard's sequence, which we have been probing through most of this chapter, to the global sequence dominated by the heroine, it is finally the significance of the return of the bloodmarked key for her, rather than for him, that comes to the fore. For her, to give back the protophallic key contaminated with woman's fluid, mirroring bloodmark is no doubt less to contest the integrity of Bluebeard's phallocentric order than it is simply to return to him the symbol of his dreadful desire. His behavior in the transmission of male desire corresponded precisely to the strategy we have seen Irigaray attribute to the sadist: foisting his desire upon woman in the form of a death wish. That wish, announced in veiled terms by Bluebeard's menacing prohibition, was revealed to her as such—as a drive toward her own death—when she encountered the object of her curiosity at the door of the crypt. In returning the key with the ineffaceable mark of the feminine, she is presenting Bluebeard with a sign of the death wish accomplished by his previous wives and, simultaneously, with the mirror formed of their blood. The mirror is their representative, inviting him to see himself in the image he has given them; in that feminine other, he sees their death wish reflected back to him as his own. Thus, in the confrontational moment when the heroine turns the protophallus back over to Bluebeard, she makes herself doubly intolerable for him: through the excess that the mark of feminine difference grafts onto his self-image, yet also, as always, through her sameness, ultimately manifested in the return of the death wish as a desire they must share.

It is this pointed awareness of the necessity of death that the heroine not only hears and—having seen the tomb—understands in Bluebeard's discourse, but—as his double—assumes and reasserts in her own. We noted earlier that the heroine, in response to the villain's death sentence, manages both to acknowledge the necessity of dying and to delay the execution in the hope that her brothers will arrive in time to save her. At this point in the story, while supposedly saying her prayers, she sends her sister up to the tower to look for their brothers, who have promised to come that day. The ensuing three-way dialogue between the heroine, her sister Anne, and Bluebeard is built around four iterations of the celebrated question she addresses to her sister: "Anne, ma soeur Anne, ne vois-tu rien venir?" (literally, do you see nothing coming?; 260–61). In the immediate context of the dramatic confrontation building toward a suspenseful dénouement, the four repetitions of "ne vois-tu rien venir?" resonate with three instances of "il faut mourir" that surround them, two in the exchange with Bluebeard immediately before "soeur Anne" appears, the third immediately after Anne's final answer, when the condemned wife presents herself in tears at Bluebeard's feet: "Cela ne sert de rien, dit la Barbe bleue, il faut mourir" (261). The sense of this last occurrence of the resolutely abstract and impersonal "il faut mourir" has to coordinate with that of the apposed clause, "cela ne sert de rien." The apposition turns upon the indefinite pronoun *rien* that we have encountered in "il n'y a rien que vous ne deviez attendre de ma colère," and that recurs in "ne vois-tu rien venir?" In the case of the proposition governed by "il n'y a rien," the evident range of the sweeping negation signified by "ne . . . rien" extends to everything and thereby includes reduction to the nothingness that *rien* signifies literally. Here, the context makes the immediate sense of "cela ne sert de rien" something like "your tearful repentance is useless," but again, in the proposition that sets the wife's pleading posture off against "il faut mourir," the literal meaning of *rien* as nothingness fits into a coherent reading: your humble submission ("cela") does not serve as ("ne sert de") the nothingness ("rien") that is required; rather "il faut mourir"—that is, only the negation produced by death will do.

The persistently impersonal form of this insight is, to the extent that leaving the specification of the victim(s) in suspense contributes to the heightening of dramatic effects, a sign of Perrault's canny narratorial skill. The studied impersonality is equally pertinent from the standpoint of the work of thematic and poetic association that the tale at large accomplishes with its elaborate evocation of death and dying. For the assertion "il faut mourir" is no less true for Bluebeard than for his wife. The structure of the reciprocal exchange of desires between husband and wife makes her gesture in returning his death wish analogous to his in giving it: transferred back to him, it is enmeshed with her wish for his death, which she also expresses in summoning her brothers. For above all the blood marking the phallus as an instrument of violence means for her that her husband is just as intolerable to her as she is to him. From her side, too, their sameness is unbearable, fatal. Hence, once again, beneath the vagueness and the poetic evocation of emptiness that are conveyed by the impersonal *rien* when it returns in "ne vois-tu rien venir?" (a vagueness and emptiness that are also evoked repetitively in Sister Anne's initial replies: "Je ne vois que le Soleil qui poudroie, et l'herbe qui verdoie"; I see only the sun through the haze and the grass turning green; 260) there is also an entirely incisive, desperately particular meaning that the heroine's brothers, whose arrival she awaits, will embody: "rien venir" alludes to the advent of death for Bluebeard as well as for the heroine. Perhaps, then, as recurring expressions of the destructive impulse Bluebeard enacts in his repetition of the wife-killing ritual, the heroine's thrice-repeated call to her sister and the returns of "il faut mourir" deserve to be treated as the text's enactment of the repetition compulsion through which, according to Freud, the work of the death instinct appears. In any case, in their dual applicability these repeated phrases sustain the rigor of a structure in which each of the main characters inescapably doubles the other: insofar as they are compulsive expressions of their speaker's death wish, they simultaneously record their wish for the death of the other; and insofar as each is fully implicated in the "il faut mourir," it articulates their mutual call for precisely the double death that the tale's dénouement stages. In the case of Bluebeard, moreover, since it is hard to imagine him restaging his sadistic scheme over and over without developing a certain fatalistic sense that he is driven to continue until his wives' relatives act to avenge them, the dénouement can hardly be a total surprise. To some degree, through his impersonal "il faut mourir," he takes into account the expression of his own death wish in his sadistic behavior.

As the moment of execution approaches, the young wife, looking at Bluebeard "avec des yeux mourants" (with dying eyes; 261), realizes that her brothers, whom Anne has seen, will arrive soon. She thus advances knowingly toward what will be either death for her and Bluebeard in turn, one after the other, or death for him alone. In these circumstances, forced to place herself under Bluebeard's raised knife, her unmitigated experience of fright in the face of death merges without transition into that of witnessing the impaling of her husband. Its effect is fatal for her precisely insofar as her fright is purgational, insofar as it disintegrates an identity dependent on her relation to him, insofar as the symbolic castration he incurs at once overturns and completes—overturns by completing—the one to which she has been subjected and, satisfying her death wish, relieves her of her past image of herself. Thus the figurative death the narrative attributes to her can be construed as the death of her former, autotelic self, liquidated in the same act that erases the parallel identity of her bluebearded foil. The death scene—the death of the doubles—delivers her from the crisis of unchecked doubling; and according to the final sentence of the story's comedic ending, this violent collapse of duplicity that reverses the antagonists' positions and frees the heroine from Bluebeard—from his multiple mirrors, from herself, from an unstable, exchangeable identity—also underlies the young woman's remarkable escape from the past.

Veritable Honnêteté

Perrault's dénouement, which provides for the most decisive and perhaps the most revealing defeat of ogredom in the *Contes du temps passé*, is an exemplary case of the recuperative salvaging that caps all of the tales except "Le Petit Chaperon rouge." Upon assuming familial authority and redistributing her ex-husband's wealth, the widow uses her share of the fortune to marry herself to another husband, another "fort honnête homme," but this time a genuine one "qui lui fit oublier le mauvais temps qu'elle avait passé avec la Barbe bleue" (who made her forget the bad time she had spent with Bluebeard; 262). The forgetting is capital in relation to Bluebeard's temptation scheme and burial vault, which reveal clearly that he could not—would not—forget; his authority, his secretive behavior, his vindictive pleasure, his very identity, depended precisely on the pursuit of the tyrannical logic requiring him not to forget the bloody past, to hold his knowledge of the secret over his wives. On what basis, however, does the tale represent the young wife's "bad time" as forgettable? In particular, by what social model or mechanism does the regimen of *honnêteté* make it possible to relegate determining events of an immediate past to oblivion?

Although the narrative is, as in most of Perrault's dénouements ("Riquet à la houppe" and "Le Petit Poucet" are the exceptions), exceedingly spare, its thrust is unmistakable. The context is set by the staging that begins in the scene with the sister, looking out from the tower onto an empty expanse where she sees only the grassy plain illuminated by the sunlight. The vision Anne shares with her

sister is gradually filled with the sighting of the approaching broth-
ers, but is interrupted when the heroine has to descend from her
bedroom and submit to her hair-raising scrape with death. With
Bluebeard's raised knife confronting her dying eyes ("yeux mou-
rants"), she is suddenly able to return her attention to her sister's
perception of the onrushing brothers and watch them carry out
their mission. Her emotionally searing trial is thus a family drama,
anchored in her communicative relation to her sister and developed
by the series of images that terminates with the transfixing spectacle
of the slicing administered to her husband by her brothers. In fol-
lowing the movement from her own short-circuited execution to
that of Bluebeard, the young woman participates vicariously in their
jointly experienced passion by taking over the role of observer from
her sister: until the end, the doubling of husband and wife remains a
visual phenomenon, and her escape from it depends on a dramatic
representation of the final explosion of castratory violence. In the
unfolding of the spectacle, the sphere of her own feelings of involve-
ment is designated by the text's telling metaphor of dying eyes. Her
attachment to Bluebeard's fate derives from the pull of identification
on a spectator immediately and irresistibly caught up in the flow of
images passing before her; the intense pressure draws her into ac-
companying him into a scene of bloodletting so horrible that it
finally becomes unendurable, shattering the visual bond and forcing
the viewer's collapse into blankness, into detachment from the real-
ity besieging her. The heroine's vicarious experience of a killing
castration is thus figured by the rending severance the swords that
pierce Bluebeard impose on her vision.

Since the heroine's brothers are cavalrymen ("l'un Dragon et
l'autre Mousqetaire"), it is possible to perceive in their intervention
another scenario like that of "Le Chat botté," in which society acts
through its agents to cleanse itself of the monstrosity represented by
ogres. But such an institutional framework does not explain how the
violent spectacle of recastration—the brothers save their sister pre-
cisely by reimposing masculine power through their victorious
brandishing of swords—can be so readily acceptable to the heroine.
Her acceptance is expressed by her immediate recourse to the very
logic of exchange in which Bluebeard had proposed to ground their
relationship: in return for their assistance, her brothers and sister
receive rewards that enable them to consolidate their positions in

society; meanwhile, her own marriage, anchored in a dowry, places her under the tutelage of the *honnête homme* who, in return, takes the lead in engineering her passage into a new and different marital relation. Thus the horizon on which this solution is possible remains fundamentally that of the family, and within the familial dynamics, the crucial relation that intervenes in the castration scenario is that of the siblings. If the brothers, by destroying the conflictual doubling and mirroring in the marital relation of their sister and her tyrannical husband, provide her with a kind of psychological *table rase*, does their wielding of the deadly phallic instrument not simply reconstitute the same order of masculine authority, the same imposing symbolism of male dominance, that fostered, in her relation with Bluebeard, an untenable case of mimetic rivalry? In what respect can the brothers' action have a re-visionary significance that goes beyond and differs from the sexual differentiation that obeys the divisive logic of castrational supplementarity?

To be sure, the exceedingly speculative drift of these nonetheless pointed and vital questions, coupled with the compact and limpid economy of Perrault's streamlined text, requires a guarded response. Within the framework of our reading of "La Barbe bleue" and "Le Petit Chaperon rouge" through the dramas of recognition and identification that they stage, the relevance of Hegel's analyses of family relations seems only too evident. In precisely the section of the *Phenomenology of Spirit* that Irigaray's account of the brother/sister relation both criticizes and echoes, in a passage unmistakably inflected by the example of Antigone, Hegel opposes this privileged relation to the conflict of husband and wife: "The brother, however, is for the sister a passive, similar being in general; the recognition of herself in him is pure and unmixed with any natural desire. . . . The moment of the individual self, recognizing and being recognized, can here assert its right, because it is linked to the equilibrium of the blood and is a relation devoid of desire."[27] As Derrida notes in his commentary,[28] such a recognition, devoid of natural desire and rivalry, hardly seems conceivable or assimilable in the Hegelian system and thus has to be interrogated as a point of difficulty. Yet with all due caveats in place, as Irigaray suggests when she writes of an ideal brother-sister relation that, devoid of disruption by desire or physical violence, ennobles the bonds of consanguinity, it is hard to deny the elemental value of Hegel's insight for relations in which the sexual difference operative in fraternal or sororal action does appear to be decisively disconnected from sexual desire. In the case of the fraternal intervention in "La Barbe bleue," moreover, the Hegelian framework that Derrida sets forth so magisterially is precisely what appears to be confirmed: the brothers, as men, come from the diurnal sphere of human society and politics to nullify Bluebeard's usurpation of their sister's role, in the nocturnal sphere of women, as the guardian of family relations and of the sepulcher. Since they carry out their castratory retaliation against Bluebeard as representatives of a blood relation that they share with their sister—a relation not yet marked as either masculine or feminine—and that satisfies her death wish rather than their own sexual desire, and since their action projects the family interests in which they are implicated into the arena of an economic and social exchange, its function as an assertion of power is to represent that power not as the masculine privilege the deficient woman has to desire, but as a prerogative of familial solidarity they enable their sister to validate concretely.

It remains evident, however, that the brothers' revenge against their sister's tormentor restores the precedence of a masculine order. The heroine's salvation occasions, no longer the resistance with which she confronted Bluebeard's marital authority, but her assent to a relationship with a true *honnête homme*. The compromise presiding over the *honnête homme*'s accommodation with, on the other hand, the aesthete's allegiance to judgment, taste, intuition, and culture, requires that crucial abstract terms of both polite and analytic discourse (such as *honnêteté* itself, which vacillates between the moral connotation of honesty and the social connotation of gentlemanliness) be left loose and underelaborated, if not simply unthought. When the *honnête homme*'s wife accedes to the regimen of castrational supplementarity, her willing subservience to him will be promoted by his example—by his willingness to gloss over the differences Bluebeard insisted on specifying with his phallic representations of knowledge and power. In other words, the familial contract that resolves the problem of sexual difference for the socioeconomic order of a phallotocracy threatened by a feminine insurgency, that enables it to recover its equilibrium and function stably, entails an implicit agreement to ignore or to forget the very grounds on which it rests. Whereas Bluebeard, having no secret, struggled to make one and secure his authority in it, the *honnête homme*, aware of differences he deems it worthwhile to overlook or suppress, will engage in a practice of dissimulation, allowing these "secrets" to be dissipated through the processes of forgetting.

Conclusion:
The End in Sight

P art I of this study examined Perrault's critical responses to three important seventeenth-century writers whose views on thought, aesthetics, and language he purported to contest. In reacting to the cornerstones of their work—to Descartes's *cogito*, Boileau's sublime, and Racine's strict classicism—Perrault came up against various forms of an age-old dilemma: how to deal with genuinely extraordinary phenomena that, while they are experienced as imposing and illuminating, stretch the mind's grasp to its limits or beyond, and force it to posit the inconceivable, the incomparable, the inexpressible. Such terms point to the need to reckon with the paradoxical and elusive quality of absolute distinction, which may be apprehended as difference, originality, otherness, or inaccessibility. On a theoretical level, this need comes to the fore in compelling foundational experiences such as the indubitable self-sensation of the soul (Descartes) or the impassioned surge of poetic inspiration (Boileau). On the level of practical, political concerns, an analogous need was brought into focus for Perrault and Racine by the transcendent presence of Louis XIV to and for his subjects.

Perrault's Compromises

Perrault's resistance to his adversaries invariably goes hand in hand with an attempt to appropriate their essential insights. This ambivalent posture results in a compromise formation that derives its coherence from the priority and authority he accords to visual representation. Rather than reject the grounding status of the *cogito* and the sublime for thought and art, Perrault denies their deep-seated origin in the order of feeling or passion. In his dismissive accounts of the profound, conceptually retorsionary experiences that underlie the demanding meditations of Longinus and Des-cartes, his strategy of sublimation and domestication is transparent: he is determined to situate the groundwork of thought and art in readily accessible experience. Vis-à-vis the concern for first princi-ples in Descartes and Boileau, Perrault's less primary *cogito* and less lofty sublime are not, then, foundational. Rather, they are derived and functional, since they emerge already ensconced in an irreduci-bly central order of representation where the Cartesian turn priv-ileging the image and the subject/object relation reigns supreme. While the Cartesian turn exerts a delineatory pressure conducive to the rational, technological outlook characteristic of Perrault and the Moderns, it stands in the way of the sublime turn, dampening its impact and restricting the space in which features of the sublime can appear. By defining the synthesizing work of *esprit* so that it em-braces the poetic impulses of spontaneity and inspiration, Perrault manages to incorporate his own muted sublime into his vision of eloquence and beauty.

In the sphere of language and rhetoric, where the primacy of image building comes to light in the tropological movement of figuration, Perrault encounters the censorship of Racine with re-spect to a culturally and historically decisive spectacle: the French monarch's all-pervasive presence to the awed peoples of Europe. In responding to Racine's criticisms of his draft epistle for the *Diction-naire de l'Académie*, Perrault appropriates the figure of preterition, an elaborate form of the Cartesian turn that Racine had used in his own historical discourse. Via the preteritional turn, Perrault molds the field of vision organized by and around the royal subject into an expressive scene in which the personal and historical dimensions can be seen together, in their interaction. Within this transcendental framework, the dauntingly complex process of forming adequate representations can be understood as the academician's ultimate compromise; it emerges as an articulation of description with narra-tion, of transfixing spectacle with the movement of history, that the exemplary image of the king at once imposes and subsumes. Given Perrault's reverential posture toward the monarchy of Louis XIV, it is hardly surprising that the prince, cast in the preeminent position of the viewed and viewing subject whose power extends into the world and is reflected back to him through vision, appears as a triumphant character in the *Contes du temps passé*. It is surely significant, moreover, that only "Le Petit Chaperon rouge" and "La Barbe bleue" fail to contribute to a representation of royal authority and felicity that can be regarded as a further, albeit discreet, imprinting of Perrault's instinctive and indefatigable inclination to cast monarchy in a favorable light.

On Reading the *Contes*: From "Peau d'âne" to Riquet's Transfiguration

In the prototypical story "Peau d'âne," the practice of royal sight that evolves quickly into love is enacted by the prince's voyeuristic gaze upon the unknown young woman whose beauty enthralls him. The youthful prince's infatuation with beauty and the motif connecting feminine beauty to visible accouterments appropriate to royalty recur in "Cendrillon," "La Belle au bois dormant," "Les Fées," and "Riquet à la houppe." The dénouements of these tales reflect their anchorage in a teleology of royal succession, investiture, and consolidation; its hold on the narrative perspective of the *Contes* is seconded, moreover, by the ties to the king achieved by the peasant heroes of "Le Chat botté" and "Le Petit Poucet." Read in tandem, the tales that replay the scenario of "Peau d'âne" by aligning the prince's attachment to beauty with the achievement of a just and happy marriage thus appear to constitute the dominant horizon of meaning in the *Contes*.

In Chapter Four we saw that "Peau d'âne" and "Cendrillon" highlight the immersion of the royal couple in the processes of sight—of seeing and being seen—with remarkable insistency. However, the story of Prince "Riquet à la houppe," the industrious hero who sharply contrasts with the lovesick voyeur of "Peau d'âne," surely supplies the collection's most incisive and conclusive statement on the import of the princely image. Riquet is unique among the princes of the *Contes* since he is not handsome. Owing to his ugliness, his task is not merely that of the other princely heroes, each of whom has to find the beautiful woman he loves and stage for the royal family her identification as wife and princess. Having fallen in love with a beautiful princess upon looking at her portrait, Riquet's heroic trial confronts him with two distinct obstacles. In their first encounter, he has to endow her with the *esprit* she needs in order to overcome her *bêtise* and become a worthy princess; when they meet again a year later, facing her resistance to keeping her promise to marry him, he has to make his own way through a comparable process of re-identification in order to acquire the image of a prince whom she can desire. His successful passage through these two trials results in the compromise formation—hinging upon the articulation of the verbal dimension of *esprit* with the visual dimension of beauty—described at some length at the end of Chapter One. In the comparative context I have introduced here by looking at the *Contes* through prototypical lenses derived from "Peau d'âne," that articulation and, concomitantly, Riquet's metamorphosis into a handsome and lovable prince correspond exactly to the process identified in Chapter Four as transfiguration. Far more for Riquet than for the other princes of the *Contes*, moreover, his marital triumph does not devolve more or less automatically from his princely station, but depends on achieving a mutually satisfying relation with the woman he loves.

Hence the significance of the relations we analyzed in Chapter One, relations that issue from the exchanges of looks and desires between the prince and princess, and in particular, from her role as the witness and agent of his transfiguration. The model for the princess's gift of *beauté* is of course provided by Riquet, whose gift of *esprit* to the princess, rather than a magical transfer from him to her of a talent she lacks, consists primarily in activating or releasing an inhibited capacity he perceives in her expressions of distress and desire. The interpersonal mechanism that he mobilizes in enabling her to discover and pursue the work of *esprit* is, fundamentally, the exchange of desire. According to the good fairy who attended his birth, Riquet is empowered to transmit his extraordinary *esprit* only to the person he loves the most. That is, his own desire for the princess furnishes the driving impetus for the "transfer"; working naturally, as it were, it induces him to sympathize with her wish for *esprit* and to integrate it to his own wishful activity as a goal he willingly seeks for her, as his desire for her to participate with him in their mutual exercise of *esprit*. Thus in their dialogue Riquet is already satisfying *their* desire; he is giving her his *esprit* to the extent that his cleverly flattering insights and formulations—his *esprit* in action—serve to put her in touch with her own spiritual potential. Her innate aptitude appears, he suggests, in her concern with her apparent lack of *esprit* and her desire to overcome that lack: "Il n'y a rien, Madame, qui marque davantage qu'on a de l'esprit, que de croire n'en pas avoir, et il est de la nature de ce bien-là, que plus on en a, plus on croit en manquer." "Je ne sais pas cela, dit la Princesse, mais je sais bien que je suis fort bête, et c'est de là que vient le chagrin qui me tue" (There is nothing, Madam, that better reveals the possession of *esprit* than the belief that one has none, and the nature of that gift is such that, the more of it one has, the more one feels lacking in it. I do not know that, said the princess, but I do know I am quite stupid, and that is the source of my mortal suffering; 282).

What, then, is necessary for the princess to overcome the repressive belief that keeps her from knowing her potential spirituality and inhibits its expression? The imperturbable Riquet's response invariably points to desire. Indeed, he plays explicitly upon the ambivalent structure of desire—understands that for each party desire is at once to desire the other and to desire the other's desire. Now that he has accepted her desire as his, she must reciprocate—"il ne tiendra qu'à vous que vous n'ayez autant d'esprit qu'on en peut avoir, pourvu que vous vouliez bien m'épouser" (you alone will determine whether you shall have all the *esprit* one can have provided that you are willing to marry me; 282)—by accepting his desire for marital union as hers. Seeing and knowing herself as Riquet sees and knows her, inspirited, will require her commitment to the relation with him specified by the verb "m'épouser": to marry me, but as the root suggests (Lat. *sponso*, to pledge solemnly; cf. the same root in *répondre*, not merely to react or answer, but to answer to, for, before, to take responsibility, provide a guarantee), in the strong sense implied by a decision to wed oneself to the principles of *esprit* that I incarnate; thus, to commit yourself to me, to my self, to drawing on the limitless store of spirit emanating from my passion.

Significantly, Riquet moves to revise his proposition by postponing the marriage for a year when the speechless princess, recoiling in the face of a responsibility she is not ready to assume, does not reply ("ne répondit rien"). Riquet's astuteness consists in allowing

her to assert her agreement—a self-commitment sufficient to pro-
duce her psychological transformation—without having to carry it
out immediately. Upon accepting his modified proposition, she un-
dergoes an immediate spiritualization that is marked by her expres-
sive self-assurance: "Elle se sentit tout autre qu'elle n'était aupara-
vant; elle se trouva une facilité incroyable à dire tout ce qui lui
plaisait, et à le dire d'une manière fine, aisée et naturelle" (She felt
quite different from before; she discovered in herself an incredible
facility for saying whatever she wished, and for doing so in a subtle,
effortless, and natural way; 282). Her promise is a viable, self-
binding performative to the extent that it enables her to assume his
perception of her, freeing her from a disabling self-conception; it
remains unfulfilled and insecure to the extent that she does not yet
accept Riquet's desire definitively, to the point of allowing him to
see himself in her.

When their final reckoning occurs a year later, the princess
whom Riquet confronts with her responsibility has become an ac-
complished practitioner of *esprit*. Their dialogue thus moves lim-
pidly through a round of highly sophisticated verbal sparring in
which he dismisses her argument that he should not hold her to a
promise she had made while still spiritless and directs her attention
to their only unresolved problem: his ugliness. Having willingly
acknowledged the bonds of spirituality she shares with Riquet, hav-
ing elicited his assurances that she can give beauty to the person she
loves, that she simply needs unreservedly to assert his wish to be
handsome as her own wish for him to become handsome, she an-
swers his wish for her wish by asserting it compliantly: "Je souhaite
de tout mon coeur que vous deveniez le Prince du monde le plus
beau et le plus aimable; et je vous en fais le don autant qu'il est en
moi. La Princesse n'eut pas plus tôt prononcé ces paroles, que Ri-
quet à la houppe parut à ses yeux l'homme du monde le plus beau, le
mieux fait et le plus aimable qu'elle eût jamais vu" (I wish with all
my heart for you to be the most handsome and lovable prince in the
world; and I make you this gift insofar as I have it in me. No sooner
had the princess pronounced these words than Riquet à la houppe
appeared to her eyes as the handsomest, shapeliest, and most lovable
man she had ever seen; 284–85). Beneath the artful simplicity of the
phrase the princess tacks onto her wish so as to articulate her gift, a
characteristically Perraldian slipperiness once again comes into play.

From the juxtaposition of the two propositions—first the wish, then the gift—it is clear that her gift is constituted by the wish. But is it simply the act of wishing, as she has assumed it within herself and expressed it, or is it is indeed the fulfillment of that wish insofar as its satisfaction lies within her power? Is the ultimate beauty of her wish and of her gift her own innate beauty, a quality comparable to Riquet's *esprit* that she carries within herself and that she is able to perceive in Riquet by virtue of its presence in her as an illuminatory principle, as embellishing light or insight she can bring to bear upon the world around her?

Perrault's narrative art at once leaves these elusive possibilities open and proceeds to indicate how the princess's craftily articulated gift of desire comes to function as an act of attribution that is carried out by sight. The shaping of Riquet's image by her desire for a visually pleasing object enables her to project the traits of beauty onto the ugly creature before her. The playful Perraldian narrator reinforces this strictly psychological account of Riquet's metamorphosis in the eyes of the princess by observing that the magical powers of the fairy godmother may have had nothing to do with it. Rather, the narrator suggests, Riquet's physique remains the same. The essential change occurs solely in the manner in which the princess elects to see her prince, to construct his image in accord with their wish, just as a year earlier her change was in her vision of herself.

The End in Sight

The transfiguration of Riquet realized by the princess's translation of her wish from speech ("La Princesse n'eut pas plus tôt prononcé ces paroles") into sight ("que Riquet à la houppe parut à ses yeux") repeats and completes her act of espousal, providing for the elevation of his princely identity into parity with hers. The heretofore dominant image of Riquet as a speaking being whose *esprit* belongs to the oral mode of discourse is now expanded and enhanced by the visual image of Riquet that she forms by sight. The term transfiguration seems especially apt in this scene since the graphic description of Riquet's ascent pointedly mobilizes references to the loci of sensation on his face. The narrative presents the genesis of the princess's visual practice—what we termed in Chapter

One the "envisualization" or "insighting" of her *esprit*—as an intellectual advance: from reflecting on "les bonnes qualités de son âme et de son esprit," which she knows thanks to the superb speech that he articulates in his mouth, she moves on to revising her perceptions of "la difformité de son corps" and "la laideur de son visage" (the misshapenness of his body and the ugliness of his face). The effects of transfiguration that endow Riquet's ugly face with the aura of her/his spirituality/beauty show up precisely in the distinctive features she sees above his mouth, "son gros nez rouge" and "ses yeux, qui étaient louches" (his big red nose and his eyes, which were cross-eyed). In them, she now perceives signs of brilliance and passion, of strength and heroism.

In the dominant, comedic sphere of the *Contes*, the story of Riquet's elevation acquires the special prominence of an exceptionally revealing, indeed exemplary adventure. In part, this has to do with his unique heroic itinerary and with a concomitant shift in the heroine's activity from royal self-representation through adornment (i.e., via garments and jewels that mark her singularity in the eyes of the prince) to an exercise of vision that takes the prince as its object. More vitally, however, as I suggested in Chapter One, the tale's special significance stems from the narrative's exposure of the reality-bending mechanism in the princess's vision. In the very scenario that, by accrediting both the prince and the princess with heroic action, takes royal distinction to its ultimate height, the construction of the hero's princely image by a heroine whose ascent precedes his requires of her a thoroughly subjective interpretation, a practice of sight that entails seeing beyond—or reforming from behind, in the spiritual eyes of the mind—the objective images that appear to her eyes. The account of her interpretive adventure in the dénouement of "Riquet à la houppe," which traces a kind of spiritualization of Riquet's body, occasions another instance of the deftly subtle ambiguity we have observed in Perrault's storywriting. In an extended period in which the narrator enumerates the figurative meanings the princess ascribes to her lover's physical deformities, the clause that evokes his eyes is perhaps the most telling example: "Ils [quelques-uns] disent encore que ses yeux, qui étaient louches, ne lui en parurent que plus brillants, que leur dérèglement passa dans son esprit pour la marque d'un violent excès d'amour" (Some also say that his eyes, which were cross-eyed, only appeared more brilliant to her as a result, that their abnormality passed in her mind as the mark of a violent excess of love). Is the active agent of sight in these two propositions Riquet's vision or that of the princess? Or is the question, as it were, undecidable?

The parallel verb sequences "ne lui en parurent" and "passa dans son esprit" function as the hinges of a marvelous descriptive shiftiness. On the one hand, Riquet's cross-eyed gaze springs into view before the princess, is the glaring subject that acts to strike a passive recipient with its bizarre effect; on the other hand, since the verb *paraître* can just as well serve to situate its indirect object in the position of the viewing subject (as in "it appears to me that"), she is the active observer who perceives the striking effects of his shifty eyes. Or again: on the one hand, the unsettling image of his gaze makes its way from her eyes into her mind, where it takes on the aura of passion; on the other hand, since "passer" can signify "have the look or sense of" for an interpreting subject, she is again the active observer of a visual disorder, to which her agile mind attributes an incisive etiology. In each proposition, then, the narrator manages to represent a person-to-person relation that can be understood to move in both directions, with the prince and the princess alike acting as viewing subjects while appearing to each other as objects.

In its cannily capacious manner, the narrator's delineation of this crisscrossing, overlapping ocular movement seems characteristic, akin to the compromise representing the crosscurrents that make the verbal order of *esprit* and the visual order of beauty interactive and interdependent. Susceptible to readings from the standpoint of either subject that do not contradict each other, these propositions manifest an openness to the process Baudelaire would term "reversibility." Their indeterminacy makes reading almost literally a dialectics, channeling the interpreter toward a bidirectional construal commensurate with the characters' ongoing exchange of insighting. The coalescent readings allow for a kind of reciprocal superimposition of each subjectivity upon the other. At any moment their union reflects no less the spirit-penetrating influence of the prince's gaze than the interpretative authority of the princess's already spiritualized sight, giving neither the upper hand. Their mutual commitment to artfully spiritualizing their views of each other presides over the comfortably ambivalent, conciliatory relation the two characters achieve.

Ogredom Revisited

"Riquet à la houppe" is, then, a drama of mutual insighting that explores the transfigurative power of the visual with extraordinary acuity. But is the temptation to treat its ending as emblematic or typical for the *Contes*, in relation to the prototypical scenario of "Peau d'âne," not immediately undermined by the tales we had to exclude from the comedic vein of the collection? That is, in particular, do the central dramas of "Le Petit Chaperon rouge" and "La Barbe bleue"—tales in which the motifs of royal authority and feminine beauty are conspicuously absent—not lie on a horizon of monstrous violence that cannot be reconciled with the universe Perrault so aptly evokes, in the first *moralité* of "Cendrillon," with the term "bonne grâce"? Still more generally, does not the reckoning with the ogres in the *Contes*—the wolf, Bluebeard, and the ogres of "La Belle au bois dormant," "Le Chat botté," and "Le Petit Poucet"—introduce a thematic countercurrent that is just as significant as the comedic vein in the work as a whole?

According to the interpretation linking "Le Petit Chaperon rouge" to "La Barbe bleue" that I sketched in Chapters Five and Six, the wolf's experience generates a question about the ogre's future to which Bluebeard's experience provides the answer. Bluebeard's fall raises, in turn, a larger question concerning the significance of society's collective action against the ogres that menace it. A first response, rapid and sketchy, but broad in scope, appears in the dénouement of "La Barbe bleue." It suggests unmistakably that the ogre's eradication makes possible the triumph of grace and virtue, of *honnêteté*, that seems dominant in the rest of the *Contes*. Surrounding this pair of tales dominated by an ogre figure, the second and third of the collection, are two others, "La Belle au bois dormant" and "Le Chat botté," in which the destruction of the ogress and ogre, respectively, enables the consolidation of royal power and marital bliss. Thereafter comes the sequence of tales of royal marriage—"Les Fées," "Cendrillon," and "Riquet à la houppe"—that can readily be interpreted in the light of "Peau d'âne." If these three tales lack explicit ogres, the ogre seems nonetheless to appear in sublimated form within the heroine's family, as a parent whose harmful action has to be overcome by a child. According to this schematic overview, then, the heroic victory over ogres and their surrogates is a step on the way to an outcome in royal marriage that stands as a social ideal presiding over Perrault's small narrative universe. But in order to shore up this integration of the tales into a single larger story about society, it remains necessary to confront two unresolved quandaries. The first, which arises in the construction of the schema itself, concerns the way in which the final story, "Le Petit Poucet," might fit into it. The second, already encountered above, has to do with "La Barbe bleue": how might its skeletal dénouement constitute a bridge leading to the crowning scenario of comedy played out in "Riquet à la houppe"?

In "Le Petit Poucet," discussed in Chapter One because of its diminutive hero's formidable *esprit*, the ogre's defeat goes hand in hand with the foiling of ineffectual parents who can be taken as ogre surrogates. Thus the plot engages the hero in a kind of double combat against the two forms of ogredom, express and implied, that we encounter in the *Contes*. In the combat with the ogre, moreover, the clever hero's deception triggers a scenario reminiscent of the extreme violence administered by the wolf to Little Red Riding Hood and her grandmother in that the ogre/father, by decapitating his daughters, inadvertently subjects his children to the fate Thumbkin's parents sought to impose upon theirs. In the aftermath of this first drama, the angry ogre chases Thumbkin and his brothers until he falls asleep, exhausted, next to the boys' hiding place near their home. Thumbkin then seals the displacement of the harmful-parent role onto the ogre by stealing first his magic boots, then his money: the salutary delivery of the ogre's wealth to Thumbkin's family recalls the ending of "La Barbe bleue," in which the heroine distributes Bluebeard's wealth to her family. Thus "Le Petit Poucet" seems to incorporate a double return to the ogreish dramas of "Le Petit Chaperon rouge" and "La Barbe bleue," blending the sequence these two dramas form into a single tale that ends, like "La Barbe bleue," in the consolidation of the family.

But maintaining the rather neat association of these three "tales of ogredom" suddenly becomes problematic in the final paragraph of "Le Petit Poucet," where the narrator resorts to a device similar to that of the alternate explanation of Riquet's metamorphosis at the end of "Riquet à la houppe." This time, however, it is an alternate dénouement that comes into play, one that denies Thumbkin's theft of the ogre's wealth and attributes the enrichment of his family

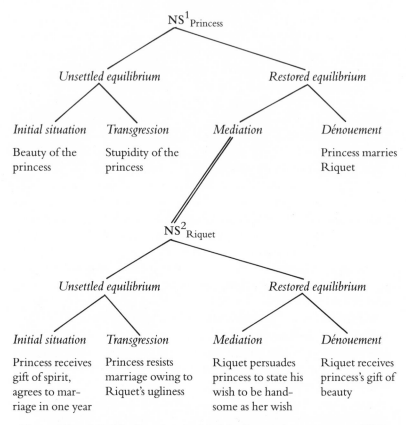

Fig. 4. The global (NS[1]) and embedded (NS[2]) narrative structures of "Riquet à la houppe."

instead to the exploitation of the magic boots on behalf of the king and his court. In this scenario, the ogre's defeat enables the hero to attain a socioeconomic success in the civilized society headed by the king, who "payait parfaitement bien pour porter ses ordres à l'Armée" (who paid handsomely for the delivery of his orders to the army; 293). This second version of the tale brings the hero closer to the itinerary of the master cat in "Le Chat botté," who also ascends from poverty into a saving association with the king that affords him wealth and comfort. The vacillation of the story between its two endings—an indecision that nonetheless culminates in the hero's social ascent—clarifies and reinforces the socially progressive principle that emerges in the passage from "Le Petit Chaperon rouge" through "La Barbe bleue." According to this simple logic, the ogre's defeat in the dénouement enables the upward movement of heroism first (in the initial version of "Le Petit Poucet") toward familial and then (in the second version) toward societal welfare.

In the narrative syntax of "Riquet à la houppe" (see Fig. 4), the two sequences situate the hero and heroine, Riquet and the princess, in a symmetrical opposition that echoes the doubling of the husband and wife in "La Barbe bleue." The comparison is all the more telling since the relationship is generated by an exchange that bears upon each character's identity: Riquet gives the princess what she desires, *esprit* (associated with speech and marked as masculine), and in return she gives him what he desires, *beauté* (associated with sight and marked as feminine). Since each character ends up possessing both qualities, they appear, just as surely as Bluebeard and his wife, to be doubles of one another. Moreover, the resemblances between Riquet and Bluebeard are striking. Each is physically repulsive and overcomes the woman's revulsion by tactics—Bluebeard's flaunting of his wealth and his secret, Riquet's use of flattery and recourse to deferring the marriage—that smack of temptation and entrapment. Like the bourgeois Bluebeard, the royal Riquet adopts the aggressive male's initiatory and negotiatory stance, conditioning the gift of (his) *esprit* upon the formal promise to marry him to which he will hold the princess. These parallels between the two tales would lead one to expect, in "Riquet à la houppe," a repetition of the mimetic rivalry, rooted in a drama of sexual difference, that "La Barbe bleue" stages; this impression seems all the more plausible since the drama in "Riquet à la houppe," like that of "La Barbe bleue," is organized around two scenes of confrontation between the central characters, the first establishing the contractual terms of the man's gift, the second addressing the woman's failure to keep her commitment.

But in the second confrontation, the twists that differentiate "Riquet à la houppe" from "La Barbe bleue" become salient. As we have noted, the second meeting between Riquet and the princess is, to a large extent, not a reckoning with a broken contract but a resumption of their first meeting, adjourned a year earlier, and its essence is a repetition of the acts of giving and of espousal-as-commitment already illustrated by the first encounter. Above all, the encounter focuses upon the princess's decision not to break the terms of Riquet's contract, but to comply with them. At a moment when her possession of both *esprit* and *beauté* gives her an advantage over her suitor, who lacks *beauté*, and when her temptation to break her promise to Riquet is reinforced by a marriage proposal from another prince endowed with every desirable quality, she nonetheless opts to match Riquet's gift with her own. Insofar as the gift she is to bestow on him is the *esprit* she received in return for accepting his desire, her judgment and decision recognize the validity of the commitment she had made while vulnerable and under pressure from Riquet. Still more poignantly, her receptive response to his invasive strabismic eyes and inflated red nose confers on them a curiously phallic aura: she finds his eyes "brillants" (thereby conjuring up the conventional symbolic connection of the eye to the radiant, blinding sun) and associates them with "un violent excès d'amour," while the nose reflects "quelque chose de Martial et d'Héroïque." The terms "violent" and "martial," in particular, convey the effects of a masculine power, symbolized by Riquet's facial organs, that the princess, in the manner of the Prince in "Peau d'âne," as it were, is prepared to drink with her eyes and then, in a gesture of generous harmony, spiritualize in her mind.

One need not succumb to the temptation to regard the princess's interpretation of Riquet's face as the feminine beautification or sublimation of an unsightly phallic order in order to read in "Riquet à la houppe" a decisive recasting of "La Barbe bleue." Riquet enables the princess to accept his gift of *esprit* on his terms and, from possessing it, to learn to love him. Thus the story skips from the point in the structure of "La Barbe bleue" just before the wife consummates her transgression to the dénouement, where the heroine achieves her satisfactory relationship with the *honnête homme*. Omitting the central drama of "La Barbe bleue" constituted by the wife's disobedience, sentencing, and brush with death, "Riquet à la houppe" offers an alternative to the persecutory action bred by Bluebeard's secret and born of an unequal exchange that permits the wife only to return the phallus, sullied by the unacceptable mark of feminine value. Whereas Bluebeard's scheme allows the young woman to contribute nothing of her own, the exchange Riquet promotes is authentic in two vital respects. First, the gift of *esprit* is definitive, entails real sharing by the two parties. Second, in giving *beauté* in return for *esprit*, the princess is not giving back a borrowed phallus; the *beauté* offered to Riquet is a quality belonging to the princess that he lacks and gratefully accepts. In the marital union Riquet thus strives to ground in reciprocity and interdependence, there is no room for a secret. Rather, the salient tactical contrast between Riquet and Bluebeard lies in the deliberateness with which Riquet tells the princess fully and clearly what he is seeking and how their exchange of gifts will work.

Insofar as Riquet's project entails a kind of discreet spiritual direction that allows the princess to discover herself and assert the value of her own spiritual presence for herself and for him, it reveals precisely the nature of the relation that the *honnête homme* in the dénouement of "La Barbe bleue" substitutes for the oppressive mastery sought by Bluebeard. So in effect "Riquet à la houppe" supplies the understanding of *honnêteté* and its power to displace the regimen of mimetic rivalry that "La Barbe bleue" evokes but leaves in abeyance. Illustrating the power of the conceptual and tropological framework of sight and vision to articulate both its characters' interpersonal relations and the conceptual interplay of *esprit* and *beauté*, the tale offers the single most probing and conclusive elaboration of the modernist teleology that Perrault's *Contes* illustrate. The characteristic turning of compromise in sublimation and spiritualization that so often resurfaces in Perrault's writing doubtless finds its most telling enactment in the reflective movement through which the princess, herself epitomizing the responsive art of *honnêteté*, draws Riquet's disturbing eyes into the uplifting perspective of her beauty. Perhaps we can capture the essential ambivalence of this doubly positive response with the somewhat precious expression of *receptive redress*: her insight both corrects her initial perception of Riquet and clothes him in an image more to her liking (a term that aptly evokes the work of likeness in this dialectics of desire). In its beneficence and self-assurance, her vision of his eyes—surely one of those powerful surges of figural condensation and articulatory reach that take on exemplary significance in an intricately orchestrated text—sums up the axiological vitality that Perrault's writing derives from placing the end in sight.

Reference Matter

Appendix

Text of the draft epistle

SIRE,

le Dictionnaire de l'Académie Françoise paroît enfin sous les auspices de VOTRE MAJESTE, et nous avons osé mettre à la tête de notre ouvrage le nom auguste du plus grand des Rois. Quelques soins que nous ayons pris d'y rassembler tous les termes, dont l'Eloquence et la Poësie peuvent former l'Eloge des plus grands Héros, nous avouons, Sire, que vous nous en avez fait sentir plus d'une fois et le défaut et la foiblesse. Lorsque notre zèle ou notre devoir nous ont engagez à parler du secret impénétrable de vos desseins, que la seule exécution découvre aux yeux des hommes, et toujours dans les momens marquez par votre sagesse, les mots de prévoyance, de prudence, et de sagesse méme ne répondoient pas à nos idées, et nous aurions osé nous servir de celui de Providence, s'il pouvoit jamais être permis de donner aux hommes ce qui n'appartient qu'à Dieu seul. Ce qui nous console, SIRE, c'est que sur un pareil sujet les autres langues n'auroient aucun avantage sur la nôtre: celle des Grecs et celle des Romains seroient dans la même indigence; et tout ce que nous voyons de brillant et de sublime dans leur plus fameux Panégyriques, n'auroit ni assez de force ni assez d'éclat pour soutenir le simple recit de vos Victoires. Que l'on remonte de siécle en siécle jusqu'à l'Antiquité la plus reculée, qu'y trouverat-on de comparable au spectacle qui fait aujourd'hui l'attention de l'Univers; toute l'Europe armée contre vous, et toute l'Europe trop foible.

Qu'il nous soit permis, SIRE, de détourner un moment les yeux d'une gloire si éclatante, et d'oublier, s'il est possible, le Vainqueur des Nations, le Vengeur des Rois, le Défenseur des Autels, pour ne regarder que le Protecteur de l'Académie Françoise. Nous sentons combien nous honore une protection si glorieuse; mais quel bonheur pour nous de trouver en même temps le modéle le plus parfait de l'Eloquence?

Vous êtes, SIRE, naturellement et sans art ce que nous tâchons de devenir par le travail et par l'étude: il règne dans tous vos discours une souveraine raison, toûjours soutenue d'expressions fortes et précises, qui vous rendent maître de toute l'âme de ceux qui vous écoutent, et ne leur laissent d'autre volonté que la vôtre. L'Eloquence où nous aspirons par nos veilles, et qui est en vous un don du Ciel, que ne doit-elle point à vos actions héroïques? Les graces que vous versez sans cesse sur les gens de Lettres peuvent bien faire fleurir les arts et les sciences; mais ce sont les grands événemens, qui font les Poëtes et les Orateurs: les merveilles de votre règne en auroient fait naître au milieu d'un pays barbare.

Tandis que nous nous appliquons à l'embellissement de notre langue, vos armes victorieuses la font passer chez les étrangers: nous leur en facilitons l'intelligence par notre travail, et vous la leur rendez nécessaire par vos conquêtes: et si elle va encore plus loin que vos conquêtes, si elle réduit toutes les langues des pays où elle est connue, à ne servir presque plus qu'au commun du peuple, une si haute destinée vient moins de sa beauté naturelle et des ornemens que nous avons tâché d'y ajoûter, que de l'avantage d'être la langue de la Nation, qui vous a pour Monarque, et (nous ne craignons point de le dire) que vous avez rendue la Nation dominante. Vous répandez sur nous un éclat, qui assujettit les étrangers à nos coûtumes dans tout ce que leurs loix peuvent leur avoir laissé de libre: ils se font honneur de parler comme ce peuple à qui vous avez appris à surmonter tous les obstacles, à ne plus trouver de places imprenables, à forcer les retranchemens les plus inaccessibles. Quel empressement, SIRE, la postérité n'aura-t-elle point à rechercher, à recuillir les mémoires de votre vie, les Chants de victoire qu'on aura mêlez à vos triomphes? C'est ce qui nous répond du succès de notre ouvrage; et s'il arrive, comme nous osons l'espérer, qu'il ait le pouvoir de fixer la Langue pour toûjours, ce ne sera pas tant par nos soins, que parce que les livres et les autres monuments qui parleront du règne de VOSTRE MAJESTE, feront les délices de tous les peuples, feront l'étude de tous les Rois, et seront toûjours regardez comme faits dans le temps de la pureté du langage et dans le beau siécle de la France. Nous sommes avec une profonde vénération, etc.

Text of the published epistle

AU ROY

L'Académie française ne peut se refuser la gloire de publier son Dictionnaire sous les auspices de son auguste Protecteur. Cet Ouvrage est un Recueil fidelle de tous les termes & de toutes les phrases dont l'Eloquence & la Poësie peuvent former des éloges; mais nous avoüons, SIRE, qu'en voulant travailler au vostre, vous nous avez fait sentir plus d'une fois la faiblesse de nostre Langue. Lorsque nostre zele ou nostre devoir nous ont engagez à celebrer vos exploits, les mots de valeur, de courage, & d'intrépidité nous ont paru trop foibles; & quand il a fallu parler de la profondeur & du secret impenetrable de vos desseins, que la seule execution découvre aux yeux des hommes, les mots de prévoyance, de prudence & de sagesse mesme ne respondoient qu'imparfaitement à nos idées. Ce qui nous console, SIRE, c'est que sur un pareil sujet les autres Langues n'auroient aucun avantage sur la nostre. Celle des Grecs & celle de Romains seroient dans la mesme impuissance, le Ciel n'ayant pas voulu accorder au langage des hommes des expressions aussi sublimes que les vertus qu'il leur accorde quelquefois pour la gloire de leur siecle. Comment exprimer cet air de grandeur marqué sur vostre front, & respandu sur toute votre Personne, cette fermeté d'ame que rien n'est capable d'ébranler, cette tendresse pour le peuple, vertu si rare sur le thrône, & ce qui doit toucher particulièrement des gens de lettres, cette eloquence née avec vous, qui tousjours soustenuë d'expressions nobles & précises, vous rend Maistre de tous ceux qui vous escoutent, & ne leur laisse d'autre volonté que la vostre. Mais où trouver des termes pour raconter les merveilles de vostre Regne? Que l'on remonte de siecle en siecle, on ne trouvera rien de comparable au spectacle qui fait aujourd'huy l'attention de l'Univers: Toute l'Europe armée contre vous, & Toute l'Europe trop foible.

C'est sur de tels fondemens que s'appuye l'esperance de l'Immortalité où nous aspirons; & quel gage plus certain pouvons-nous en souhaitter que vostre Gloire, qui asseurée par elle-mesme de vivre eternellement dans la memoire des hommes, y fera vivre nos Ouvrages? L'auguste Nom qui les deffendra du temps, en deffendra aussi la Langue, qui aura servi à le celebrer, & nous ne doutons point que le respect qu'on aura pour une Langue que vous aurez parlée, que vous aurez employée à dicter vos resolutions dans vos Conseils, & à donner vos ordres à la teste de vos Armées, ne la fasse triompher de tous les siecles. La supériorité de vostre Puissance l'a desja renduë la Langue dominante de la plus belle partie du monde. Tandis que nous nous appliquons à l'embellir, vos armes victorieuses la font passer chez les Etrangers, nous leur en facilitons l'intelligence par nostre travail, & vous la leur rendez necessaire par vos Conquestes; & si elle va encore plus loin que vos Conquestes, si elle se voit aujourd'huy establie dans la plupart des Cours de l'Europe, si elle reduit pour ainsi dire les Langues de Païs où elle est connuë, à ne servir presque plus qu'au commun du Peuple, si enfin elle tient le premier rang entre les Langues vivantes, elle doit moins une si haute destinée à sa beauté naturelle, qu'au rang que vous tenez entre les Rois et les Heros.

Que si l'on a jamais deu se promettre qu'une Langue vivante peust parvenir à estre fixée, et à ne dépendre plus du caprice & de la tyrannie de l'Usage, nous avons lieu de croire que la nostre est parvenuë de nos jours à ce glorieux point d'immutabilité, puisque les livres & les autres monumens qui parleront de VOSTRE MAJESTE, seront tousjours regardez comme faits dans le beau siecle de la France, & feront à jamais les delices de tous les peuples, & l'estude de tous les Rois.

Notes

For full authors' names, titles, and publishing data on the works cited in short form in the Notes, see the Bibliography. Unless otherwise noted, all citations to Perrault's *Contes* in the text and the Notes are to Marc Soriano's 1989 edition.

Chapter 1

1. For short tales like "Le Miroir," I have chosen to indicate only the inclusive pages (in this case, 84–95) rather than encumber the commentaries with a raft of numbers for quotations that can be easily tracked down.

2. The source I cite for the *Parallèle* (Slatkine Reprints, 1970) reproduces four of the original pages on a single large page. Accordingly, I shall generally provide two sets of numbers: the original volume and page number in vol. 3, followed by the Slatkine pagination. The first of these numbers correlates systematically with the pagination reproduced in the very useful 1964 edition of the *Parallèle* published by Hans Kortum, which includes a noteworthy introductory essay by H.-R. Jauss.

3. In expanding upon this analogical definition with great insistence by invoking the painter's techniques, the Abbé studiously omits any reference either to the doctrine of *ut pictura poesis* or to contemporary discussions of the doctrine of imitation.

4. For a probing critical account of the Freudian view, see Irigaray, *Speculum*, especially the treatment of the male gaze as the source of phallomorphic metaphors (in "Another 'Cause'—Castration," 46–55).

5. Descartes, *Oeuvres philosophiques*, 1: 651.

6. Descartes, *Méditations*, 78. This and other quotations are translated from the Latin text in the widely available Garnier-Flammarion paperback edition. I have benefited from the recent Livre de Poche edition by Michelle Beyssade, who supplements the Latin text and the 1647 translation by the Duc de Luynes with her own retranslation in modern French.

7. Descartes, *Méditations*, 90, 92.   8. Ibid., 94; my italics.

9. Ibid., 96–98.   10. Ibid., 110.

11. Heuristic considerations—the essay provides a conveniently compact distillation—prompt me to cite this account of Heidegger's line on the *cogito*, rather than the much more elaborate one set forth in his two-volume study on Nietzsche.

12. Heidegger, "Age," 133.

13. Ibid., 149–50.

14. Descartes, *Méditations*, 86; my italics.

15. Henry, *Généalogie*, 27. For my purposes, Henry's exceptionally emphatic resistance to a representationalist recuperation of the *cogito* has the advantage of marking the oppositions with maximal clarity. Aside from others (Derrida, Nancy) who resist the slippage to which Henry objects in Heidegger's reading, he is hardly alone in commenting on the apperception of feeling in the *Traité des passions* (see, e.g., Beyssade, *Philosophie première*, 202–14). On the interesting difficulties of Henry's reading see Borch-Jacobsen's probing essay "The Unconscious, Nonetheless," in *The Emotional Tie*, 123–54.

16. Henry, *Généalogie*, 28–29.

17. Ibid., 31.

18. See Descartes, *Passions de l'âme*, para. 5, 19, 26.

19. Ibid., para. 17. See also paras. 21, 25.

20. See Henry, *Généalogie*, 72–74.

21. Ibid., 82–86.

22. Descartes, *Oeuvres*, 3: 118.

23. Neither in the *Parallèle* nor in the *Pensées chrétiennes* does Perrault display an awareness of the irony of a "modern" appealing to the classificatory scheme of the neo-Platonic Porphyrus (remembered primarily as the editor of Plotinus's works, but also as a student of Longinus).

24. The modern reader needs to distinguish the relatively slight interest of Perrault's lightweight discourse on the *cogito* or on the proofs of the existence of God from the considerable interest and importance of the man/animal distinction. In part, the interest stems from the fact that Perrault pursues the question with remarkable vigor and tenacity, and in part it has to do with the historical significance of efforts to replace Descartes's mechanistic model of animal behavior at a moment when the "life sciences" were about to emerge. See Foucault, *Mots et choses*, chap. 5, "Classer"; and Roger, *Sciences de la vie*.

25. Descartes, *Méditations*, 164.

26. Ibid.

27. The name Riquet is commonly treated as a diminutive of Richard, which incorporates components (rich + ard) that evoke a rich man. For a

discussion of the name and its connotations see Marin, *Food for Thought*, 165–68.

Chapter 2

1. See La Bruyère, "Des jugements," in *Les Caractères*, 12: 107.

2. Perrault's commitment to the glorification of Louis XIV seems not to have been shaken either by his own experience of falling into relative disfavor or by the following explanation of degeneration he encountered in reading Boileau's translation of *Le Traité du sublime*: "Mais nous, continuoit-il, qui avons appris dés nos premieres années à souffrir le joug d'une domination legitime, qui avons esté comme enveloppez par les coûtumes et les façons de faire de la Monarchie . . . : ce qui arrive ordinairement de nous, c'est que nous nous rendons de grands et magnifiques Flatteurs" (But we, he continued, who have learned from childhood to suffer under the yoke of a legitimate domination, who have been, as it were, enveloped by the methods and customs of monarchy . . . : what ordinarily becomes of us is that we turn into grand and glorious flatterers; Boileau, *Oeuvres complètes*, 400). Perrault did, to be sure, take note of the paradoxical position that he occupied in praising his adversaries: "D'excellens hommes de nostre temps que j'ay loüez & dont j'ay cité les ouvrages comme des preuves incontestables de la superiorité de nôtre siecle, ont mieux aimé se fascher de l'injustice qu'ils pretendent que j'ay faite aux Anciens, que de me sçavoir gré de la justice que je leur ay renduë" (Excellent men of our time whom I have praised and whose works I have cited as incontestable proofs of the superiority of our century, rather than being grateful to me for having given them their due, have preferred being angry with me for the injustice they claim I have done to the Ancients; *Parallèle*, 4: preface; 281–82).

3. See, in particular, Fénelon's *Lettre*, pt. IV, "Projet de rhétorique" (38–61). It suffices to read Fénelon's famous letter to Louis XIV (*Oeuvres*, 541–51) to see that his work presents an extraordinary case of dissidence from the prevailing view of the century. See, for example, the intriguing discussion of *Les Aventures de Télémaque* by Philippe-Joseph Salazar, in Citti, *Fins de siècle*, 173–85.

4. Boileau, *L'Art poétique*, chant 1, in *Oeuvres complètes*, 159. Traditional literary scholarship, as exemplified by A. Adam's introduction to the Pléiade edition, recognizes the high level of subtlety and strategic compromising that Boileau achieved in *L'Art poétique*, as well as his sustained attentiveness to the sublime and the role of sentiment in aesthetic judgment. It is therefore surprising to find in Luc Ferry's recent work *Homo Aestheticus* a hopelessly reductive account of Boileau's classicism, along with a free-

wheeling view of Dominique Bouhour's dialogues that patient readers will find simply amazing.

5. Jacques Le Brun's introductory note to the Pléiade edition dates the composition of Fénelon's dialogues (which were not published until 1718) between 1677 and 1681, that is, after *L'Art poétique* and before the flare-up of the quarrel between Boileau and Perrault in 1688.

6. Dominique Bouhours, *Les Entretiens d'Ariste et d'Eugène* (1671) and *La Manière de bien parler dans les ouvrages de l'esprit* (1687); René Rapin, *Les Réflexions sur la poétique de ce temps et sur les ouvrages des poètes anciens et modernes* (1677).

7. Fénelon, *Oeuvres*, 26.

8. See the introduction and chap. 1 of Khibédi-Varga, *Rhétorique et littérature*.

9. Since the version of the treatise provided by Boileau's translation and its account of authorship are centrally at issue here, I have elected to follow the convention of those commentators who continue to refer to the anonymous author as Longinus.

10. Boileau, *Oeuvres complètes*, 338. All page citations in the subsequent discussion are to this Pléiade edition, but for the occasional reference to a chapter, I use the numbers that are followed uniformly in modern editions of *On the Sublime*.

11. Ibid., 340.

12. Ibid., 336.

13. Note, for example, the correspondence between the first two paragraphs of Longinus's chap. 2 (Boileau, *Oeuvres complètes*, 342–43) and the first half of the title Boileau gives the chapter: "S'il y a un art particulier du sublime; et des trois vices qui luy sont opposez" (Whether there is a special art of the sublime, and of the three vices opposed to it).

14. Ibid., 337; my italics.

15. Needless to say, Boileau's adaptive practice of translation, while making the text eminently readable, produces numerous unfortunate side effects. The essential account of the Boileau-Longinus relationship is provided by Brody, *Boileau and Longinus*. For a brilliant analysis of issues pertaining to the translation of Longinus and helpful retranslations of key passages on the sublime, see Michel Deguy, "Le Grand-dire," in Nancy, ed., *Du sublime*. The implications of translation are further illuminated in the remarkable essay by Philippe Lacoue-Labarthe, "La Vérité sublime," in the same volume.

16. Hertz, *End of the Line*, 7.

17. Boileau, *Oeuvres complètes*, 357; my italics.

18. Ibid., 550.

19. The poem is reprinted in the appendix to vol. 1 of Perrault's *Parallèle* (Slatkine ed., 79–85).

20. Boileau, *Oeuvres complètes*, 546ff. Reflection 10 takes up the objections to the *Traité du sublime* published in 1709 by Jean Le Clerc, who cited a long letter containing the criticisms authored by the erudite bishop Pierre-Daniel Huet (known principally as an outspoken defender of the Bible against philological and philosophical interpretations ventured by the likes of Spinoza). Boileau had first responded to Huet's objection to the line from Genesis in his original preface to the treatise, some 35 years earlier.

21. Ibid., 551–52.

22. For a summary view see Marin, "On the Sublime."

23. Boileau, *Oeuvres complètes*, 366, 368.   24. Ibid., 370.

25. Ibid., 369.   26. Ibid., 370.

27. An exceedingly capacious reading of Longinus's account of the effacement of figures, close in its general outlines to the one I have sketched, is offered by Philippe Lacoue-Labarthe (in Nancy, ed., *Du sublime*, 139–45). I have left aside here pursuit of the connections between the analysis of the play of light and the presence of the monarchic witness in whose sight the visibility of figures is compromising. An attempt to appreciate the status of the discourse of flattery in the work of Boileau, Perrault, and others would need to return to this passage in Longinus and to ask, for example, how it illuminates the senses of truth in a strong and sophisticated text such as Boileau's ninth *épître*, the nuances of which appear to escape Luc Ferry (*Homo Aestheticus*, 54–60).

28. Boileau, *Oeuvres complètes*, 392.

29. The Abbé is forceful in underscoring the centrality of metaphor in Perrault's vision of rhetoric. Consider, for example, this criticism of a long quotation from Demosthenes: "Rien n'est plus sec ny plus despourveu d'ornemens, il ne s'y rencontre pas le moindre tour d'Eloquence, non pas mesme une seule metaphore, figure si necessaire à tout discours un peu soustenu, que sans elle l'Eloquence n'y sçauroit subsister dans l'étenduë de deux periodes" (Nothing is drier nor more deprived of ornaments; there isn't the slightest sample of eloquence, and not even a single metaphor, the figure so necessary to any sustained discourse that without it eloquence could not be stretched across two periods; 2: 162–63; 134). In order to describe the rule of metaphor (to use Ricoeur's term) in Perrault's dialogues, one would have to connect this understanding of its role as the figurative tissue of imaginative discourse with the unconceptualized metaphorics I have sketched here in a very rudimentary fashion. This would entail, in turn, taking into account my discussion of Perrault's treatment of vision, sight, lenses, and mirroring in Chapter One. The operation of the transferential system of metaphor, governed by the imagery of light, conforms with the now classic account set forth in Derrida, "Economimésis."

30. Perrault doubtless has in mind the tradition of *dialogues des morts*, revived by his ally in the Quarrel, Bernard le Bovier de Fontenelle, in the

Nouveaux dialogues des morts (1680). In the early 1690s, Fénelon was composing his *Dialogues des morts* (originally published in 1711), with their extremely engaging dialogues of Cicero and Demosthenes (dialogues 31–33).

31. Boileau, *Oeuvres complètes*, 361.

32. Ibid.

33. Ibid., 363.

34. Perrault's stance on the decadence of rhetoric is curiously elusive. Whereas the very possibility is dismissed by the Chevalier (2: 177; 138), the thrust of the following mocking and oddly incoherent discussion of Quintilian (2: 198–226; 143–50) appears to be that accusations of decline are not to be taken seriously.

35. Boileau, *Oeuvres complètes*, 353.

36. The opposition between Perrault and Boileau over the sublime dovetails, however, with their conflicting views on *le merveilleux* in opera, of which the Abbé offers a nicely schematized summary (3: 282–84; 267–68).

37. The *Parallèle* also appropriates, inevitably, the broad expressive range of *esprit* that accounts for its capacity to underwrite the rationalization (or sublimation) of the *merveilleux* and the sublime. In the *Contes*, however, the manipulation of the term is far more studied and concerted.

38. *Les Hommes illustres* provides a clear indication of the extent to which Perrault reduces the factors of genius and passion to a minimal role in his account of artistic production. The one striking case in which he appears to recognize something akin to sublime authorship is Corneille, whom he treats as the French Homer and to whom he ascribes "grandeur de génie" (grandeur of genius; 1: 77). The other noteworthy case is the forceful attribution to La Fontaine of "le talent merveilleux que la Nature luy donna" (the marvelous talent that Nature gave him; 1: 85).

39. Perrault's view, expressed in his many comments on translation into French, is made explicit in the *épître dédicatoire* he composed for the *Dictionnaire de l'Académie française* (1694) and is echoed in the portrait of Corneille noted above: "Si le François est devenu le Langage de tous les honnestes Gens de L'Europe, la France n'en est pas seulement redevable à la gloire du Prince que le Ciel luy a donné, mais au desir qu'ont eu tous les Peuples de gouster les beautez des Pieces de ce grand Poëte dans leur Langue naturelle" (If French has become the language of all the right-thinking people of Europe, France owes this not only to the glory of the prince heaven has given her, but to the desire of all peoples to perceive the beauties of this great poet's plays in their natural language; *Hommes illustres*, 1: 78).

40. The quick dismissal of criticism via an ironic allusion to censorship is of course an exceedingly commonplace and facile device. Perrault spells

out its principle succinctly with respect to Balzac's letters: "Elles eurent aussi leurs Censeurs en grand nombre, elles estoient trop belles pour en manquer" (They also had a profusion of censors; they were too fine to be wanting for them; *Hommes illustres*, 1: 71).

41. In studying *Les Hommes illustres* as an important early work of French literary and cultural history, one would need to ask not simply what (or to what extent) principles of inclusion and exclusion inform Perrault's selections, but what values inform the judgments he expresses in individual portraits. It is evident that he remains vigilantly attentive to the long-standing conflict of the Ancients and the Moderns. The only ready source of cohesion that he perceives appears to be the role of Louis XIV—his inspiring influence and the benevolent effects of his subsidization of artists—in the cultural sphere. For those who are caught up in the monumentality of the king's reign, Louis's longevity is surely, as we have noted, a crucial obstacle to periodization and to writing that discusses end-of-century realities objectively.

Chapter 3

1. Soriano, *Brosse*, 52.

2. The two-dozen-odd figure is based on the Pléiade volumes edited by Raymond Picard; see especially vol. 2, sec. 6, pts. 2–4, which include texts omitted from other "oeuvres complètes" of Racine. On the other hand, some of Racine's editors do include the annotations of Perrault's draft epistle and the published piece. See, for example, the introductory note and the two texts in the 1961 single-volume edition in the Seuil "L'Intégrale" series, 422–25. Texts of the draft and published epistles are reproduced in the appendix.

3. Soriano, *Brosse*, 90 (n. to p. 60).

4. Ibid., 60. The following quote is from p. 61.

5. Ibid., 66.

6. See Soriano, *Contes de Perrault*, 275.

7. Viala, *Racine*, 113.

8. Ibid., 117.

9. Other editors use the same numbering. Of the five segments that I do not place in this category, three (7, 23, 28) have to do with logic and argument and one (26) with the conception of the dictionary. I excluded the fifth (14) hesitantly; it states approval, but then points malevolently toward a possible, albeit unlikely, misconstrual, thus implying that a more scrupulous stylist would have turned the phrase differently. I should note that Soriano recognizes the primacy of remarks on "la propriété des termes et le style de Perrault" (*Brosse*, 51–52), but whereas I am pointing to a

position on language that the annotations develop cumulatively, Soriano's emphasis is indeed on Perrault's style, and especially on the parallel between flaws detected by Racine and two stylistic tendencies—"une tendance à la duplication . . . et une tendance contraire—inconsciente ou mal contrôlée—à inverser le sens de ce qui est dit" (a tendency toward duplication and an opposite tendency—unconscious or ill-controlled—to invert the meaning of what is said; 51) that Soriano traces to the experience of twinship.

10. Ibid., 48.

11. It is somewhat curious that Soriano's chronology, designed to furnish background on the disputes between Perrault and Racine, omits from the period 1675–76 an episode in the Quarrel of the Ancients and Moderns that specifically concerned a proposal in the academy, advocated by Perrault but rejected, to modify the lagging dictionary project.

12. See Viala, *Racine*, 244–45.

13. Polemical appropriations of the phrase "langues de bois" in the discourse of contemporary French politics would, I surmise, exemplify such abuse. I would suggest concomitantly that the term *propaganda* has stood up well in historical studies, and that the background provided by scholarly work on propagandistic discourse is a significant reason for preferring it to the abstract expression "langue de bois" ("une langue dans la langue" connotes an orientation or cast put on the full range of the language, rather than a special idiom, a language or discourse peculiar to a particular group of users or object of representation). By contrast, the term propaganda (a) does not draw attention away from the occasional nature of the texts (Perrault's, Racine's, the academy's) designed to carry out a highly overdetermined discursive act, and (b) maintains the premise that the subject who writes and/or signs a text is responsible for it as a particular use, but not a distinct version, of the national language in which it is composed—in this case, spectacularly, the French language as registered in the work the epistle dedicates. Propaganda implies compliance with a position, but not necessarily the mindless repetition of doxological propositions. For discussion of the analytic concept of ideology that is widely used in contemporary social science and is in my view a necessary safeguard if one is to risk the kind of judgmental intellectual history that Soriano advocates, see Dumont, *Essais*; and for an extremely helpful account of propaganda's role in the analysis of discourse, see Angenot, *Parole pamphlétaire*. For a superb account of the evolution of the propaganda machine under Louis XIV, see Apostolidès, *Roi-machine*.

14. Picard, *Carrière*, 338. For Soriano's denunciation of Picard's editorial stance, see *Brosse*, 11.

15. Soriano, *Brosse*, 70.

16. Ibid., 71.

17. Todorov, *Morales*, 280. The following quote appears at p. 290.

18. A curious omission: Todorov mentions no source for this distinction between revelation and representation, the history of which can be traced back at least to Plato, and the fortune of which in contemporary thought is, to say the least, very prominent. It has been particularly important as a lever for deconstructive analysis in the orbit of Heidegger, Derrida, Lyotard, and others—that is, in a vein of inquiry that Todorov appeared to value for its exegetical power in some of his early work, but that he now classifies as "Nietzschean philosophies of difference" and anathematizes.

19. For an economic and useful exposition of the terminological framework that underlies much of this essay's commentary on the text of the dedicatory epistle, see Patillon, *Eléments de rhétorique classique*. On the evolving understanding and use of rhetoric in seventeenth-century France, Khibédi-Varga, *Rhétorique et littérature*, is an invaluable resource. My understanding of the larger communicative framework operative within explanatory discourse derives directly from Khibédi-Varga's illuminating discussion in chap. 2, "Le Discours," of his *Discours, récit, image*.

20. Following Khibédi-Varga, Louis Marin, and many others, I take for well established two operative premises that will quickly become evident here: (a) both the terms and the viewpoints of classical rhetoric are particularly relevant to the analytic study of writers like Racine and Perrault because they put us directly in touch with a conceptual framework in which they were schooled and to which they devoted a great deal of critical reflection; (b) it is almost inevitable for modern scholars to use the marvelous *summa* produced by Pierre Fontanier early in the 19th century as a basic source of descriptive concepts in conducting analyses of stylistic or evolutionary phenomena of the type I venture in this essay. I am also indebted to many probing discussions of these concepts in Morier, *Dictionnaire de poétique*.

21. "Discours prononcé à l'Académie française à la réception de M. l'abbé Colbert," in Racine, *Oeuvres complètes* (Pléiade ed.), 342. For a brilliant reading of this text, see the chapter entitled "Stratégies raciniennes," in Marin, *Portrait du roi*, 130–43 (*Portrait of the King*, 105–17).

22. Fontanier, *Figures du discours*, 143.

23. On the special significance of the spectacle in the environment of Louis XIV's court, see Apostolidès, *Roi-machine*, 135–59. In commenting on the words "spectacle" and "attention," my intent is to underscore the work of the Indo-European roots *spek-* and *ten-* in the organization, not only of the portrait, but of the conceptual apparatus that Perrault's writing deploys. The function of terms built upon the Latin *specere* (speck, specta-

tor, spectrum, specular, spectral, etc.) and the metathetical form that yields the Greek *skopos* (scope, scopophilia, telescope, skeptic, spectroscope, etc.) has been amply elucidated by feminist critics of our time. The case of *ten-*, which appears in the Latin *tendere* (tend, tender, tent, attend, pretend, ostensible, etc.) and the Greek *teinein* (epitasis, protasis, hypotenuse, tendon, tone, etc.) is all the more worthy of investigation, since it also enters the Latin family based on *tenere* (tenable, tenet, tenor, contain, retain, pertain, etc.). In French, the question has to do with the potential for interplay between *tendre* and *tenir*, that is, conceptually, between presence and possession.

24. "L'hypotypose peint les choses d'une manière si vive et si énergique, qu'elle les met en quelque sorte sous les yeux, et fait d'un récit ou d'une description, une image, un tableau, ou même une scène vivante" (Hypotyposis depicts things so vividly and energetically that in a sense it puts them under our eyes, making a narrative or description an image, a picture, or even a living scene). Fontanier, *Figures de discours*, 390.

25. In the passage of portraiture developed via hypotyposis and preterition that we are reading with some patience here, the conjunction *mais* is almost certainly not used in the adversative or contrastive sense to which we are accustomed in modern French. Although it does mark distinction and opposition vis-à-vis the preceding clause, its principal function is that of a reinforcing connective that marks intensification. In translation, "yet" or "moreover" rather than "but."

26. The choice of qualifiers—among *conceptual, argumentative, thematic, semantic, enthymematic, demonstrative*, etc.—is delicate here. Within the passage, the construction of the portrait, which is clearly figural, is much more concerted and transparent than the reflection on language and expression. The latter, which extends across the entire paragraph, can be situated on various levels, ranging from the most immediately practical to the highly theoretical. My intuitive sense, which is based on diverse discussions in Perrault's *Parallèle des anciens et des modernes* and which must be stated very reservedly, is that Perrault's approach lies in the middle between the extremes. Hence the choice of "conceptual," which does imply an attempt to sustain within the construction of the portrait an explicit attention to the problem of expression that it resolves.

27. See, in particular, Marin's introduction and first chapter (7–46) and *finale* (263–90).

28. "L'enthymémisme . . . consiste dans un rapprochement vif et rapide de deux propositions ou de deux termes, d'où résulte dans l'esprit une conséquence vive et frappante qui le saisit et l'entraîne d'une manière victorieuse" (*Enthymémisme* consists of two propositions or terms brought together in a lively or rapid manner, so as to instill the mind with a vivid

and striking result that seizes and captivates it). Fontanier, *Figures du discours*, 382–83. The figure is obviously not to be confused with the Aristotelian category of enthymematic or deductive reasoning (see Barthes, "Ancienne Rhétorique," B. 1.6–1.17).

29. Earlier I used the term *metonymic condensation* to characterize the image of Europe stylistically, that is, in the discursive architecture of the epistle, as a figure that resumes presidentially, so to speak, both the part of the letter that precedes it and the part that follows. The process of association makes it possible for the name *Europe* to function as a metonym insofar as it embraces, on the one hand, the theater of Louis XIV's presence (e.g., Europe armée = the several European countries aligned against France in the War of the League of Augsburg), and on the other hand, the components of his biography ("Europe trop foible" = the scene of many conquests). But technically, the status of the image in the passage—even when we do not extend the exegetical effort to include the reference to concrete history (i.e., the strained military-political position of France in 1694)—is a good deal more complicated than my guarded account suggests. In essence, the rhetorical weave of the passage is such that a whole range of figures and tropes are activated in and around the phrase "toute l'Europe armée contre vous, et toute l'Europe trop foible." I have mentioned parataxis, *enthymémisme*, interrogation, narration, preterition, hypotyposis, apposition, and ellipsis (without yet even noting the effect of ellipsis created in the image itself by the qualification of the second "toute l'Europe," which is limited to the adjective *faible*). The tropical intersection/condensation would have to include as well: simile (through the elaborate comparison constructed by the sentence the image finishes), metaphor (i.e., the construction of European geography as a metaphoric representation of Louis's power), personification (through the exchange set off by the opposition of "l'Europe armée" to "vous"), and perhaps synecdoche (l'Europe armée = the inhabitants of Europe taking up their arms, the whole thus naming the parts). In the course of further analysis, it would be interesting to bring up the long-standing question of whether any benefit can be gained from distinguishing the operation of synecdoche from that of metonymy: does the indecisive demarcation of the figures correspond (a) to the insurmountable duplicity built into the image and (b) to the indecisive position the analysis would have to integrate upon considering the referential content of this Europe, represented as the theater of Louis's triumph but in terms that also reflect the military stalemate of the 1690s?

30. Marin, *Portrait du roi*, 51–107.

31. Quoted in ibid., 50.

32. Although contorted, this formulation is by no means farfetched. Consider, for example, the academy's understanding of the dictionary

project as it is set forth by Racine at the end of the same speech welcoming l'abbé Colbert into the academy that we considered earlier: "Et ce travail même qui nous est commun, ce dictionnaire qui de soi-même semble une occupation si sèche et si épineuse, nous y travaillons avec plaisir. Tous les mots de la langue, toutes les syllabes nous paraissent précieuses, parce que nous les regardons comme autant d'instruments qui doivent servir à la gloire de notre auguste protecteur" (And this very work that is our common task, the dictionary that seems, in itself, to be such a dry and thorny occupation, is work we pursue with pleasure. All the words of the language, all of its syllables, seem precious to us because we regard them as so many instruments that should serve the glory of our august protector). Racine, *Oeuvres complètes* (Pléiade), 343–44. Alain Rey aptly terms the phenomenon in question here "linguistic absolutism." We can contrast Perrault's hyperbolic vision with the realistic view of the dictionary's future value that Fénelon would set forth in his "Lettre à l'Académie" some twenty years later ("Quand notre langue sera changée, il servira à faire entendre les livres dignes de la postérité qui sont écrits en notre temps. . . . Un jour on sentira la commodité d'avoir un Dictionnaire qui serve de clef à tant de bon livres"; When our language is transformed, it will serve to transmit the books of our time that are worthy of survival. . . . A day will come when we shall appreciate the usefulness of having a dictionary that is the key to good books). *Lettre*, 25–26. Pursuit of the inquiry I suggest in my conclusion would usefully compare the representation of the king in Fénelon's celebrated letter of remonstrance to Louis XIV (December 1693 or January 1694) to the generous portrait of the king he offered less than a year earlier (March 1693) in the concluding paragraphs of his "Discours prononcé dans l'Académie française."

33. A text worthy of special consideration here is René Rapin's *Le Magnanime ou l'éloge de Louis de Bourbon* (Paris: Jeremie Bouillerof, 1690), which begins by elaborating a multifaceted distinction between *l'éloge* and *le panégyrique*. See also France, *Politeness*, chap. 1, especially 15–18.

Chapter 4

1. Simonsen, *Conte populaire*, 26–27.

2. The essential points on the author/audience relation are well presented in Barchilon, *Conte merveilleux* (see especially the discussion of effects indicative of the writer's *clin d'oeil*, 31–36), and nicely summarized by Zipes in his introduction to his translation of Perrault's tales.

3. The broad framework of Lévi-Strauss's study is succinctly sketched in *L'Origine des manières de table* as follows: "En ajoutant d'autres dimensions au modèle, on intégrera les aspects diachroniques, tels ceux qui concernent l'ordre, la présentation et les gestes du repas. . . . Ainsi peut-on

espérer découvrir, pour chaque cas particulier, comment la cuisine d'une société est un langage dans lequel elle traduit inconsciemment sa structure, à moins que, sans le savoir davantage, elle ne se résigne à y dévoiler ses contradictions" (If further dimensions were added to the model, it could be made to include diachronic aspects, such as the order and presentation of meals and behavior during them. . . . Thus we can hope to discover how, in any particular society, cooking is a language through which that society unconsciously reveals its structure, unless—just as unconsciously—it resigns itself to using the medium to express its contradictions); *The Origin of Table Manners*, tr. John and Doreen Weightman, 495. In the rest of this chapter I shall, with some reluctance, use the English translations of the works by Lévi-Strauss and Louis Marin.

4. Lévi-Strauss, *Origin*, 489.   5. Ibid., 420.

6. Ibid., 498, 499.   7. Ibid., 499.

8. To my knowledge, the first strong appropriation of Elias's theses in studies of the fairy tale occurs in Jack Zipes's pathbreaking book, *Fairy Tales and the Art of Subversion* (1983). On Perrault and 17th-century France, see especially chaps. 1 and 2.

9. Elias, *Civilizing Process*, 1: 127. On "fork rituals" see 1: 126.

10. Ibid., 120–21.

11. Marin, *Food for Thought*, 131. The translator of *La Parole mangée* retains the French term *transsignifiance* in English, perhaps hoping to preserve thereby the particular connotation of the term *signifiance*, as distinct from *signification*, *signifié*, and *signifiant*. *Signifiance* usually refers to the power or capacity to signify, to signifying potential or "signifiability," whereas the other three terms refer to aspects of the sign or the act of signification. I shall use *transsignifiance* only in italics, designating thereby the French term. But in most cases I have preferred the neologism "transignification," referring not to signifying potential but to the process or activity of signification.

12. Of the various 17th-century definitions of the "sauce Robert," the most precise is the one in Pierre Richelet's *Dictionnaire français* (1680): "C'est une sauce avec des oignons, de la moutarde, du beurre, du poivre, du sel et du vinaigre, qu'on met ordinairement avec du porc frais rôti" (a sauce with onions, mustard, butter, pepper, salt, and vinegar that one ordinarily serves with freshly roasted pork; cited in Collinet's edition of the *Contes*, 321–22). France, *Politeness*, 33, describes the ogress's desire to eat her granddaughter "à la sauce Robert" as a curious detail "which seems to poke fun at the notion of cannibalism, though without really undermining the macabre effect of these pages." From my vantage point and that of Louis Marin, this detail points cagily to the phenomenon I treat more concertedly in Chapters Five and Six, Perrault's artful construction of ogres and ogresses as ambiguous, partially acculturated figures.

13. Marin, *Food for Thought*, 145; my italics. I have slightly altered Jhort's translation.

14. Lévi-Strauss, *Pensée sauvage*, 139.

15. Marin, *Food for Thought*, 126.

16. Ibid., 128.

17. Ibid., xix.

18. See, in particular, Perrault's *Pensées chrétiennes*, in which he expresses his religious convictions with confidence and fervor. The place of the Eucharist as a referent in Perrault's thought is evident in paras. 29 and 54.

19. Marin, *Food for Thought*, xviii.

20. In its simplicity, Jesus's transfiguration, as presented in the gospels of Matthew, Mark, and Luke and in the second epistle of Peter, can be regarded as a model. The biblical narratives associate the disciples' vision of Christ's shining glory with a transformation of his identity, the nature of which is specified by the voice of God asserting that Jesus is his son. In its most immediate, elemental aspect, the figure is the face that is expressive of profound identity. In Luke's version (9: 28–36), this visible expression of glory is reinforced by the illuminative whitening of Jesus's garment.

21. Marin, *Food for Thought*, 46.

22. Type 510A for "Cendrillon," 510B for "Peau d'âne," in the extremely elaborate system exposed in *The Types of the Folk-tale*. In addition to the background presented in the basic works by Delarue and Soriano, Simonsen's *Perrault: Contes* provides very useful, concise accounts of the source material for each tale.

23. Gilbert Rouger, in his edition of the *Contes*, provides a persuasive justification of the reading "pantoufles de verre," as opposed to the claim of some readers (Balzac, Littré, Gide) that the homonymic "pantoufles de vair" (fur slippers) makes better sense. The line of insight developed here would reinforce the arguments of Rouger and his predecessor, Paul Delarue, with two points: (a) a slipper made of fur would be flexible, less well suited than the rigid glass for the shoefitting contest that Cendrillon wins; (b) a glass slipper, perceived as a refined artifact (one that may be light-conducting and thus capable of revealing what it delicately covers), makes a rather more appropriate object for the Prince's gaze than would a fur slipper (which could have masking, animalizing effects like those of the ass's skin).

24. My schematic representations of narrative structure are based on Thomas Pavel's proposal for a generative account of narrative syntax. At each structural level, the basic movement from disturbed equilibrium to restored equilibrium follows the same sequence: an initial situation is modified by a transgression that requires a corrective effort (mediation) by the hero or heroine leading to the dénouement, which can be either a success

or a failure. Subordinate narrative structures, such as NS^2, are actualizations or elaborations of the function under which they appear in the higher-level structure (NS^1). Thus, in the cases of "Cendrillon" and "Peau d'âne," NS^2 is an elaboration of the mediation function in NS^1. Each sequence conforms to the basic actantial or agential structure that Pavel takes from the work of A. J. Greimas. The abstract term *actant* refers to a role or function that is most commonly filled by a single character, but can also be occupied by composite agents (a couple, family, or group). Greimas identifies six actants that interact in a narrative sequence as follows: the *dispatcher*, identifiable as the object of the transgression, "sends" the *subject* (hero or heroine), who may be aided by an *ally* or hindered by an *opponent*, to seek an *object* (or reach a goal) for a *receiver* (or beneficiary). The name of the sequence is that of the character(s) in the dispatcher function.

Chapter 5

1. For a brief explanation of the tree diagram, see n. 24, Chap. Four.

2. Although the feminist allegory Hélène Cixous sketches in "Castration or Decapitation" is improvised and positioned at the antipodes of systematic criticism, it traces an extraordinarily incisive line of interpretation. Cixous treats the red hood of sex as a defiant exposure of the clitoris (i.e., of the organ of feminine sexuality that women are supposed to keep under cover). The wolf who ensnares Little Red Riding Hood deals with a threat to the masculine order by luring the girl back into the proper place of the exemplary woman, whose passivity is emblematized by "La Belle au bois dormant" when she is in bed asleep.

3. The set of associations that derive from the "head metaphor," as it were, is elaborated in Plato's *Timaeus*. Among the sexual connotations that the hood might have for certain readers, I should doubtless mention one that runs directly counter to Cixous's reading: might the red hood not allude to Paris's famous Phrygian cap and thus serve as a phallic symbol that is shocking to men since it is displaced onto the head of a woman? I should also point out the semantic interest that *chaperon* as a term and name brings into play via its root, *caput*: through its permutations, the "head metaphor" also presides over the vast semantic field of the term *capital*.

4. Bettelheim, *Uses of Enchantment*, 214–17.

5. Soriano, *Contes de Perrault*, 150ff. In his interesting and complex discussion of "Le Petit Chaperon rouge," Soriano makes less than is his wont of motifs in the folkloric sources that are suppressed in Perrault's version, notably a scene in which the wolf has Little Red Riding Hood cook some of her grandmother's flesh and blood, and another in which he has her remove her clothes garment by garment and throw them into the fire. Simonsen, *Perrault: Contes*, 59–62, suggests that Perrault's moderniza-

tion eliminates essentially the sequences that represent the initiation of women into their traditional familial roles.

6. Perrault's translation (Gabriel Faërne, *Cent Fables en latin et en français*) appeared in 1708 in a collection called *Lettres choisies de messieurs de l'Académie françoise*. The Bibliothèque nationale has separate editions of this short work published in 1725 and 1744; there have been no modern editions.

7. Didier, "Perrault féministe," 112. The frontispiece to the 1695 edition and the question of narrative voice are treated in another fine contribution to the special issue of *Europe* devoted to Perrault, in which the Didier article appears (739–40, Nov.–Dec. 1990): Louis Marin, "Préface-image: le frontispice des Contes-de-Perrault," 114–22.

8. For a lucid introduction to the problematics of consciousness and desire, see Borch-Jacobsen, *Lacan*, 81–90.

9. Ibid., 187.

10. For an interesting literary-historical discussion of ogres and Perrault's role and intentions in introducing them, see France, *Politeness and Its Discontents*, chap. 2.

Chapter 6

1. See Fig. 2, p. 168. For another account of the narrative structure that insists on two parallel dimensions over which the respective protagonists preside, see Flahaut, *Interprétation*, 87–88.

2. In Soriano's *Contes de Perrault*, see 165–70. See also Simonsen, *Perrault: Contes*, 66–68, and Velay-Vallantin, *Histoire*, 45–50.

3. Jean-Marie Apostolidès, in a brilliant realist reconstruction of the motives of Bluebeard and his wife ("Des choses cachées dans le château de Barbe-bleue," in *Marvels and Tales*, 5.2 [Dec. 1991]: 179–99), perceives in their union an allegorical representation of a failed marriage between representatives of two classes. Bluebeard, as Jacques Barchilon and Catherine Velay-Vallantin, among others, have suggested, is apparently a commoner who may well have amassed his riches through the speculative activity of a financier. One can presume that his goal is to attain ennoblement through an alliance with an impoverished aristocratic family, and Apostolidès treats his defeat as a momentary victory of the embattled class of nobility, carried out in the tale's comic ending by the family's use of his riches to reconstitute itself (196–97). While my reading can readily allow the conflict between the protagonists of the two narrative sequences to embrace such an opposition between bourgeois and aristocrat, it debouches in a somewhat more ambivalent view of the dénouement. In the light of the Perraldian posture of compromise that informs the *Contes* as a corpus, and noting, as does Velay-Vallantin (*Histoire*, 71), that Perrault refrained from specifying Bluebeard's apparently bourgeois and bastard origins, but left

them elusive and implied in his text, I take the ending to be less a last-gasp victory of a declining noble caste than a further, definitive sign of the aristocracy's drift into complicity and accommodation with the power and values of an ascendant bourgeoisie. Apostolidès, too, picks up on this ambivalence, blending it trenchantly with the motif of social contamination: "En un sens, la caste aristocratique ne peut survivre que par l'argent du crime, l'argent du sang, à condition qu'elle en taise l'origine douteuse" (In a sense, the aristoracy can survive only through the money of crime, of blood, and even then only by suppressing its suspect origin); "Des choses cachées," 197.

4. Apostolidès sets up an opposition of two secrets: Bluebeard's ("Des choses cachées," 185–88), which he treats hypothetically as a shameful past anchored in acquiring riches from the wives he took in and killed for their dowries, and the young wife's (189–93), which he imagines to be her deflowering. Her shameful descent into prohibited sexual behavior might have occurred, he speculates, during the week, mentioned at the beginning of the tale, of frolicking with her friends at Bluebeard's country house. As Apostolidès contends, this would provide a strong and pointed explanation of her willingness to marry Bluebeard that is missing in Perrault's text. Her entry into the forbidden chamber could then be construed in Freudian terms as a compulsive repetition of that first loss of innocence. Among the difficulties with this hypothesis, two seem paramount. First, it rests on a tenuous claim that a plausible motivation for the heroine's conduct cannot be derived from her position as a member of an impoverished family, needing and desiring Bluebeard's wealth, and perhaps deciding to risk the marriage as well on the basis of the kind of strategic calculation that many readers attribute to the heroine in the second half of the story, where she and her sister eventually appear to have prepared and staged the salvatory ending. Second, if we accept the thesis of a deflowered girl being shamed into marriage, the series of entrapments Bluebeard carried out with his previous wives then becomes quite eccentric. This time his basic motive would be the acquisition of his wife's social status, not his possession of her as an object of (sexual) desire. Instead of following readers of the 17th-century public who, according to Velay-Vallantin, *Histoire*, 72–76, linked Bluebeard to the legendary childkiller Gilles de Rais, our psychologically realistic rereading would tend to perceive in him less the aggressive perversion of an authentic ogre—a sadistic hero who has given himself over to forcing guilt upon innocent victims and reveling in the repetition of his wife-killing ritual—than the somewhat fatuous conniving of a bourgeois opportunist who actually covets social integration and seeks to use the young woman's secret to secure wifely obedience. My reading here will place the repetition compulsion primarily on the side of Bluebeard (whose self-imaging instantiates a phallocratic doubling that transfers it onto his

feminine foil) and, after Freud, will link it to his taste for violence and the playing out of the death instinct.

5. Flahaut, *Interprétation*, 88–93, links Bluebeard's prohibition and his wife's consequent desire to the founding prohibition within the nuclear family, the child's exclusion from the parents' bedroom and the ban on sexual relations with the mother and father. Thus, following Bettelheim and other commentators oriented by psychoanalysis, he tends to see the underlying narrative in "La Barbe bleue" as a presentation, only a bit more subtle than that of "Le Petit Chaperon rouge," of the heroine's initiation to sexuality. In violating Bluebeard's prohibition, the heroine would be symbolically looking into the parents' bedroom. See also Flahaut, "Barbe-Bleue et le désir de savoir."

6. For a formidable meditation on the signifying power of the key, which is also a remarkable example of keenly subjective, autobiographically oriented criticism, see Leclerc, *cle*.

7. With respect to the symbolism of identity, the domestic setting of the story and also Bluebeard's appearance invite a comparison with "Le Petit Chaperon rouge." See, for example, my discussion of the heroine's headpiece at note 2 of Chap. Five; and on the significance of the blue highlighted in the protagonist's beard and nickname, see the magnificent commentary by Velay-Vallentin in *Histoire*, 69–71.

8. On the euphemizing of the tomb in general, see Durand, *Structures anthropologiques*, 255.

9. The semantic range of *sacer* is treated in Benveniste, *Vocabulaire*, 2: 187–92.

10. On the role of *contes de fée* in the *bibliothèque bleue*, see Chartier, "Livres bleus," 66off.

11. On the letter *f* as a sign of the feminine, introducing the opposition of the masculine (*clé*) and feminine (*clef*) into the graphic texture of the variable term *clé/clef*, see Leclerc, *cle*, 27. Leclerc also points out that the three capital letters *C, L,* and *E* can be combined to form the image of the object they designate: a large *L* is turned on its side, with its top attached to the bottom-right curl of the *C*; a small *E* is then nestled into the right angle formed by the two spokes of the *L*. In Leclerc's fanciful reading, the graphological play of *clé/clef* heightens the little word's semantic magic.

12. Figures are called tropes, according to Fontanier, "parce que, quand on prend un mot, dans le sens figuré, on le *tourne*, pour ainsi dire, afin de lui faire signifier ce qu'il ne signifie point dans le sens propre" (because, when one takes a word in the figurative sense, one turns it, so to speak, in order to make it mean what it does not mean in the proper sense; *Figures du discours*, 19; my italics).

13. Flahaut uses the same biblical analogy to show how the association

of desire with guilt is established by the lawmaking authority. He under-scores in particular the difference between Yahweh's right to impose his prohibition and Bluebeard's corrupt need to impose his, "parce qu'il a lui-même transgressé une loi fondamentale" (because he himself has broken a fundamental law). *Interprétation*, 95.

14. See Freud, *Interpretation of Dreams*, 6.E: 385–439.

15. The first *moralité* treats the curious woman as a female stereotype; the second, more interesting one evokes the modern woman who has almost become her husband's equal.

16. Irigaray, *Speculum*, 157 (126). Though this work has been translated into English, my analysis required a more literal rendering of the cited passages than Gill provides. Thus here and below, I cite the French original and give the page in the published translation in parentheses. On the connotations of blood in popular tales and songs that could carry over into Perrault's tale, see Velay-Vallantin, *Histoire*, 62–66.

17. Ibid., 158 (126–27).　　18. Ibid., 266 (214).

19. Ibid., 274 (220).　　20. Ibid., 63 (54).

21. Ibid., 101 (83).　　22. Ibid., 36 (33); my italics.

23. See the essay "La Signification du phallus" in Lacan's *Ecrits*.

24. Ibid., 692.

25. Within the frames of a certain Freudian discourse on sexuality that underlies the account of relations between the sexes ventured here, one can ask if Bluebeard is not reverting from an economy of anal eroticism that is bonded and structured for expressive sublimation by the phallus and its substitutes, to an economy of sadomasochism that pays short shrift to symbolic exchange, that suppresses the mediation of desire and pleasure by representation in favor of direct, impulsive realization. Is he not thereby expressing an obscure wish to break out of his own entrapment in the sexual/dialogical order of representation? In hiding away the blood and corpses in his private vault, does he not seek desperately, but futilely, to clear for himself a refuge in the narcissistic reflection afforded by the splen-did mirrors on his castle walls?

26. Here the light that Bluebeard's itinerary sheds on the fate of the wolf in "Le Petit Chaperon rouge" is particularly poignant. If, as I have suggested, the wolf is an animal or instinctual prototype of the ogre, if his experience foreshadows that of full-blown humanized ogre figures like Bluebeard, his future has to be imagined as one fueled by an irrepressible desire that drives a ceaseless renewal of his aberrant search for humanity. The term "aberrant" is as appropriate in the one case as the other, since neither ogre shows any interest in a viable compromise between the life and death drives, i.e., since their searches are always superseded by the enactment of the incorporative violence of sadism and/or masochism, by

the intense pleasure of release (*jouissance*) that ultimately binds *eros* to *thanatos*. No doubt one could also develop in this context a speculative comparison. It would suggest that one can no more readily differentiate animal being from human being on the basis of the human's being unto death or fulfillment in death than one can differentiate them on the basis of a primitive desire for the other in which an inchoate sense of self comes to itself. See Borch-Jacobsen, *Lacan*, 15–16; and on the death drive in "La Barbe bleue," Flahaut, *Interprétation*, 107–9.

27. Hegel, *Phenomenology of Spirit*, 275.

28. Derrida, *Glas*, 208–30 (left-hand pages).

Bibliography

Aarne, Antti. *The Types of the Folk-tale*. Tr. and enlarged by Stith Thompson. Helsinki. Suomalainen Tiedeakatemia, 1928.

Angenot, Marc. *La Parole pamphlétaire*. Paris: Payot, 1982.

Apostolidès, Jean-Marie. *Le Roi-machine: spectacle et politique au temps de Louis XIV*. Paris: Minuit, 1981.

Barchilon, Jacques. *A Concordance to Charles Perrault's Tales*. Norwood, Pa.: Norwood Editions, 1977–79.

———. *Le Conte merveilleux français de 1690–1790*. Paris: Champion, 1975.

———. *Perrault's Tales of Mother Goose*. 2 vols. New York: Pierpont Morgan Library, 1956.

Barchilon, Jacques, and Peter Flinders. *Charles Perrault*. Boston: Twayne, 1981.

Barthes, Roland. "L'Ancienne Rhétorique." In *L'Aventure sémiologique*. Paris: Seuil (Points), 1985.

Benveniste, Emile. *Vocabulaire des institutions européennes*. 2 vols. Paris: Minuit, 1969.

Berg, Elizabeth. "Recognizing Differences: Perrault's Modernistic Aesthetic in the *Parallèle des anciens et des modernes*." *Papers in Seventeenth-Century French Literature* 18 (1983): 135–48.

Bettelheim, Bruno. *The Uses of Enchantment: The Meaning and Importance of Fairy Tales*. New York: Knopf, 1966.

Beyssade, J.-M. *La Philosophie première de Descartes*. Paris: Flammarion, 1979.

Boileau, Nicolas. *Oeuvres complètes*. Paris: Pléiade, 1966.

Borch-Jacobsen, Mikkel. *Lacan: The Absolute Master*. Tr. Douglas Brick. Stanford, Calif.: Stanford University Press, 1991.

———. *The Emotional Tie*. Tr. Douglas Brick and others. Stanford, Calif.: Stanford University Press, 1992.

Bouloumié, Arlette. "L'Ogre dans la littérature." In Pierre Brunel, ed., *Dictionnaire des mythes littéraires*, 1071–86. Paris: Editions du Rocher, 1988.

Brody, Jules. *Boileau and Longinus*. Geneva: Droz, 1958.

Carbone, Geneviève. *La Peur du loup*. Paris: Gallimard, 1991.

"Charles Perrault." *Europe* 739–40 (Nov.–Dec. 1990): 3–172.

Chartier, Roger. "Livres bleus et lectures populaires." In Roger Chartier and Henri-Jean Martin, eds., *Histoire de l'édition française, 2: Le Livre triomphant*, 657–73. Paris: Fayard, 1984.

Citti, Pierre, ed. *Fins de siècle*. Bordeaux: Presses universitaires de Bordeaux, 1990.

Cixous, Hélène. "Castration or Decapitation." *Signs* 7.1 (1981): 41–55. Originally published as "Le Sexe ou la tête" in *Cahiers du GRIF* 13 (1976).

DeJean, Joan. *Fictions of Sappho, 1546–1937*. Chicago: University of Chicago Press, 1989.

Delarue, Paul. *Le Conte populaire français*. Vol. 1. Paris: Erasme, 1957.

Delarue, Paul, and Marie-Louise Tenèze. *Le Conte populaire français*. Vol. 2. Paris: G.-P. Maisonneuve et Larose, 1967.

Derrida, Jacques. "Economimésis." In *Mimésis désarticulations*. Paris: Aubier-Flammarion, 1975.

——. *Glas*. Paris: Galilée, 1974.

Descartes, René. *Méditations métaphysiques*. Ed. J.-M. and M. Beyssade. Paris: Garnier-Flammarion, 1981.

——. *Méditations métaphysiques*. Ed. M. Beyssade. Paris: Livre de Poche, 1991.

——. *Oeuvres philosophiques*. Ed. F. Alquié. 3 vols. Paris: Garnier, 1963–73.

——. *Les Passions de l'âme*. In *Oeuvres philosophiques*, vol. 3. Paris: Garnier, 1973.

Dictionnaire de l'Académie française. Paris: J.-B. Coignard, 1694 (1901 facsimile).

Didier, Béatrice. "Perrault féministe." *Europe* 739–40 (Nov.–Dec. 1990): 101–13.

D'Oria, Domenico. "La Structure de la société française au XVIIe siècle dans les dictionnaires de Richelet, Furetière, Académie Française." In *Dictionnaire et idéologie*. Fasano: Schena, 1988.

Dumont, Louis. *Essais sur l'individualisme*. Paris: Seuil (Points), 1983.

Dundes, Alan, ed. *Little Red Riding Hood: A Case Book*. Madison: University of Wisconsin Press, 1989.

Durand, Gilbert. *Les Structures anthropologiques de l'imaginaire*. Paris: Presses universitaires de France, 1963.

Elias, Norbert. *The Civilizing Process*. Vol. 1: *The History of Manners*. Vol. 2: *Power and Civility*. Tr. Edmund Jephcott. New York: Pantheon, 1978–82.

Fénelon, François de Salignac de La Mothe-, l'abbé de. *Oeuvres*. Vol. 1. Paris: Gallimard (Pléiade), 1983.

——. *Lettre à l'Académie*. Ed. Ernesta Caldarini. Geneva: Droz, 1979.

Ferry, Luc. *Homo Aestheticus: l'invention du goût à l'âge démocratique*. Paris: Grasset, 1990.

Flahaut, François. "Barbe-Bleue et le désir de savoir." *Ornicar* 17–28 (1979): 70–87.

——. *L'Interprétation des contes*. Paris: Denoël, 1988.

Fontanier, Pierre. *Les Figures du discours*. Paris: Flammarion, 1968.

Foucault, Michel. *Les Mots et les choses*. Paris: Gallimard, 1966.

France, Peter. *Politeness and Its Discontents*. Cambridge, Eng.: Cambridge University Press, 1993.

Freud, Sigmund. *The Interpretation of Dreams*. Tr. James Strachey. New York: Avon, 1965.

Hazard, Paul. *The European Mind: The Critical Years 1680–1715*. New Haven: Yale University Press, 1953.

Hegel, G. W. F. *Phenomenology of Spirit*. Tr. A. V. Miller. Oxford: Oxford University Press, 1977.

Heidegger, Martin. "The Age of the World Picture." In *The Question Concerning Technology*. Tr. William Lovitt. New York: Harper & Row, 1977.

Henry, Michel. *Généalogie de la psychanalyse*. Paris: Presses universitaires de France, 1983.

Hertz, Neil. *The End of the Line*. New York: Columbia University Press, 1986.

Holbek, Bengt. *The Interpretation of Fairy Tales: Danish Folklore in a European Perspective*. Helsinki: Suomalainen Tiedeakatemia, 1989.

Irigaray, Luce. *Speculum de l'autre femme*. Paris: Minuit, 1974. Translated into English as *Speculum of the Other Woman* by G. Gill. Ithaca, N.Y.: Cornell University Press, 1985.

Kantorowicz, E. H. *The King's Two Bodies*. Princeton, N.J.: Princeton University Press, 1965.

Khibédi-Varga, Aron. *Discours, récit, image*. Paris: Pierre Mardaga, 1989.

——. *Rhétorique et littérature: Etudes de structures classiques*. Paris: Didier, 1970.

La Bruyère, Jean de. *Les Caractères ou les Moeurs de ce siècle*. Paris: Gallimard (Folio), 1975.

Lacan, Jacques. *Ecrits*. Paris: Seuil, 1966.

La Fontaine, Jean de. *Fables*. Ed. Jean-Pierre Collinet. Paris: Folio, 1991.

Leclerc, Annie. *cle*. Paris: Grasset, 1989.

Lévi-Strauss, Claude. *The Origin of Table Manners*. Tr. John and Doreen Weightman. New York: Harper & Row, 1978.

——. *La Pensée sauvage*. Paris: Plon, 1962.

Litman, Théodore. *Le Sublime en France (1660–1714)*. Paris: Nizet, 1971.

Marin, Louis. *Food for Thought*. Tr. Mette Jhort. Baltimore: Johns Hopkins University Press, 1989.

———. *La Critique du discours: sur la "Logique de Port-Royal" et les "Pensées" de Pascal*. Paris: Editions de Minuit, 1975.

———. *La Parole mangée et autres essasi théologico-politiques*. Paris: Méridiens Klincksieck, 1986.

———. "On the Sublime, Infinity, Je ne sais quoi." In *A New History of French Literature*. Cambridge, Mass.: Harvard University Press, 1989.

———. *Lectures traversières*. Paris: Albin Michel, 1995.

———. *Le Portrait du roi*. Paris: Seuil, 1981. Translated into English as *Portrait of the King* by Martha Houle. Minneapolis: University of Minnesota Press, 1988.

———. *Le Récit est un piège*. Paris: Minuit, 1978.

Marvels and Tales 5.2 ("Special Issue on Charles Perrault," ed. Catherine Velay-Vallantin) (Dec. 1991): 154–520.

Morgan, Jeanne. *Perrault's Morals for Moderns*. New York: Peter Lang, 1985.

Morier, Henri. *Dictionnaire de poétique et de rhétorique*. 4th ed. Paris: Presses universitaires de France, 1989.

Nancy, Jean-Luc, ed. *Du sublime*. Paris: Belin, 1988.

Patillon, Michel. *Eléments de rhétorique classique*. Paris: Nathan, 1990.

Pavel, Thomas. *La Syntaxe narrative des tragédies de Corneille*. Paris: Klincksieck, 1976.

Perrault, Charles. *Contes*. Ed. Marc Soriano. Paris: Flammarion, 1989.

———. *Contes*. Ed. Gilbert Rouger. Paris: Garnier, 1967.

———. *Contes*. Ed. Jean-Pierre Collinet. Paris: Gallimard (Folio), 1981.

———. *Contes*. Ed. François Flahault. Paris: Livre de Poche, 1987.

———. *Les Hommes illustres qui ont paru en France pendant ce siècle*. 2 vols. Paris: Antoine Dezallier, 1697–1700. Cited from reproduction (Geneva: Slatkine Reprints, 1979).

———. *Mémoires de ma vie*. Ed. Antoine Picon. Paris: Macula, 1993.

———. *Parallèle des anciens et des modernes*. 4 vols. Paris: Jean-Baptiste Coignard, 1692–97. Cited both by the original pages and by the pagination of the single-volume reproduction (Geneva: Slatkine Reprints, 1970).

———. *Parallèle des anciens et des modernes*. 4 vols. Ed. Hans Kortum. Munich: Eidos Verlag, 1964.

———. *Pensées chrétiennes*. Ed. Jacques Barchilon. Paris: Biblio 17, 1987.

Picard, Raymond. *La Carrière de Jean Racine*. Paris: Gallimard, 1961.

Racine, Jean. *Oeuvres complètes*. Vol. 2 (prose). Ed. Raymond Picard. Paris: Gallimard (Pléiade), 1966.

———. *Oeuvres complètes*. Paris: Seuil (L'Intégrale), 1961.

Rey, Alain. "Linguistic Absolutism." In *A New History of French Literature*. Cambridge, Mass.: Harvard University Press, 1989.

Roger, Jacques. *Les Sciences de la vie dans la pensée française du XVIIIe siècle.* Paris: A. Colin, 1963.

Serres, Michel. "Les Métaphores de la cendre, ou introduction à la féerie expérimentale." *Critique* 23.6 (Nov. 1967): 906–11.

Simonsen, Michèle. *Le Conte populaire français.* Paris: Presses universitaires de France, 1986.

——. *Perrault: Contes.* Paris: Presses universitaires de France, 1992.

Soriano, Marc. *La Brosse à reluire sous Louis XIV: "L'Epître au Roi" de Perrault annotée par Racine et Boileau.* Fasano: Schena, 1989.

——. *Les Contes de Perrault: culture savante et traditions populaires.* Paris: Gallimard, 1968.

——. *Le Dossier Charles Perrault.* Paris: Hachette, 1972.

Todorov, Tzvetan. *Les Morales de l'histoire.* Paris: Grasset, 1991.

Velay-Vallantin, Catherine. *L'Histoire des contes.* Paris: Fayard, 1992.

Viala, Alain. *Racine: la stratégie du caméléon.* Paris: Seghers, 1990.

Zipes, Jack. *Breaking the Magic Spell: Radical Theories of Folk and Fairy Tales.* Austin: University of Texas Press, 1979.

——. *Fairy Tales and the Art of Subversion.* New York: Wildman, 1983.

——, ed. and tr. *Beauties, Beasts, and Enchantment: Classic French Fairy Tales.* New York: Meridian, 1991.

Index

In this index an "f" after a number indicates a separate reference on the next page, and an "ff" indicates separate references on the next two pages. A continuous discussion over two or more pages is indicated by a span of page numbers, e.g., "57–59." *Passim* is used for a cluster of references in close but not consecutive sequence.

Library of Congress Cataloging-in-Publication Data

Lewis, Philip E. (Philip Eugene)
    Seeing through the Mother Goose tales : visual turns in the
writings of Charles Perrault / Philip Lewis.
        p.   cm.
    Includes bibliographical references and index.
    ISBN 0-8047-2410-5 (cloth : alk. paper)
    1. Perrault, Charles, 1628–1703—Criticism and interpretation.
2. Criticism—France—History—17th century.   I. Title.
PQ1877.L49   1996
841'.1—dc20   95-18795
                                                             CIP

♾ This book is printed on acid-free recycled paper.

Original printing 1996
Last figure below indicates year of this printing:
05 04 03 02 01 00 99 98 97 96